Searching for the Light

SEARCHING
FOR THE
LIGHT

Essays on Thought and Culture

NORMAN BIRNBAUM

New York   Oxford
OXFORD UNIVERSITY PRESS
1993

Essay Index

Oxford University Press

Oxford   New York   Toronto
Delhi   Bombay   Calcutta   Madras   Karachi
Kuala Lumpur   Singapore   Hong Kong   Tokyo
Nairobi   Dar es Salaam   Cape Town
Melbourne   Auckland   Madrid

and associated companies in

Copyright © 1993 by Norman Birnbaum

Published by Oxford University Press, Inc.,
200 Madison Avenue, New York, New York 10016

Oxford is a registered trademark of Oxford University Press

Library of Congress Cataloging-in-Publication Data
Birnbaum, Norman.
Searching for the light : essays on thought and culture /
Norman Birnbaum.
p.   cm. Includes bibliographical references and index.
ISBN 0-19-506889-0
1. Sociology—United States. 2. Marxian school of sociology.
3. Education, Higher—Political aspects. I. Title.
HM22.U5B47 1993 301—dc20 92-33018

2 4 6 8 9 7 5 3 1

Printed in the United States of America
on acid-free paper

For Timothy S. Healy, S.J.

Preface

To what extent do these essays, written between 1971 and 1984, possess any consistency of theme? They do record, if not a progression, a change. In the articles republished as the first part of the book, "Sociology and Its Fate," I was attempting to come to terms with the sociological legacy. More precisely, I was trying to decide what to do with my own disciplinary inheritance, my concern with the historical substance and political uses of theory. I concluded that the idea of a sociology independent of historical analysis, philosophical assumption, and political predisposition was untenable. The title of one of the essays, "An End To Sociology?," ends with a question mark, but by the time I wrote it, I had answered the question. My own engagement in the discipline was indeed over. I turned my attention, as citizen and scholar, to other matters.

The section on "Marxism and After" points to some of these—the question of secularization and the persistence of religions in many forms; the challenge posed by Freud and psychoanalysis to the belief in the human capacity for self-transformation; the question of the direction of modern politics. The rather brief essay "Are We Entering a Post-Marxist Age?" may be casual in its style. In substance, it is the central and connecting element in the entire anthology. Written in 1984, it certainly anticipated much of what was about to happen in the neo-Stalinist societies—and, for that matter, in our own.

Can thought really apprehend the movement of our societies, or is it bound to limp (or run, as the case may be) behind history itself? More, can ideas alter our sense of possibility—and our practise? In an essay written for the Carnegie Commission on Higher Education, "Students, Professors and Philosopher Kings," devoted to the political role of our universities, I considered the question from the perspective of the institutionalization of knowledge. Of course, in our universities, much is institutionalized which is decidedly extraneous to the pursuit of learning, or simply hampers it. Looking back on the excitements of the sixties, in 1972, I concluded that universities were both improbable and unsuitable as sites for revolutionary mobilization. They were (and, alas, are) more likely to produce apologetics and technologies of domination than critical social ideas. However, I did insist that universities provided protected space for the development of these ideas—if larger circumstances allowed. The essay was written just as what was to become the current argument about multi-culturalism was beginning. I am struck by how much of the argument, on all sides, is irrelevant to the major problems of our nation. While many in the American intelligentsia were preparing for their long descent into academic encapsulation, many of our French contemporaries were readying themselves for government. Did not M. Jacques Delors at the time publish a book under the compelling title, *Changer?* The final essay, on the cultural conference convened by President François Mitterrand and his Minister of Culture, Jack Lang, in 1983, was rather well received in France. The Socialist government was still relatively new in office and French hopes for a union of power and spirit were not extinguished. My essay suggested that it might pay to settle not for a union but for a limited alliance. Since then, in the western nations (and in central and eastern Europe, too) that also seems, however sober, at least as much a hope as an expectation.

Some of what I have learned since writing these essays is to be found in *The Radical Renewal, The Politics of Ideas in Modern America* (Pantheon Books, New York, 1988.) May I suggest that those who enjoyed that book may find the present collection interesting—and that others may find it worth their while to move from the essays to the book?

(Readers of an earlier anthology, *Toward a Critical Sociology,* published by Oxford University Press in 1971, will notice that I have again included my account of the international sociological meeting held at Varna in Bulgaria in 1970. I have done so because the event did cause me to reconsider in terms expressed in the subsequent essays in the first part of the present collection. I also suspect that a newer generation of sociologists will hardly have had the kinds of contact with Neo-Stalinism available at Varna—hardly a pleasure, but instructive.)

I do express my appreciation to my editor, Sheldon Meyer, for his continued confidence and support. Before too long, I plan to entrust to him the resutls of an inquiry on the prospects of western socialism and its presently diminished American counterpart, American social reform, in historical circumstances very different from the ones which engendered these essays. Perhaps, however, there is more continuity in our setting than we now see. If so, that is justification enough for the present volume.

Washington, D.C.   N. B.
June 1992

Acknowledgments

The author and the publisher are grateful to the following for permission to reprint the essays in the anthology.

The Editors, *Social Research:* "Sociology: Discontents Present and Perennial," *Social Research,* Volume 38, Number 4, Winter 1971; and "An End to Sociology?," *Social Research,* Volume 42, Number 3, Autumn 1975.

The Editors, *Partisan Review:* "Circus at Varna," *Partisan Review,* Volume 38, Number 1, Spring 1971.

The Editors, *Review:* "The *Annales* School and Social Theory," *Review,* Volume 1, Number 3/4, Winter/Spring 1978.

Professor Robert J. Lifton: "Critical Theory and Psychohistory," from Robert J. Lifton and Eric Olsen, Editors, *Explorations in Psychohistory, The Wellfleet Papers,* Simon and Schuster, New York, 1974.

Professors Charles Y. Glock and Phillip Hammond: "Beyond Marx in the Sociology of Religion," from Charles Y. Glock and Phillip Hammond, Editors, *Beyond the Classics in the Sociology of Religion,* Harper and Row, New York, 1973.

The Editors, *Commonweal:* "Are We Entering a Post-Marxist Age?," *Commonweal,* 5 October 1984. Copyright © Commonweal Foundation.

The Carnegie Commission on Higher Education: "Students, Professors and Philosopher Kings," From Carl Kaysen, Editor, *Content and Context,* McGraw-Hill, New York, 1973.

Contents

I

SOCIOLOGY AND ITS FATE

The title of one of the essays, "An End to Sociology?," sets the theme for the others as well. The question mark might well have been dispensed with, since the burden of the four papers is that sociology's claims to analytic distinctiveness, to a special conceptual mission, can no longer be sustained. Sociology came into being as an attempt to depict the inner structure of a new historical formation, industrial society. That society has changed, so much so that even the mid-twentieth century seems very remote. What some termed "late capitalism" (without quite knowing what would succeed it) entails fusions of culture and economy, market and policy, society and state, which cannot be analyzed in terms of the classical sociological texts. Meanwhile, intellectual developments as varied as the complex historiography of the *Annales* school and the psychoanalytical account of the psyche oblige us to see how linear, how inextricably bound to an idea of progress, much of the sociological tradition was. That impression has been reinforced by compelling evidence: the historical pluralism of cultures and their unwilling servitude to a world market that unifies nations, peoples, societies in quite contradictory and conflicting ways. We have learned that the role of ideas (what the *Annales* historians would call *mentalités* and an antecedent tradition would term ideologies) in society is differentiated and subtle as well as, at times, explosive and omnipotent. We can summarize by saying that the fragmentation of our historical experience has been accompanied by a fragmentation of our perspectives. No one discipline can claim privileged access to the movement of society, and no one theory can totalize disparate accounts of an historical setting itself rent by discontinuity and dissonance.

Written somewhat after the excitements of the 1960s, these essays also evince considerable skepticism about the intellectual and moral value of subordinating social thought to political conviction, especially if conviction is defined programmatically. Politics counts enormously in these essays—as the search for the possible social foundations of a transformed common life. That search takes the form of what I refer to in the texts, variously, as the effort to articulate a metahistory or a metatheory. By that I mean a critique of our historical existence, which certainly influences both our politics and our thought by providing a vision and a sensibility (it cannot be described as a rhetorical grammar, but at times it may come close to one). It is from sensibility and vision that particular projects of inquiry and the categories and orders of theory are derived—if in no mechanical manner. Social theory, then, makes sense as an effort to master historical

and philosophical perplexities and not primarily as an attempt
to construct a model of the social world, natural-science-like in
its capacity to predict. The regularities a science of society is supposed to discern may, after all, simply not exist.

These themes also characterize the other two sections of the
anthology, which treat contemporary Marxism and its fate, and
the social uses of culture and the university. The report on the
International Sociological Congress at Varna in 1970 deals with
immanent difficulties of sociological inquiry, but it also points to
our political miseries. It serves, then, as a bridge to the next
section, as well as evidence for the irreducible political content
of sociological inquiry. In my description of the sociology of the
state socialist societies, there is some evidence of the small lati-
tude provided by the Brezhnev period and much more evidence
of the large strains that were to result twenty years later in the
self-destruction of the post-Stalinist Communist regimes. Meanwhile, the West appeared at Varna with a bifurcated consciousness. The party of sixty-eight (sixty-nine in Italy) was confident
that its attack on the ossification of liberal capitalism anticipated
political and spiritual triumphs to come—and was quite unaware that the only thing that was to come was its own ossification. The party of liberal capitalism triumphant saw little need
to defend itself at Varna, but was present in the caricatured form
of broken renderings of a flat historical landscape. How wrong
we were in many of our ideas! Perhaps, however, the critical
sensibility at work in the report is the sort of thing we need if
we are to persist in the effort to make sense of society, or rather,
to understand its lack of sense.

1

Circus at Varna

What could be more attractive than a conference—the eighth postwar World Congress in Sociology—in Varna, a sea resort set in olive groves on the Black Sea coast. To the attraction of nature was added the prospect of the first large, public encounter between "bourgeois" sociology and its orthodox Marxist counterpart, against the backdrop of a "developing" state socialist society. The whole thing, however, was a barely mitigated disaster. But it all can best be understood in the context of the course of sociology since 1945.

The dizzy postwar expansion of sociology as an academic field (I hesitate to use the term "discipline," for good philosophical reasons) is reflected in the attendance figures for successive international gatherings. The first one I attended, at Liège in 1953, had some 300 participants. At Amsterdam in 1956 there were already about 500 sociologists, and at Stresa in 1959 there were over a thousand. At Washington in 1962 the number was higher still, and by the time the Evian conference was held in 1966 there were over 2,000 present. Even though the Bulgarians threw in by official count 501 persons, many of them ridicuously unqualified, the throng at Varna numbered 4,000.

Over the past twenty-five years sociology has grown in the U.S.A. and Western Europe from similar roots. Initially, the catastrophes of fascism and war and the problems of reconstruction gave rise to a general political introspection. But the constriction of postwar western politics and the suspension of disbelief in the capitalist machine turned introspection into apologetics. Instead of asking how society could be

5

made whole and rational, sociologists portrayed its fragmentation and senselessness as inevitable. Those who sought something else were dismissed as "utopians" by those who fancied themselves in possession (or about to come into it) of immutable laws of behavior, of higher insight into the necessary and beneficial constraints of social structures. Rapidly emptied of critical ideas, sociology soon lost all intellectual content: it became a set of techniques for gathering data. The techniques were useful, not least to those in command of those corporate and government bureaucracies which set such narrow limits on our political choices. Sociologists became minor ancillaries of the administrative technologists: they presented their instruments of inquiry as aspects of a pure science, if a nascent one, even though their work served very impure purposes.

Not all of sociology, however, was self-consciously technical. Serious efforts were made in the United States to develop abstract criteria for sociological analysis and general models of society, though these, too, were subject to political assumptions. The abstract criteria often dealt with social constraints as "functions," as mechanical necessities imposed on men and not as historical forms which could be criticized and changed. In fact, the models frequently presupposed a consensus which they had helped bring about. In Europe, a serious and desperate search to relate the Marxist tradition to contemporary social and political phenomena began as soon as it became clear that wartime antifascism had not been the prelude to a socialist Europe. The reluctance of the European working class to assume a revolutionary mission led to studies of psychic coercion: briefly, the process of alienation was now seen not only in the fragmentation of man as citizen and producer but in the willed servitude of a new generation of consumers. Meanwhile, phenomenologists looked beyond politics for a human essence. They sometimes found it, not just beyond politics, but beyond community, and so reduced social existence to a giant charade.

The multiplicity of Western sociology had a saving philosophical virtue: political ideas might infuse sociological notions, but they did so in mediated fashion. Sociologists could, and did, argue about their assumptions, but they also argued about the social world. Ultimately, what diminished the appeal of the doctrines of consensus and function is the historical evidence that consensus no longer exists, that institutions no longer work.

The state socialist regimes have allowed, by and large, no such public corrections of social thought. A flourishing pre-Bolshevik Russian sociological tradition was eradicated, and as Stalinism replaced the frequently adventurous Marxism of the early revolutionary years, a dogmatized and impoverished "Marxism-Leninism" was all that could be heard in the Soviet Union. The promulgation of "laws" of social development of an entirely invented kind had one clear aim: the point was not to understand the world or to change it, but to justify it. The implantation of Stalinism in Eastern Europe by the Red Army had the same effect in countries like Poland, Czechoslovakia and Hungary. Only in Yugoslavia did a sociology autonomous of state and party control emerge. Marxist and critical, theoretic in substance but empirical in focus, Yugoslav sociology had to defend itself against inane denigration in the East and incomprehension in the West.

In the last decade, the decomposition of Stalinism and the growth of productive capacity in the state socialist regimes have altered the situation. In Poland and Czechoslovakia a suppressed sociological tradition often Social Democratic in inspiration was reborn. In Hungary, while the aging Lukács labors away at his treatises, his younger disciples do empirical sociology. The crosscurrents of Communist politics at times silence a sociology which has refused to become a sloganized exegesis of party programs, but the intellectual territory liberated by the sociologists has not all been lost. Paradoxically though, the resilience and honesty of sociology in Eastern Europe owes much to the Communist technocrats' need for reliable information as a mode of extending and consolidating their rule. The increasing complexity of administration, distribution and political manipulation in societies now entering the advanced stages of industrialization, and the need for reliable data on consumer preference, educational and occupational discipline and political opinion, leave the technocrats little choice but to encourage certain kinds of sociology. Once merely housed in Moscow in the Institute of Philosophy of the Academy of Sciences (an Institute not so long ago notorious among the learned in the Soviet Union as an assemblage of ideological hacks), sociology now has found other quarters. Moscow now also has an Institute of Concrete Social Research. In Akadamsgorod, near Novosibirsk, computerized and mathematical models of behavior are advanced with an ardor we saw in this country two decades ago. The technocratic cultivation of sociology, however, is a constant internal threat to the Soviet Union's intellectual controllers: suppose the sociolgists do not confine themselves to the execution of technocratic directives for data collection but begin, instead, to think critically about society? This is what happened in Czechoslovakia, Hungary, and Poland. Indeed, the Varna Congress was a gigantic mechanism of defense against this possibility.

The first line of defense was left to the Bulgarians. The organization, if it can be dignified by that word, of the Congress did not seem to come from Moscow (many Soviet colleagues were revulsed by the local arrangements). The Bulgarians, among the most retrograde of regimes in Eastern Europe, probably acted instinctively. The impression of openness had to be given, but the effects of genuine oppenness had to be minimized, since they could not be entirely eliminated. Masterful only in their disorganization, lack of coherence and inability to deal with simple matters, our Bulgarian hosts may indeed have acted largely in good faith. The result was as good as purposeful sabotage.

Even a great satirist could barely do justice to the scene. The participants from Eastern Europe were lodged mostly in hotels ten kilometers distant from the resort town of Gold Strand, where the rest of us were housed. There was no list of participants with their local addresses, although there was under the counter of a Balkantourist desk a preliminary list of bookings arranged by hotels—an inaccurate one. Only one hotel had telephones in its rooms, and in any event receptionists and clerks at the other hotels were usually unable to find the names of their guests on their registers. A bus service did shuttle back and forth between Gold Strand and the Congress meeting sites at the Palace of Culture and Sport and the University in Varna. The Eastern Europeans, however, had buses only at the beginning of sessions and mealtimes. It was not easy for them to get to Gold Strand for those extracurricular talks which frequently constitute the life of a scholarly conference.

The participants had been instructed, in the strictest terms, to ship their papers in advance to the Bulgarian organizing committee. Many who did never saw their papers again. Some never arrived, others were given out at random, so that none were left for the sessions for which they were intended, and still others were strewn in such disorder that hours of their authors' searching were required to extricate them from the pile. Four out of every five summaries in the printed volume of abstracts were by authors from Eastern Europe. The daily Congress Bulletin, issued in Bulgarian, French and English, invariably stressed the contributions from Eastern Europe. The Bulletin outdid itself, however, on the second day. There was no space, its anonymous editors explained, for conveying changes of room, modifications of programs and other notices—these were too numerous. We were favored, instead, with the full text of the address of greeting delivered the day before by His Excellency, the Prime Minister of the Bulgarian People's Republic.

To these difficulties of communication were added others. The Italians who constituted the secretariat of the International Sociological Association negotiated for several days during the Congress to obtain a bulletin board in the Palace of Culture. Their request had been agreed to by the Bulgarian organizers, but the Palace personnel simply removed it. The gallery was stacked during the opening address by the Prime Minister with persons who wore Party membership buttons, but local students and the local populace could not attend the discussions: entrance to the buildings was by congress badge only. Meanwhile, room allocations were constantly shifted about, two groups were sometimes assigned to one room and at one point Adbul Malik, the distinguished Egyptian sociologist currently in exile in Paris, had to convene his group on the floor of a corridor. Large groups were given small rooms and small groups found themselves in large ones.

There were other episodes. The Prime Minister had invited some 300 of the participants (chosen from among session chairmen, rapporteurs, and so on) to a closed reception, but the Organizing Committee had printed the time and place of the event on the program. Bulgarian police and plainclothesmen took the invitations at the foot of a hotel staircase (some were promptly handed over the bannister behind their backs to uninvited sociologists) and pushed back hundreds of others. A British university lecturer was thrown down the staircase and a German teaching assistant who remonstrated with the police was rather thoroughly roughed up. No apologies were tendered, but the Bulgarian sociologists did plead with their foreign colleagues to treat the incident as a "provocation." By this time, however, the irritation and disgust of many of the participants with the course of the Congress were quite audible, and even the least perceptive of our hosts began to wish us gone. The International Hotel, where the reception was held, returned to its daily routine before the sociologists had left. An earlier set of guests had been thrown out of their rooms and transferred to other hotels upon our arrival (scheduled, after all, only two years in advance). Now a curious mixture of German tourists and stocky native big shots filled its lobby. The latter were well protected: the detectives I'd first seen around the Prime Minister were very visible. Their comportment was such as to suggest that the "defense of socialism" was consonant with Turkish manners: they made themselves conspicuous by shoving aside women at the elevators. The Bulgarian elite enjoyed ostentatious privileges and showed hopelessly provincial and petit-bourgeois taste. The big shots drove about with motorcycle police escorts who compelled all traffic on broad and empty roads to stop while they passed. Their limousines had white chintz curtains. Pathetic Bulgaria? Like many nations once ruled by the Turks, its people seemed broken in culture and spirit. And to Orientalism was added Stalinism.

Was there any scholarly value at all to the conference? A considerable number of sociologists had doubted it ahead of time, and stayed away. Aron, Bell, Bendix, Bottomore, Casanova, Dahrendorf, Etzioni, Gellner, Gouldner, Lefebvre, Habermas, Pizzorno, Supek and Worsley were among the absentees. Adam Schaff, apparently swept aside by the recent Polish campaign against "revisionists" (and Jews), was missing. His Warsaw colleague Zygmunt Bauman had chosen the road of exile—or return—to Tel Aviv and did not travel to Bulgaria. The absences were very regrettable. Some of the missing scholars are neo-Marxists, and their encounter with a dogmatic orthodoxy would have been educational for the younger sociologists from the state socialist regimes, who were present in great numbers. Some are decidedly ex-Marxists, and the sharpness of their positions would have enlivened the Congress. Instead, discussion was befogged, and I had the impression of swimming in a gelatinous substance. Talk was cheap but genuine controversy was rare.

In no country are sociologists conspicuous for their reluctance to speak, and the relative absence of conflict at Varna remains to be explained. Harangues there were aplenty. A pseudo-Marxist aggressiveness marked the contributions of many of the participants from Eastern and Central Europe, who seemed quite unable to distinguish between intellectual polemic and a level of discourse which would have stupified Agitprop cadres at a party school. We also had to bear with those who, in the middle of discussions, read from totally irrelevant prepared texts. Chairmen who had prepared their sessions for months in advance were at the last minute asked to accomodate just another few more Soviet or Bulgarian papers.

What I have called pseudo-Marxism is less an ideology than it is a catechism or an incantation. It is also a sociological phenomenon. The groups from the state socialist regimes were quite profoundly divided, and that division was in itself a mitigating element at the Congress. There were, to begin with, differences of intelligence: not even all the varieties of Stalinism and Brezhnevism have been able to alter genetic variations. I had the impression that the more dogmatic representatives from the eastern societies were actually the less gifted ones. Factors of social inheritance also played their part. Many of the Bulgarians, the Communist Germans and some of the older Russian recruits to "intellectual" activity from Party organizations were quite obviously not from academic or professional families, not offspring of the intelligentsia, but sons and daughters of manual workers. Upward social mobility, in state socialist regimes as well as our own, extracts its own cultural price: the crudity and historical shortsightedness of the pseudo-Marxists expressed a lack of education, an inability to work with the complexities of a tradition—even their own. I recall a moment when Alain Touraine reminded a session that not all revolutions were made by Leninist-type parties: the French had not been. Cultural and intellectual isolation must also have played their part in engendering vulgarity: the Poles, the Czechs and some of the Russians have traveled widely, as have the Rumanians. The Communist Germans rarely get to the Sorbonne or Berkeley, and most of them have not been to Frankfurt, Goettingen or West Berlin. Their more sophisticated spokesmen (Hahn, Steiner, Braunreuter and others) were interesting. The others should have been told by a regime jealous of its international standing to shut up.

Intellectually, pseudo-Marxism consists of a few elementary propositions, repeated compulsively, and mostly false. The theme of the Congress was "Contemporary and Future Societies, Prediction and Social Planning." The pseudo-Marxists insisted on a rigid distinction between state socialist and other societies. The "laws" of development applicable to the one type could not be applied to the others. None speculated that there are not any "laws" of social development, but simply successions of historical structures with different degrees of responsiveness to concious historical will. This was surprising, since their conception of "law" in their own societies presents their respective Communist parties as the sole legitimate and effective incarnations of human historical will. To this was linked the assertion that the working class (exceedingly vaguely defined) in fact exercised power and held productive property in these societies. I did ask a Communist German how we could understand this last claim: were there not, as mediating factors, state, party, the division of labor, authority structure in the work process and differential allocation of the social product? The answer was brief: the question was a "theoretical and not an empirical one." As I heard it, I could not help but think of the German phrase, *auf die Gesinnung kommt es an,* it all depends on your point of view.

The "laws" of development for the state socialist regimes determined the interpretation of their empirical research. Since these societies were "victoriously" developing their productive and moral capacities, they had no conflicts. Occasional problems in development meant only insufficient assimilation of the official social morality. Critical studies of bureaucracy were few, although the Vice-Rector of the Komsomol Academy in Moscow did report on a study of popular attitudes to local bureaucracy which suggested something other than complete satisfaction. The pseudo-Marxists used empirical research to "verify" laws which were nothing but projections of their own dogmatic minds. There was no Marxist analysis of production relations, of superstructure, in their own regimes. Contradiction central to Marxist theory as a category for apprehending history did not exist for them.

In these circumstances, the pseudo-Marxist contribution to administrative technology in their own countries was nil. States and societies cannot be governed by recourse to a few elementary dicta, particularly when the dicta are false. This difficulty did contribute an opportunity for the more serious sociologists in these countries. I would divide them into two groups, although it was sometimes difficult to tell them apart. We did meet no small number of colleagues who were overtly or covertly critical of, even opposed to, the exercise of power in state socialism. One distinguished younger Soviet colleague told me, "Marx died a long while ago; much has happened since then, not least in what some refer to as 'bourgeois' thought." From another country, a participant explained his silence: "Under present political conditions at home, I cannot speak my mind, and I will not say things I do not believe." Criticism, for those sociologists, consists in describing social reality. They cannot, in general, deal with it as a political totality—but they can and often do say enough to illuminate the whole by dealing

with its parts. The Poles and the Czechs were, as we might have expected, masters of the art: there is evidence that they are being joined
by an increasing number of sociologists from the Soviet Union.

What kind of studies do come from those with a minimally critical
attitude? I heard, or read, accounts of social mobility in the socialist
societies which left no doubt as to the existence there of a stratified
system of social relations—a class system based on state property. There
was an intelligent Polish contribution on workers' participation in economic planning as a goal of Polish socialism which left no doubt that
the goal was very remote of attainment. An inquiry on religion in the
Soviet Union pointed to its decline, but also left open the question of
the universality of religious aspiration. Studies of this sort were distinguished from the pseudo-Marxist harangues not only by their attention
to nuance and detail, but by a superior intellectual level, a realization
of the difficult relationship between theory and fact, a refusal to assimilate reflection to political exhortation. There are, of course, limits beyond which they cannot as yet go.

But as they succeed in developing more valid methods of sociological inquiry will they not contribute to the consolidation of the state
socialist technocracy by making it more efficient? The answer, unfortunately, is yes. Of the two groupings of sociologists in Eastern Europe
who inhabit our world of discourse, the second is not so much critical
as pragmatic. Some, to borrow a term from von Hayek not heard much
recently, are "scientistic." The enormous development of the culture
of mathematics and the physical sciences in the Soviet Union has induced some sociologists there (the parallels with our own recent academic experience are striking) to experiment with mathematical and
formal descriptions of social process. There's a new Soviet version of
Lenin's famous dictum, that socialism equals the Soviets plus electrifi-
cation—socialism equals the Soviet state equipped with computers. In
a regime which has not begun to solve enormous problems of bureaucratic ossification, the reduction of some of those problems to terms
soluble by computers is obviously a political priority. The Communist
Germans, too, have made much of computerization: the aged Ulbricht
himself, some years ago, took a three-day crash course in program-
ming. They cannot yet, however, begin to relinquish the notion of controlling all social processes from the center. The Soviet interest in computerization of social research seems to reflect a political decision—
however contested and uncertain—to allow some areas of society a
relative autonomy. It is of a piece with economic decentralization and
the conscious development of a socialist market. The appearance for
the first time at a World Congress of Sociology of Soviet sociologists of
this type went largely unremarked. It is a phenomenon which may in
the end be more significant than the crudities inflicted upon us by
some of their colleagues. The establishment of a framework for the

study of these processes presupposes a prior intellectual decision that they are relatively independent. The license to study them implies a political decision to use manipulative rather than coercive means of control. In fact, those regimes with an intelligentsia closer to contemporary Western culture are precisely those which have been persuaded to move toward the cultivation of empirical sociology—and for technocratic reasons.

What about the Western sociologists? Many of our stars were there, and they were accompanied by a good many intellectual footmen. The diversity of topics covered by the western papers was immense: family, community, social psychiatry, work and organization, politics, methodology and much more. Indeed, there was no single Western sociology represented at the Congress, as a fragmented social world has been reflected in a fragmented social science. The papers were full of conflicting assumptions about social nature, its malleability and manipulability—all to the good, for pluralism is a good thing, no doubt. But there was very little debate about the nature of our society, which cast some doubt on our intellectual seriousness. In some sense, we were the exaggerated antithesis to the absurd simplifications of our state socialist brethren. There a terrifying uniformity, here an intolerable confusion. Perhaps, however, the confusion is willed: a certain kind of categorical pluralism allows every man his own sociology. In the final analysis, this is a caricature of a free market—though the market society has long since disappeared, replaced by its technocratic and bureaucratic successors. But, despite the confusion, Western sociology has redeeming elements. Bureaucracy and technocracy themselves have become the objects of inquiry for those who seek to bring up to date the sociological tradition that investigated early industrial society. Inquiry of this sort, of course, inevitably becomes political: the pluralism of sociology cannot justify a flight from politics.

During the Congress, political voices were not entirely silent. Some, like myself and a few allies, attempted to engage the pseudo-Marxists and above all the authentic Marxists from the state socialist regimes in some kind of dialogue. Publicly, this proved almost impossible. Privately, over Slivovitz, we made out better. At the very least, we managed to trade our books and articles for caviar and vodka: the Soviet as well as the general Communist demand for printed matter was very great. A note of political pathos was added by the group of younger sociologists who managed to hold a few meetings—on the sociology of sociology. Was international sociology at the service of the internatinal power elite, they asked? The answer is that, in general, it has very little to offer to that elite. Nevertheless, the younger Dutch, Germans and Americans who organized the meeting struck a responsive chord. Hundreds of colleagues rushed to inscribe themselves on their mailing list. I asked about their coordinating committee and learned that of its five initial members, one was a young Bulgarian and one a student from Niger attached to a Bulgarian university. This was certainly one of the first international new left groups to have not one but two representatives from Bulgaria on it: the "helpfulness" of the Bulgarian was in the circumstances a bit surprising.

I would have wished for much more criticism of technocracy—in the neocapitalist and state socialist regimes—on the Congress program, but it was good to see the critical sociologists break through. Their level of rationality contrasted favorably with that of the radical caucus at the September annual meeting of the American Sociological Association, at which professors were denounced for writing radical books, for "not doing anything," and one leaflet declared that radical sociologists were henceforth to be considered the main enemies of radicalism. Reminders of the inanities of the American scene were not, however, entirely missing. One younger American described Manson as an exemplar of a new communal way of living, and the "fat people's liberation movement" and the "gay people's liberation movement" as part of the avant-garde in America. The chairman of the session did interrupt to ask that the terms be explained: he lived in Paris and knew what they meant, but he doubted that they were current in Bulgaria.

My last image of the Congress was at the airport in Sofia. Sixty of the French had been bumped off an overbooked flight to western Europe and had been told that they would have to spend the night in Sofia while alternate routings were found. They made a terrible fuss, and in the end Bulgarian Airlines whistled up a special jet to fly them directly to Paris that night. I congratulated them on their success: it was no doubt the first demonstration in Sofia in decades, and probably the last for a long time.

Our own plane was a Lufthansa Boeing, with drinks and newspapers available before we had crossed the border: an airborne fragment of our own reality, but a perfectly representative one, crowded, hurried, efficient in small things and tinny. Perhaps, I thought, society has begun to resist even analysis and reflection, to say nothing of mastery. The early sociologists were political philosophers and philosophers of history. They looked to society for the fulfillment of human nature, for the possibility of a better life. Our own generation has renounced these aims; we regard empirical sociology as a gloss on a reality we do not believe we can change. Max Weber, asked early in this century why he studied society, said that he did it to see how much he could stand. *("Wieval ich auschalten kann.")* We lack even this ironic acknowledgement of individual moral purpose, and our search for a new public good has been halting and ineffective when we have indulged it. The word *indulged* is frightening, but I shall let it stay. What was once the strongest force behind intellectual activity is now a mere psychological oddity, a matter of personal whim, a moral idiosyncracy. The most desperate and the least satisfactory aspect of our Congress was, however, perhaps the most valuable one, insofar as we tried to go beyond the picture of things as they are to find a moral and political vocabulary to describe an irrational and oppressive world. But this did not get very far. For the self-designated party of revolution in the state socialist societies has become a party of the institutionalized revolution, an apologist for old tyrannies in new form, whose most intelligent and rational subjects are agonizingly aware of their servitude. For our part, we do not embrace our injustices, but we do not seem to be transcending them. Our own younger revolutionaries think that they can start from scratch, and so fall easy victim to its old traps. A happier solution may await us in the future, but international conferences appear to be the last place to work toward one.

2

Sociology: Discontent Present and Perennial

I dislike repeating myself; I dislike, even more, repeating others. When the editor did me the honor of requesting a contribution to this symposium, my first inclination was to decline. I had just sent to the press a collection of my recent work, a large expression and specification of my own discontents with our discipline.[1] Moreover, Robert Friedrichs and Alvin Gouldner had just published critiques of American sociology at once remarkably dissimilar and remarkably convergent.[2] Finally, I had—on my bookshelves—a number of recent contributions to the debate,[3] partially read, partially unread. Under the circumstances, was it

[1] Norman Birnbaum, *Toward a Critical Sociology*, New York: Oxford University Press, 1971.

[2] Robert W. Friedrichs, *A Sociology of Sociology*, New York: The Free Press, 1970. Alvin W. Gouldner, *The Coming Crisis of Western Sociology*, New York: Basic Books, 1970.

[3] Dorothy Emmet and Alasdair MacIntyre (eds.), *Sociological Theory and Philosophical Analysis*, New York: Macmillan, 1970. Michel Foucault, *L'Archeologie du savoir*, Paris: Gallimard, 1969. Jurgen Habermas and Niklas Luhman, *Theorie der Gesellschaft oder Sozial-Technologie*, Frankfurt: Suhrkamp, 1971. Paul Lazarsfeld, *Qu'est-ce la Sociologie?* Paris: Gallimard, 1970 (also published in UNESCO, *Tendances Principales de la Recherche dans les Sciences Sociales et Humaines—I: Sciences Sociales*, Paris-The Hague: Mouton, 1970). Henri Lefebvre, *Au-delà du structuralisme*, Paris: Anthropos, 1971. Gian Rusconi, *Teoria Critica della Societa*, Bologna: Il Mulino, 1968. Finally, what we may think of as a reasonably official statement by American sociology about itself: the report on sociology prepared for the Behavioral and Social Sciences Survey of the National Academy of Sciences and

not best to get on with the doing of sociology or, if that was unpromising, of something better? If, in the end, I offer this sketch to my colleagues, it is not simply a consequence of that omnipresent intellectual disorder, literary narcissism. It is because I think that I see, a bit more clearly, the elements of our difficulties. Somewhat arbitrarily, I propose to select and discuss four sources of our recent discontents: political, practical, theoretical, and what—for want of a more satisfactory term—I designate as cultural.

The readers of *Social Research* require no lessons from its contributors in cosmopolitanism. Clearly, a critique of sociology limited to the United States leaves much to be desired. I offer no such critique—but I wonder whether I may err in an opposite direction. The national characteristics of American sociology are obvious, including its provincialism. (Was it not only a few years ago that the official organ of the American Sociological Association, the *American Sociological Review*, solemnly announced that it would henceforth review no foreign books?) Yet a rootedness in a national culture, an immersion in national political problems may also be preconditions of the integration of general ideas with the tasks of analysis. Perhaps the difficulty with American sociology lies, curiously, in its insulation from much in our national intellectual tradition and national life. American historians, economists, novelists, philosophers and film-makers—to name but a few who like ourselves, promulgate images of society—seem closer to both, less abstracted from either.[4] If our task lies, in no small measure, in the integration of European thought with the American sociological tradition, we shall have to develop a firmer grasp, a new evaluation, of our tradition.* If, on the other hand, that tradition is either exhausted or rests on foundations that are fragile or worse—if we have to begin anew— we had best be sure precisely where it failed. I am unable to develop this point at length in these pages, but the very mention of it provides a qualification (and a challenge) to many of the points I do make.

I

I have written of political discontents with sociology, as distinguished from practical ones. Anticipating a bit, we may say that political criticism of current sociology insists that it is too close to current practice,

the Social Science Research Council, Neil Smelser and James A. Davis (eds.), *Sociology*, Englewood Cliffs: Prentice-Hall, 1969.

[4] Christopher Lasch, *The New Radicalism in America, 1889–1963*, New York: Knopf, 1963 and *The Agony of the American Left*, New York: Knopf, 1969.

* The author wishes to thank the John Simon Guggenheim Memorial Foundation for a Fellowship which gave him the time to set down these observations.

whereas practical criticism of it insists that it is too remote. Put in these terms, the antithesis is too schematic; it will do as a beginning point. Most of the political criticism of sociology comes, of course, from currents which identify—in one way or another—with the traditions of the left. Their basic positions are clear enough. Sociology in its present form has irreducible ideological components; the burden of its findings tend to legitimate the current social order, by inducing approval or resignation in those who take them seriously. These ideological components are closely related to practical elements: sociologists have become ancillary agents of power, by performing intelligence services for elites who in turn use sociological intelligence for purposes of domination, exploitation and manipulation. Two correctives are needed. One would entail an ideological purification, or reversal; the other would entail a change in alliances so that sociologists would not serve elites but other, hitherto dominated groups.

Upon examination, the ideological critique of sociology is equivocal. Part of it insists that sociologists pay too little attention to certain salient facts: inequalities in power and property. Another part argues that sociologists are insufficiently utopian or visionary: Precisely by sticking too closely to the facts, sociologists blind themselves to alternative possibilities of social order. The demand for a reversal of alliances is no less equivocal. In its simple form, it leaves unanswered the question of the modality of the new relationship between sociologists and new, or different, publics. Are these to set the tasks of the sociologists, or are new forms of cooperation between those with knowledge and those striving for power to be developed?

Stated in these terms, the political discontent of the left with sociology is both compelling and strangely unconvincing. For one thing, it is not new. It is difficult to find an argument in the recently published anthology, *Radical Sociology*,[5] which is not to be found in Robert Lynd's *Knowledge for What*, published in 1939.[6] Indeed, a good deal of the criticism by the present sociological left embodies a net decline in intellectual quality compared to the works of earlier generations of academic radicals (Lynd was preceded by Veblen, after all) and more recent ones (like Paul Sweezy and, of course, C. Wright Mills). Perhaps the chief difficulty with the positions I have just summarized, however, is their unmediated and unreflected quality.

By unmediated and unreflected, I mean that these positions—in the main—do not entail an encounter with, or assimilation of, either a tradition of critical social thought or the central academic tradition in the social sciences. Harold Rosenberg (an art critic who, interestingly

    [5] J. David Colfax and Jack L. Roach, *Radical Sociology*, New York: Basic Books, 1971.

    [6] Robert Lynd, *Knowledge for What*, Princeton: Princeton University Press, 1939.

enough, is a member of the Committee on Social Thought at the University of Chicago) wrote a book entitled *The Tradition of the New*. There is a tradition of the left in social thought. Its origins may be set, variously, with Heraclitus, Joachim de Fiore, the protagonists of the Putney Debates, or Jean-Jacques Rousseau. The existence of evil in the world was not first remarked by the generation which entered the American universities in the 1960s; the problem of transcending an unjust, rigidified, and corrupt society is not new. The problems of the relationship of social thought to action,[7] of relatively static conceptual models to historical movement,[8] even of the relationship of thinkers to publics,[9] have not recently come upon us.

I have insisted on the superficiality of much of the current radical critique of sociology for radical reasons. A generation that wishes to immunize itself from the intellectual consequences of advancing age (a slower ideological metabolism, theoretical sclerosis, and—on the psychic plane—a compulsion to repeat its fathers' errors) will have to prepare itself for a long-term struggle. Indeed, if we think of sociologists rendering service to new publics, we shall have to ask if these sociologists are the intellectual equals of their (putatively) conservative opponents. I find it striking that a certain amount of radical energy has been expended, recently, in criticizing Alvin Gouldner.[10] The force, nay power, of Gouldner's book is directly proportional to his ability to analyze the premises of conventional sociology from within. If the work of Talcott Parsons is a contemporary American version of a far older attachment of sociology to the party of order, then our understanding of that party (and above all, of the interaction between its institutions and its ideology) will not be served by ignoring his work. What accounts for radical discomfort at Gouldner's book is, I think, its author's interest in a theoretical understanding of the world.

The embarrassment of some of the sociological left in the presence of theory merits closer attention. In *Radical Sociology*, David Colfax strikes some very ambivalent notes.[11] Theory has its uses, if I understand his

---

[7] Weber's "Science as a Vocation," *From Max Weber* (Hans Gerth and C. Wright Mills, eds.), New York: Oxford University Press, 1946, is the usual reference. It is interesting to compare Weber with Durkheim. Emile Durkheim, *La Science Sociale et l'action*, Paris: Presses Universitaires Françaises, 1970.

[8] This is a problem within Marxism itself, unless I have misunderstood Karl Korsch, *Marxismus und Philosophie* (Erich Gerlach, ed.), Frankfurt: Europaische Verlagsanstalt, 1966. The Korsch work was part of a discussion now available in English. Georg Lukács, *History and Class Consciousness*, Cambridge: Technology Press, 1971.

[9] Lewis Coser, *Men of Ideas*, New York: The Free Press, 1965. See also the excellent German statement, Karl Markus Michel, *Die sprachlose Intelligenz*, Frankfurt: Suhrkamp, 1968.

[10] See the review of Gouldner in *Ramparts* by Jeffrey Schevitz.

[11] "Varieties and Prospects of 'Radical Scholarship' in Sociology," *Radical Sociology*, pp. 81–92.

argument correctly, and so do radical academicians—but the real vanguard will be found on, or very near to, whatever barricades are up at
the moment. I have elsewhere said that in a society which increasingly
utilizes knowledge for administrative and productive ends, a particularly critical social function falls to those with theoretical knowledge.[12]
Sharing a common education and something of a common culture with
technocratic elites and professional-technical workers, they are in a
position to undermine the morale of the former, and crystallize the
discontents of the latter. Before the Bastille was stormed, the advance
work for the French Revolution was done by bourgeois intellectuals in
aristocratic salons.[13] There are senses, however, in which theory has a
political use apart from the immediate texture of conflict in a society.
Politics, the living of a common life, demands theory as an aspect of
human self-reflection. The humanization of industrial society is unlikely to be accomplished soon; it may, indeed, never be accomplished.
The dignity of theory will remain unimpaired, even should an utopian
politics prove impossible of realization.

It is at this, I think, that a good many in the radical party in sociology bridle. Their revulsion for the academicization of theory—in the
pejoritave sense, in which it loses theoretical as well as practical value—
is so great that they fail to recognize the indispensability of theory to a
radical politics. The European case is a striking contrast. In some countries, (France, the German Federal Republic and Italy) a clear division
of labor between theoreticians and those engaged in political practice
has been accepted by radical social movements. Paradoxically, this has
made it easier for theoreticians to engage in politics—and for those
involved in practice to contribute to theory. It is quite true that the
familiar debate on the cooptation of the academic intellectuals, on the
university as a "knowledge factory," has extended to Europe. Here,
too, a sector of the university left has abandoned the university and
sought literal fulfillment of the early Marxist demand that philosophy
become practice. What is more impressive, at least in the fall of 1971,
is the way in which the experience of the European New Left has
begun to be integrated into a tradition of theory which finds a home
in the universities.[14]

[12] "The Vanguard," *Partisan Review*, Vol. 36, No. 2, 1969.

[13] Daniel Mornet, *Les origines intellectuelles de la revolution française*, Paris: Colin,
1933, and Alain Touraine, *Post-Industrial Society*, New York: Random House, 1971. This
is an appropriate place to mention, as well, Thomas Bottomore's new version of his
Sociology: A Guide to Problems and Literature, New York: Pantheon, 1971. Bottomore has
attempted—with considerable success—to integrate recent political reflection with the
perennial problems of sociology.

[14] See the forthcoming translation of Svetozar Stojanović's book, *Between Ideals and
Reality: A Critique of Socialism and Its Future*, New York: Oxford University Press, 1973.
Also: Nicola Badaloni, *Il Marxismo degli anni sessante*, Rome: Editori Riuniti, 1971.

It may be objected, at this point, that my discussion has been confined to a very general plane, that it has hardly dealt with the specific structures, content and practice of social theory at all. Quite so, but neither does the theoretical critique developed to date by most of radical sociology in the United States. The strength of the radical critique appears to me to lie exactly in the area chosen for a critique of sociology by the technocratic center and the conservative right—in the relationship of sociology to political practice.

II

Economists, lawyers, political scientists, and, to some degree, psychologists have experienced little difficulty in entering the realm of political and administrative practice. To be sure, to some degree, the practitioners from these disciplines are drawn from sectors of their fields which codify practice. They may develop technical critiques of the agencies for which they work, but this is a part of the reflective process of the agency—not a large-scale application of knowledge, from without, to its work. The one conspicuous exception to this assertion is a large one: the familiar Keynesian revolution in economics, which has so altered public policy in capitalist politics over the past generation. Here, however, a political decision on the part of the elites (to generate full employment) preceded, or accompanied, their decision to seek technical advice from the Keynesian economists.

One very clear reason for the minor role played by sociologists in public policy is that we possess little operational knowledge to pass on to those with power. There is no sociological equivalent of the Keynesian Multiplier. Even in spheres like the planning of welfare functions or educational development, our wisdom is very much a matter of historical hindsight. The notion that the expansion of educational opportunity is the *via regis* to increased social mobility is, in its pure form, certainly true. The efficacy of policy recommendations based on that notion depend, however, upon a continuation of expansion in those sectors of the economy which employ new graduates. Moreover, a general expansion of educational opportunity creates conditions—within and without the educational system—which constitute a genuinely new historical situation; the old models cease to apply, in effect, once they are taken seriously.[15] Further, the application of certain kinds of sociological knowledge would entail long-range planning, a diminution of

---

[15] I am unaware of any systematic effort to study the consequences, for our knowledge of the social function of the social sciences, of the recent enlistment by policy makers of economists and sociologists in the service of programs of educational expansion.

political and social resistances, for which our institutions are simply not prepared. We have only to recall the tangled interrelations of social scientists and recent American attempts to deal with our racial and ethnic problems to see that the practical implementation of sociological knowledge calls into question the content of our knowledge itself.[16] Briefly, sociological analyses of the American racial situation seem to involve prior ethical and political decisions which shape the sociologists' categories. We find ourselves forever inside a circle.

It is not surprising, then, that three sorts of discontent have arisen from this situation. I shall term the first type conservative discontent. The conservatives have noted that, to say the least, sociology has been oversold: We know far less than we claim, and our techniques for establishing new knowledge do not appear to represent striking advances on more or less conventional wisdom. Worse yet, we arrogate to ourselves moral functions which should properly fall to society as a whole. Apart from recommendations as to modesty, however, the conservative critique fails to provide any hope of an immediate exit from this impasse. Indeed, the burden of the critique is that there is no exit and that, if there were one, it should be locked or guarded. Note that the conservative critique implies (and sometimes states) an entire set of propositions about the proper, as well as the possible, relationships between knowledge and power. Additionally, it seems to assume that no major purposeful alterations in the balance of forces in our society are likely in the near future. What the sociologists cannot do, no one else can do, either.[17]

A second type of critique may be termed technocratic. The distinction between this and the conservative critique is not total, and that indispensable house organ of the American technocrats (or those who would be technocrats), *The Public Interest,* at times speaks in both voices. This critique suggests that some of the responsibility for the relative feebleness of sociology lies in its abstention from undertaking public responsibilities. Some of the advocates of the creation of a national Council of Social Advisors to the President, a hypothetical counterpart to the Council of Economic Advisors, suppose that contact with the demands of what we may term administrative reality will eventually strengthen the social sciences.[18] The technocratic critique seemingly proposes to bring sociology down from the heaven of theory to the earth of institutional functioning. It proposes, however, no alteration in our conceptions, in our positivistic schema for enquiry; it simply

[16] References will be found in my "On the Sociology of Current Social Research," in *Toward a Critical Sociology.*

[17] See Daniel Patrick Moynihan's *Maximum Feasible Misunderstanding,* New York: Free Press, 1969.

[18] Henry W. Riecken, "Social Science and Contemporary Social Problems," *Items,* The Social Science Research Council, Vol. 26, No. 1, March 1969.

urges that we change our vantage point, and leaves the epistemological consequences to chance.

A third sort of discontent with sociology's relationship to practice is radical—its house organ may be *Social Policy*. For a large number of advocates of a changed relationship to practice, no particular epistemological consequences follow from their position. Like the technocratic critics, they propose (or assume) an extrinsic relationship between sociology and those who utilize its knowledge. New publics, or new clients, do not on this account entail new sociologists—only old sociologists, addressing themselves to different purposes. Some go further, and advocate a fusion of roles: the sociologist as institutional innovator.[19] What is radical in all of this is the notion that sociology should serve the oppressed and disadvantaged, although some of the current radical literature may well underestimate this component in the American sociological tradition. The radical critique of that tradition argues that its consensual concepts stem from its implicit adherence to elite-dominated models of society, but the critique is strongest where it is most negative. What would a sociology not only of, but for, the oppressed look like? The discussion remains exceedingly programmatic; we do not know. Some obvious points may be made. Sociologists who have embraced the notion of the cultural specificity of the oppressed—who denounce as the intellectual equivalent of genocide attempts to induct the oppressed or excluded into our own version of high culture—are not entirely silent. Yet it is difficult to imagine a new culture erected on a *tabula rasa*, and it is implausible that we might attain new wisdom by negation—by refusing rather than assimilating two millennia of social thought.

III

Both political and practical considerations, then, lead us back to theory. The political critique of theory and the practical one, each in its several varieties, have far more to say about the use of sociology than about its inner structures. This is not the place for a restatement of sociological theory, although I am reminded of the late Theodor Adorno's remark about his colleagues in philosophy. Where previous generations of philosophers had deemed it sufficient to work on philosophical questions by criticizing their predecessors and contemporaries, some modern philosophers seem to suppose that they can create the world anew in their texts. Might it not be time to reestablish continuity in sociology, precisely for the purpose of finding solutions to the prob-

[19] Henry Etzkowitz and Gerald Schaffander, *Ghetto Crisis*, Boston: Little, Brown 1969.

lems that beset us? The remarks that follow are, I know, excessively programmatic—like all programs, this one will have to be modified as it is put into effect. It has the virtue, at least, of drawing upon work that is already in process.

The first sort of work in process may be thought of as our collaboration with our predecessors. The historians have long since discovered what we are now experiencing: The past requires constant reinterpretation. The traditions of social thought, the narrower or more specific history of sociology, do not lie before us like an open book. The text, in effect, is subject to rereading on every page. Consider the exegetic controversies that attach to the writings of Marx, or of Weber (I hardly need cite references), and which are beginning to focus on Durkheim as well. Consider the revival, if that is the term, of sociologists long unread: Michels and Scheler, and Mauss. I anticipate, shortly, a wave of interest in early American thinkers like Ward. Any but the most superficial reading of these texts will show that the problems these thinkers were attacking are, with all allowance for differences of idiom and social context, very much with us.

An immanent critique of sociology, however, has very little chance of success. The point of an encounter with tradition is that new questions, new problems, are posed to it. We know full well that politics and social practice, generally, are a major source of these problems. The time has also come to acknowledge that the boundaries of our field are totally indistinct. I do not propose another effort to redefine sociology, to give it status by asserting its claims to conceptual independence. The nature of a discipline is that it is in constant transformation.[20] It is time to open up sociology once again, to recognize that we are not only dependent upon our social context for inspiration, but that we are obliged to make far greater use of our intellectual context as well. I propose to argue this point with reference to our relations with three disciplines: philosophy, history and psychoanalysis. It is true that each of these, in its way, is in as much perplexity and uncertainty as we are—but the very perplexities of another field may illuminate our own.

Sociology grew out of philosophy and, in some national settings, has remained closely connected with it. Recently, the relationship of American sociology to philosophy has been constricted by developments within philosophy itself. The narrowing of empiricism and positivism made of philosophy a set of commentaries on the operations performed elsewhere: Philosophy no longer described a world, nor did it enunciate the principles by which we know our world. Rather, it

---

[20] See my essay, "The Arbitrary Disciplines," *Change in Higher Education*, Vol. 1, No. 4, 1969. And, of course, Thomas Kuhn, *The Structure of Scientific Revolutions*, Chicago: University of Chicago, 1962.

adumbrated the process by which other disciplines apprehended reality; philosophy relegated itself to the epistemological sidelines. This act of self-renunciation was accomplished for ascetic, even noble purposes; it remained an act of renunciation. More recently still, American sociology has begun to be influenced by currents which are now running strongly in academic philosophy itself: existentialism, Marxism, and phenomenology. These afford, each in its own way, a broadening of perspective in sociology: New possibilities for interpreting data—indeed, new possibilities for identifying data—new conceptions of human possibility emerge when we abandon the terrain to which a natural science conception of sociology confines us. Here, I write programmatically of a program. With rare exceptions (as in the influence of Alfred Schutz on thinkers as diverse as Harold Garfinkel on the one hand and Peter Berger and Thomas Luckmann on the other), the American votaries of an antipositivistic philosophy have as yet to convert philosophic currency into sociological cash. The Marxists are an exception, but they could build on an earlier assimilation of Marxism in American social thought. Characteristically, the American school of Marxism or Marxist-influenced sociology is strongest in the concrete description of social structure, weakest in the development of a total social theory. Viewed in another way, perhaps the weakness is a strength: What would have become of Marx had he spent all of his time commenting on the writings of Hobbes, or the Encyclopedists? That is precisely what a certain Marxist exegesis proposes; Yankee pragmatism may, after all, have some advantages.

I have termed this a program, but a glance across the Atlantic will show that the program is eminently capable of realization. The notion that sociological categories are also answers to philosophical questions does not require much defense in the European universities. Neither does the proposition that sociologists, instead of doing philosophy *malgré eux-mêmes,* should acquire the rudiments of a philosophical education. A serious objection may be raised at this point. Granted that Jean-Paul Sartre's *Critique de la Raison Dialectique* is essential reading for an educated contemporary, granted that our conceptions of social action must be modified after we have read Merleau-Ponty, granted that the Frankfurt School's critique of the direct transposition of natural science models to sociology has considerable validity—what follows for our daily work as sociologists? Two very different sorts of answer have to be given.

The first is that much can follow, or very little. Metatheory as well as theory are at stake. The functions of metatheory are to direct discourse toward clusters or types of problems; to fragment inert totalities, the unity of which has become artificial; in short, to remind us that the world may be constructed differently than convention would allow. More specifically, metatheory enables us to see convention (sociological convention as well as the social convention it purports to depict) as the reified embodiment of old metatheories. Theory, a more direct attempt to conceptualize society in its concreteness, fuses imperceptibly with metatheory. Let me put it this way: Metatheory is the critique of historical existence; theory is its description. Can a correct description of a historical process be attached to a defective metatheory? Probably, and vice versa. At some point, however, the tension between the two must explode. Most sociology is conducted in some considerable degree of unawareness of this tension; a discipline originally intended to enlarge our understanding may, by its very partial successes, restrict it. The latency of this sort of philosophical discussion enables us to function day by day; it also mires us in routine.

That is the first answer. The second is rather less schematic. The contemporary philosophical discussion, as it impinges on sociology, casts into doubt two aspects of our assumption. The first concerns the historicity of the propositions we assert, the second concerns the meaningful structure of the actions we undertake. A recourse to the disciplines of history and psychoanalysis, even with their lacunae and contradictions, may not enable us to solve the problems posed by philosophy (or by the metatheoretical derivatives of philosophy in sociology). But it will broaden our perceptions.

It is a familiar enough dictum that sociology is a historical discipline. What, exactly, does this mean? That our generalizations are historically specific, no one would deny; comparative work and historical sociology have been called upon to make them less narrowly so. Suppose, however, that our concepts are historically specific as well. A case can be made that the analytical apparatus of sociology is in fact a derivative of a set of philosophical and empirical observations on the emergence of a distinctive social type—industrial society—in the 19th and 20th centuries. If so, profound changes in that society would confound our observations by making obvious the deficiencies of our categories. If I have understood the sense of a good deal of post-Marxist sociology, in particular that of Raymond Aron, it is this enterprise on which it is engaged.[21] It is here that post-Marxists and neo-Marxists meet, in the effort to wrest new concepts from the (dimly perceived) long-term movement of history. Now that American sociology is beginning to take serious account of the Frankfurt School, it is not too

---

[21] Aron's Inaugural Lecture at the *Collège de France* returns to this theme and to the metatheoretical status of sociological theory. I am aware that he would not put it in this way, but if he will forgive the phrasing: the message is clear. Raymond Aron, "De la condition historique de la Sociologie," *Informations sur les Sciences Sociales*, Vol. 10, No. 1, February 1971. No one is second to myself in scepticism about the notion of a post-industrial society, in particular as developed by Daniel Bell. (See his essay in *Survey*, Vol. 16, No. 1, 1971 and the ensuing discussion in Vol. 17, No. 2, 1971.) Nevertheless, the attempt to employ a new vocabulary is a genuinely theoretical one, and merits both attention and respect.

much to hope that we will shortly pay attention to one of the most original of 20th-century Marxists—if not the most original—Antonio Gramsci. Gramsci's rootedness in Italian historical soil enabled him to combine the abstract categories of Marxism with a delicate sense of the particularities of Italian history. His critique of sociology, at the same time a critique of a rigidified or northern European Marxism, shows what intellectual energies may be released when historical categories are confronted and overcome.[22]

Not every sociologist, of course, can play Prometheus—bringing new warmth and light to the intellectual community. However, there remain entire areas of social experience, easily accessible in archives, in the works of our colleagues in history which can widen our ordinary perspectives. The profound questions of time series and demographic scale defy a historical statement, and nothing can be done with these in the absence of immense amounts of historical data.[23] Social structures are historically transitory, their content is infinitely variable, their modes of cohesion, change and supersession no less so. A concretistic view, devoid of an appreciation of the meaning of the term, structure? Perhaps—but the only way in which the claims of structuralism, in any of its varieties, can be evaluated is by recourse to detailed historical work. Here, too, the theoretical import of history is very great.[24]

Finally, I turn to psychoanalysis. Successive waves of interest in this discipline have beat upon our shores—and subsided. There was a period in which psychoanalysis was supposed to supply the categories for understanding the mechanisms of compliance. There was yet another in which the processes of socialization were viewed as something like the internalization of social structure—and in which social structure, in turn, was to be explained as a form of exteriorization of an inner psychological logic. For reasons which I do not understand, this last phase was allowed to ebb away, the problems it posed largely unresolved.[25] In this country, Erikson unswervingly pursued the deeper dimensions of human history—joined later by a new group of psychohistorians.[26] The term is in itself suggestive of an interest in histor-

[22] Antonio Gramsci, *Quaderni del Carcere, I. Il Materialismo Storico,* Turin, Einaudi, 1966.

[23] Fernand Braudel, "La Longue Durée," *Annales,* No. 4, 1958. A very different statement comes from the report on *History* to the Behavioral and Social Sciences Survey, edited by David Landers and Charles Tilley. *History,* Englewood Cliffs: Prentice-Hall, 1969.

[24] Claude Lévi-Strauss, *La Pensée Sauvage,* Paris: Plon, 1962 and Lucien Sebag, *Marxisme et Structuralisme,* Paris: Payot, 1964.

[25] See Clyde Kluckhohn, Henry Murray and David Schneider, *Personality in Nature, Society and Culture* (2nd ed.), New York: Knopf, 1953. See also the critique of this development by Alex Inkeles and Daniel Levinson, *Handbook of Social Psychology* (Gardiner Lindzey, ed.), 1954, 1969.

[26] Erik Erikson, *Childhood and Society* (2nd ed.), New York: Norton, 1964; *Young*

ical movement which has superseded interest in the maintenance of fixed social structures. In Germany, the alliance between Mitscherlich and the Frankfurt School has given us the beginnings of yet another systematic effort to work through the theoretic implications of the uneasy coexistence of our two modes of discourse.[27]

Perhaps we do deal with two very different types of discourse, conceptualizing social phenomena so differently that their only fruitful collaboration rests on recognition and acceptance of the differences. The solution is elegant, but unconvincing. The clinical practice of psychoanalysis has established, as commonplace observation tells us, that symptomatology has changed over the past generations. Startling shifts in sexual morality, sexual role differentiation, and general impulse expression; unimaginable outbursts of aggression; pathetically unfulfilled communal-libidinal drives—all of these are commonplace eruptions in contemporary society. Indeed, the phrase *eruption* suggests an underlying stability of structure for which there is increasingly little evidence. Part of the difficulty in the clinical practice of psychoanalysis may be due to the decreasing fixity of social structure.[28] All of this raises grave questions of philosophical anthropology which touch the Freudian legacy deeply. It also raises questions about our own reliance, as sociologists, on largely uncriticized notions of psychic function, human plasticity, and human impulse. The fact that some of us are, in effect, routinized Freudians is no consolation; Freudian routine is breaking down in its own heartland.[29] I must confess to bewilderment, even dismay, at the prospect of having to take up thorny theoretical issues again which offer so little hope of immediate solution. Even a relative failure in an attempt to rethink our relationships to psychoanalysis may contain a measure of success; we shall have gained a clearer vision of our own technical limitations.

IV

Here terminology fails me, if argument does not. I have said that there are cultural dimensions to discontent with sociology, and what I have

Man Luther, New York: Norton, 1958; *Ghandi's Truth*, New York: Norton, 1969. See also Robert J. Lifton, *Boundaries*, New York: Random House, 1969.

[27] Alexander Mitscherlich, "Psychoanalysis and the Aggression of Large Groups," *International Journal of Psychoanalysis*, Vol. 52, Part 2, 1971. Also: Alfred Lorenzer, Helmut Dahmer, Klaus Horn, Karoli Brede and Enno Schwanenberg, *Psychoanalyse als Sozialwissenschaft*, Frankfurt: Suhrkamp, 1971. A different view is taken by Neil Smelser and Robert Wallerstein, "Psychoanalysis and Sociology: Articulations and Applications," *International Journal of Psychoanalysis* 50: 693–710, 1969.

[28] I am indebted to Dr. Charles Fisher for discussing these matters with me; he has taught me much.

[29] Anna Freud, *Difficulties in the Path of Psychoanalysis*, New York: International Universities Press, 1969.

to say is painful. It may well be that we are at the end of a long and important state of cultural history, which may be thought of (crudely) as the period of bourgeois culture.[30] Op art, mixed-media *chefs d'oeuvre,* McLuhanism in all of its aberrations seem to have superseded the reflectiveness and relative autonomy of aesthetic experience in its previous forms. Nevertheless, we are the inheritors of a considerable cultural legacy, and our capacity to understand the present, as well of course as the perennial symbolic structures of human existence, depends upon our mastery of that legacy. Most work in sociology proceeds in not quite sublime disregard of the legacy. It is flatter, less imaginative, even more philistine as a result. It should not be thought that I am arguing for a complete interchangeability of sociologists with art historians, or historians of literature, or aestheticians. Far from it— but the discipline and sensibilities required by profound work in these fields seem to mobilize human capacities which we allow to lie unused in ourselves.

Let me give two, very different examples. Our distinguished French colleague, Edgar Morin, is the author of a serious study of mass culture, a valuable community study in Brittany, a spot inquiry on a proto-medieval antisemitic disturbance in Orleans, and of a remarkable analysis of the French student revolt. He has recently published a diary of his stay in California—impressionistic, aphoristic, perhaps even wrongheaded.[31] But he is able to seize the moment both in its contemporaneity and historicity. Another colleague, the German historian of thought Hans Blumenberg, some years ago published a philosophical inquiry into the origins and structure of modernity.[32] The book's title, *Die Legitimät der Neuzeit,* bespeaks an excitement fully conveyed in its pages. Not surprisingly, Blumenberg not only uses a full range of historical texts, but also deals seriously with Bertolt Brecht's profound play about Galileo.[33] As a sociologist who has put some energy into the study of religion, I found the text—if the word can be forgiven—a revelation. Blumenberg demands that we rethink, entirely, the concept of secularization which we use so casually in our enquiries. And if we take his work seriously, our categorical apparatus for the study of "rationalization" will have to be profoundly revised. Only historical depth can generate a new historical view; if we shut ourselves off from sources of this kind, our work is bound to be impoverished, even sterile.

As I write, I can look out of a window in Turin on the River Po. The scene is not arcadian. Between myself and the Po there lies the city's exhibition hall, crowded at the moment with visitors to an ex-

---

[30] See the chapter on "Culture" in my own *The Crisis of Industrial Society,* New York: Oxford University Press, 1969. And, of course, Lionel Trilling, *Beyond Culture,* New York: Viking, 1968.

[31] Edgar Morin, *Journal de Californie,* Paris, Seuil, 1970.

[32] Hans Blumenberg, *Die Legitimät der Neuzeit,* Frankfurt: Suhrkamp, 1966.

[33] *Materielen zu Brechts "Leben des Galilei,"* Frankfurt: Suhrkamp, 1963.

position of technology. And on the river itself, fog and industrial smog mix. Some few blocks away, the southern immigrants are crowded into northern slums. Goethe's Italy is no more; neither is E. M. Forster's or, for that matter, Roberto Rosellini's, and American Express seems to earn more from investment banking in Milan than tours in Florence. Meanwhile, I turn the pages of a book full of sociological insight and analytical rigor: a report on the election fought in Naples by a Communist candidate, in the form of letters to a French friend (the Marxist philosopher Louis Althusser).[34] Maria Antonietta Macciocchi's book was not enthusiastically received by some of the Italian Communist Party; she was accused of snobbism because she employed literary references. Perhaps; but I know of very few works in political sociology, community study, or the sociology of development which are its equal. The future of industrial society is as uncertain as its present is dismaying; if we are to deepen our understanding, much in our work will have to change.

[34] Maria Antonietta Macciocchi, *Léttera dall' Interno del P.C.J. a Louis Althusser,* Milan: Feltrinelli, 1969.

3

An End to Sociology?

No international sociological congress I have attended (and I have been at every one since 1953) has neglected the question, is there a crisis in sociology? Upon occasion, the question has pervaded, even dominated, formal congress discussion. Upon others, it has constituted a substratum of criticism, in contrast with the certainties expressed in the official proceedings. We may doubt our methods of social observation, despair of our interpretative ideas, deplore the use (or nonuse) society makes of our work. No matter, we may console ourselves with obsessive self-concern. The participants in panels of this kind may change (although some, like their answers, may grow more familiar). The societies and types of regime they represent may vary. Their rhetoric, the saliency of some rather than other issues, may alter. We have now institutionalized the crisis. Systematic introspection, nay inversion, is a legitimate (and certainly recognizable) disciplinary specialty. In this, we are not entirely alone. Economists, historians of literature, historians *tout court*, philosophers can be heard discussing their own work in what appear to be similar terms. Aestheticians ask if art has ended, and some of psychiatry has become antipsychiatry. The difficulties within our field partake of a general crisis in the human sciences. Profound historical change and its (distorted) reflection in thought seem inextricable.

It apparently remains only for all of us in the human sciences to look enviously at the natural scientists, whose problems of conceptual discontinuity seem to offer happier resolutions. Perhaps our envy is closely related to our unfamiliarity with these sciences, themselves undergoing deep and rapid transformation. Perhaps, as we shall see, the analysis of these transformations may tell us something about ourselves. But *Schadenfreude* over the fate of colleagues whose concerns are near to ours, envy of those whose discourse seems entirely different, are equally easy, even cheap. What is hard, and necessary, is another examination of our own difficulties. And chief among these is our propensity to suppose that our crisis has a solution. We would do well to begin by thinking of it historically, and asking if it has a beginning and a middle: the end may be different from any we can envisage ahistorically. To anticipate a bit, many of us had hitherto supposed that the trouble was that sociology had the wrong ideas. Consider, however, the possibility that the idea of sociology as a separate discipline is in itself wrong.

Origins and Progression

Sociology developed in the nineteenth century as a response to the deficiencies of the traditional modes of apprehending society. Political philosophy often (think of Rousseau and Burke, De Maistre and Mill) entailed models of society, images of comportment, analyses of motivation. Its strength was, however, its weakness. The abstract qualities of the tradition of political philosophy allowed the historical concreteness of modern social development to escape. Of course, it pervaded political philosophy—by reflection and refraction. However, themes like the antithesis between tradition and emancipation were addressed with contemporary reference subordinated to the analysis of principles.

The abstract quality of political economy was, by contrast, an advantage. It is customary for moralists (and others) to denounce political economy for obsessive concern with *Homo economicus*. In a society in which new forms of production and exchange converted much of society into an appendage of the market, this concern was a precondition for intellectual achievement—as Marx saw. Sociology, in the work of Comte and Spencer, and later of Toennies and Durkheim, inquired into the consequences of that transformation. In doing that, however, the new mode of inquiry often detached itself (by a curious intellectual anesthetization) from a concern with the market.

The claim of history to be the totalizing discipline par excellence (even in epochs in which a political historiography was dominant) cannot be discounted. However, history's mode of totalizing a description of society was concrete—a single historical situation examined, brought into focus. Moreover, historians were interested in the past as a precondition of the present; they very rarely described the present as a result of the past. Marx, it will be recalled, disclaimed credit for the discovery of the importance of social classes in modern history—attributing that to the liberal Guizot. Sociology, with its sense of the uniqueness of the emergent industrial and capitalist society, might have understood itself as a form of contemporary history. (Tocqueville's self-understanding was approximately that.) Instead, the analysis of that society schematized history. In the effort to fix the outlines of a new epoch, the presence of the legacy of the past was overlooked.

Finally, there were *Political Arithmetk, Kameralistik, la Physique Sociale*—the efforts to quantify observable social regularities. Much of the historical energy concentrated in these new forms of thought was to end in political economy. The response to quantification of the first generations of sociologists was not unequivocal. Some treated these developments as techniques, useful ancillaries to social interpretation. None, not even Comte, supposed that the total quantification of sociological analysis was now possible. Even those most influenced by the natural sciences (Comte and Mill) concentrated on the development of very general categories which could subsume qualitative data. I refer to matters like the construction of theories of consensus and cohesion, attributions of motivational sequence. Spencer, of course, used evolutionary (biological) models. Let us take seriously the familiar argument that it was Malthus's model of population that influenced Darwin, conceptions of nature imitating ideas of society and not the other way around. It was as an idea, not as a rigorous model of discourse, that the notion of natural limits entered sociology. If Weber, for instance, was a social Darwinist, metaphor and not technique infused his work.

Sociology, then, was from its inception an exceedingly synthetic discipline. It brought political philosophy up to date by attempting to objectify some of the moral dilemmas which preoccupied that sort of inquiry. That is, it historicized conflicts which were once depicted as immutable. From political economy, sociology drew the idea of the novelty, the magnitude, of the market. History gave it a sense of movement, of sequence. Social statistics, finally, supplied the elements of a concrete description of the armature of the new society. We may put the matter in another way. Sociology attempted a description of a new social formation *sui generis*. That description, however, was fused to analysis—which derived statements about the new social formation from general principles of social behavior and social process. These principles, however, were often enough expressions of conceptions historically specific to the new nineteenth-century society. The synthesis, briefly, rested upon the delicacy and justice of the historical perceptions of the first sociologists. We should not be surprised that, no sooner promulgated, the synthesis began to break down.

The breakdown was, conceptually, very nearly complete by the time sociology was admitted to the academy. I am unconvinced that the resistance to the introduction of sociology in the universities (very recently overcome in the case of the ancient British universities, about which I know a bit) was due to trivial academic interests. It had two sources, and only a thinker committed to simplistic reductionism would attribute primacy to one or the other. The first was the movement of thought. The methodological or philosophical assumptions, the substantive concepts, the techniques of observation and analysis, of the human sciences may and did exhibit a near-chaotic diversity. They also constituted a field of considerable intellectual riches, few of which sociology seemed capable of appropriating. Think, for instance, of the fact that our field has never really assimilated, psychoanalysis or (more recently) structural linguistics.

The second was the movement of society. The lineaments of industrial society having been seized, they changed. New densities, new mechanisms, new institutions emerged. No one account (or model) seemed able to encompass these. Further, in contemporary politics, ideas of and about society were political artifacts. Conflict within sociology expressed, often in distorted or foreshortened form, conflicts of a political kind. The scientific pretensions of many sociologists, and even more their scientific perspectives, compelled them to flee the implications of this condition. At its inception, sociology sought to complete the task of political philosophy. During its (spurious) maturity, it abandoned that task. Where, as a result, sociology was not morally and intellectually impoverished, it was historically disoriented. Viewing things *sub specie aeternitatis*, sociologists lost their capacity to see them in their historical specificity.

In the middle period of sociology, after the generation of Durkheim, Pareto, Weber, there were three central tendencies. The first, certainly quantitatively the most important, was a concentration on specific sectors of modern society. Stratification (not class), urban and rural sociologies, analyses of the family, industrial studies became the central matter of sociological investigation. Whereas previous generations had used data of this sort as material for the construction of ideas of society in its totality, a new asceticism now made its appearance.

Comte was attached to scientific method (or scientistic, in the view of intelligent detractors like von Hayek) but insisted that he had a view of the social totality. His twentieth-century descendants claimed that they would generate a view of the whole after an indefinite series of specific inquiries. There was no agreed conception of the scope of these inquiries. Some envisaged the testing of general hypotheses on social behavior and process. Others thought of concentration on specific sectors of society, depicted as more (or less) central to the functioning of the whole. All agreed that a sociological utopia lay in the future. At some point, the discipline would promulgate valid knowledge of society as a whole.

The utopia to be constructed in this way certainly represented an identification of sociology with the process of rationalization. Every bit of metaphysical pathos was banished from the field. The ancient chores of political philosophy were assigned to other specialists, themselves often all too eager to abandon them.

The third tendency was another—a secular—substitute for political philosophy. A series of general, if contradictory, characterizations of the epoch was produced by sociologists self-consciously engaged in historical commentary. The names Mannheim and Sorokin will suggest the varied scope of the enterprise. We can look back and see that Weber, himself an historical commentator of great power, provided precept and example for the enterprise. The separation of judgment of fact from judgment of value, the dizzying discrepancy between his conceptual analysis of human action and his historical work, suggest that Weber accepted as ineluctable the fragmentation of sociological vision.

Contemporary sociology is the legatee of this progression. Certainly, most of its effort continues in the area of sectorial studies of modern society. Appearance and reality are different. It appears that sociologists study matters ignored by others (other disciplines, the general public). In fact, sociology has a peculiar sensitivity to changes in the mood of the technocratic directorates who dominate (as best they can) our epoch. In the United States, to take three recent instances, the exacerbation of the problem of blacks and other minorities, the complex of questions around impoverishment, the protest of students and youth were not anticipated by sociologists. Attention was given to these matters when they attracted political attention. Much of modern sociology (and this is as true in the state-socialist societies, if not more so) makes of it a data-gathering component of a highly fallible social technology. The scientific utopia of which I spoke fools almost no one. The technocratic interest in contemporary sociology is due not to its putative capacity for large-scale social description but to its actual ability to eschew that in order to collect administratively useful knowledge.

The making of social theory continues, nevertheless. It increasingly resembles that preoccupation with an historically contentless totality, a model of all possible societies, anticipated by Durkheim. Interestingly, recent work on Durkheim shows how this was a pendant to his own belief in a social technology. What is so striking about social theory today is its abstracted capacity. A *machine à tout faire*, it serves everyone and no one. The epoch of functionalist domination of social theory is over, at least for the United States (perhaps it is just beginning in the Soviet Union, where an enforced consensus is a political fact). We have, instead, a mélange of methodological argument, alternative categorical systems, competing images of society. But wait: Have I not just insisted on the abstracted quality of contemporary theoretical discussion, with the implication that it contained at least one of sociology's recent traditions, the flight from political philosophy? Do not competing images of society, if my term has any meaning, imply the return of political discussion? Indeed they do. I will not write of a return of the repressed, since it is unclear that this particular return is actually a therapeutic recovery. It may be what the psychoanalysts term acting out.

The element of historical commentary in contemporary sociology is the *via regis* for the incorporation of a kind of political philosophy in our work. Statements on the possibilities and limits of development of our society, upon analysis, are frequently statements of political choice. (Consider the controversy on the specificity of a postindustrial society. Bell and Touraine *inter alia* identifying it in entirely different ways.[1]) Politics, of a sort, even saturates the data-gathering operations of those who think of themselves as technologists of research, as pure empiricists. Ideas of our historical location (and therewith ideas of the kind of polity we can attain) set the limits, and often fix the content, of the categories in which data are recorded. Indeed, the categories form the data. The long debate in another part of sociology which opposed conflict theorists to consensual ones ought not to be dismissed as a poor successor to medieval scholasticism. Historians of scholasticism, after all, tell us that even technical argument on points of minor detail evoked structural differences within and between medieval philosophical systems. We can understand that debate as a form of political controversy. That some of the participants in it did not dare utter its name is regrettable, but not of overwhelming account.

The Ineluctable Crisis

The distinquished members of the panel have indeed agreed that there is a crisis in sociology. They are agreed neither on its dimensions, precise historical causes, nor philosophical and political meanings. For every sociologist, a crisis: The discipline which claimed at the beginning to adumbrate a new social-historical totality ends in a plurality, if not an infinity, of opinions. A metaphysical bang ends with a methodological whimper. Surely, more can be said; it follows.

The differences expressed here are important, not because they are easy of resolution, but because they may not be. One element of the crisis in sociology seems clear—we ask too much of it. How can a single discipline integrate all of contemporary knowledge in the human sciences, give an exact account of the inner movement of contem-

[1] Daniel Bell, *The Coming of Post-Industrial Society* (New York: Basic Books, 1973); Alain Touraine, *La Société post-industrielle* (Paris: Denoël, 1969), Eng. trans. *The Post-Industrial Society* (New York: Random House, 1971).

porary world history, provide the idea of a good or fulfilled human community, derive the sociopolitical techniques which would bring that community into being, and resolve every contradiction and difficulty in the contemporary theory of knowledge.

A simple solution presents itself: Ask less. That would be simple, but inelegant. Each problem on the list has this characteristic—it entails every other. Limiting the central problem of sociology to one is not a way to avoid any of the others: What we do need at first is a process of clarification, in which we could become aware of the systematic interrelations among these problems. Therapeutic clarification for individuals takes the form of educating them to assume inner responsibility for their acts as a preliminary to any change in their behavioral pattern. A conceptual therapy for sociologists would invite them to recognize that they cannot escape responsibility for the intellectual consequences of their interests. I propose to proceed by sketching the universe of discourse sociology entails. I will then ask what assistance, if any, we may ask of other sorts of inquiry; there is much that we have to learn. Finally, I will consider the idea of crisis again; by then, an answer may be less difficult.

Left and right, the party of change and the party of order, have marched their armies across our stage for so long that we have lost sight of something; their struggle is often illusory. Lecture-room Metternichs and literary Robespierres have this in common—a penchant for pursuing theoretic discussion of politics *ad absurdum.* Reading some sociological polemics, one might think that society as a whole had entrusted custody of political ideology exclusively to committees of sociologists (or, at least, academics). It would follow that everything sociologists do has political implications. That is, perhaps, true—but not in the way it is commonly understood. Political clarification in sociology takes the form of self-clarification, looking for the political implications of sociological analysis. Would it not be more efficacious to add to this a different sort of effort, to understand the political implications of ostensibly apolitical aspects of social process? This might well imply two sorts of analysis. One would deal with the interpenetration of politics and ordinary institutions. The phrase is cumbersome: politics is not a separate institutional sphere in modern societies, and there are in any event no ordinary institutions. I do not refer to the struggle for power within institutions, taken discretely, but to the ways in which these struggles combine into a pervasive politics. All of politics, additionally, is not struggle: the constraints which canalize conflict in one rather than another direction, mobilize or immobilize energies, are as important as overt antagonisms. A total system of social constraints, therefore, sets limits on the polity. What these limits are, and how they could be extended, are important questions for a sociology that would think of itself as political.

I have said that, until now, historical commentary has been the usual mode of integration of political philosophy with sociology. Would it not be more economical to attempt that integration, which now proceeds in haphazard and unreflective fashion, in a more direct way? Some prefer an advocacy social science, with social scientists taking the side of hitherto oppressed or disadvantaged groups. I do not consider it a denigration of the enterprise to suggest that it entails but one interpretation of politics and of knowledge. A technocratic politics of the left, very little different in texture from that of the right, may be a result. In any case, an image of political community as a vacuum into which competing interests rush accepts, and perhaps reifies, contemporary political structures in the liberal capitalist societies. Suppose, alternatively, that sociology were to concern itself with different models of political community, new forms of representation, new sorts of public education and exchange of opinion, qualitative conceptions of the public interest. Neither all nor much of this need point in the direction of decentralization: our societies present problems in the identification, as well as the control, of centralized power. It is surprising how little that is not schematic sociologists have to say about these problems. Our idea of technobureaucratic society is unilinear, presupposing the alternation of uninterrupted growth of a central steering apparatus and spasmodic guerrilla actions against it. A useful relationship between our conceptions of political possibility and our philosophical notions of political ends requires a dialectical confrontation.

Is this a way of asking that sociologists become political philosophers? I do not think so, but it is a way of asking that we take stock of the political philosophical component in our thought. That is a matter larger than our taking sides in present conflicts. It involves critical reflection on the range of analytic discourse to which our fascination with immediate structures of conflict restricts us. We will have to recognize that different conceptions of human substance, of sociability itself, may involve amended or new analytic categories. The kind of thought at issue need not exhaust itself in the construction of utopias. We would do well to recognize that the imagination required for utopian thought may be a working element in any sociological thinking that would go beyond our parochialisms. History does generate changes in consciousness: it is time that, instead of running after history, we anticipated somewhat.

Historical anticipation obliges us to explore the developmental possibilities of our political structures. The analysis of possibility, in turn, sends us back to the subtle transformations of power in our society, in which form and content have come apart. Some part of the uneasiness of the advanced societies comes from the sense that they are out of control. There is a pervasive bad conscience among politicians and their intellectual servitors which bespeaks their awareness of the discrepancy between their world-historical pretensions and their dwarflike practice. A sociological analysis of power will have to relate dialectically to these tempers and distempers, as the bad conscience of their bad conscience. The search for new models of political community, however, cannot legitimate itself through its intentions. It will have to be judged on the plausibility and precision of its arguments.

Upon examination, philosophical openness calls for historical specificity. Larger systems of sociological interpretation have treated the successive transformations of bourgeois society in condensed fashion, distilling its experience into categories. We now know three things, if we know anything. Within these societies, the forms and substance of bourgeois domination are ending. We have reason to suspect that the conventional historical periodization is wrong: different time scales, and other processes than those that dominated bourgeois self-depiction, have shaped that progression whose outlines we thought we comprehended. Meanwhile, the global power exercised by the bourgeouis nations has been drastically reduced. There is something quaintly archaic, indeed, about the term bourgeois to describe a historical formation we now suspect was at the intersection of a number of lines of development. I may put the problem in a different way, which connects with my discussion of political community. That the ideas of Aristotle, Augustine, Hobbes, Rousseau, and Hegel have entered sociology, not by direct appropriation but by incorporation in a tradition of social theory of which we are the heirs, is not surprising. What is surprising is that sociologists should suppose that our categories are universal whereas others are historically specific. Just as our society is historically stratified, and can be read like an archaeological site, our thought bears the imprint of its origins.

It is customary to treat this problem under the rubric of ethnocentrism, rather as the political component of sociology may be depicted as a form of partisanship. The situation is much more complex. There can be no immediate leap from ethnocentrism to a pure universalism, just as there can be no total transition from political bias to value neutrality. Indeed, a pure universalism may not be value neutral, since it may well entail judgments on our part as to the direction in which social history should tend. We find ourselves in the midst of a historical and cultural process by which the elements of a new universalism are being developed or—more precisely—argued and even fought about. A falsely totalizing discipline in its present form, sociology can at least accept the burden of constructing provisional totalizations of reflection. It is with some care that I have chosen the word reflection. Unless it is to claim to be that universal science uniting thought about society and thought about nature the emergence of which Marx predicted, sociology (or, rather, sociologists) must make more modest claims.

I have connected the analysis of our historicity and the depiction

of political community, and I would justify the connection in this way.
The decreasing degree of autonomy of function of separate societies,
the situation of polycentric global conflict into which they have moved,
gives us a world history as a series of increasingly interconnected particular histories. The spread of industrialization and ideas of citizenship
might seem to suggest the Westernization of the world (a phrase which
is embarrassing in connection with the Chinese Revolution). It by no
means suggests its modernization, a term which implies that our own
societies are at the apex of human development. The specific historical
forms of industrialization, the new political systems being developed
in large parts of the world, more fundamentally can be read as evidence for the end of the Western preponderance in world history. By
analogy, the enormous increase in the functions of the modern state is
by no means synonymous with an extension of its power. The interpenetration of state and society endows the state with a greatly enlarged task of coordination. It also enables a system of power contained in the market to integrate itself, in turn, with the state.

The phrase "provisional totalization of reflection" needs explication. The provisional quality of sociological discourse would consist of
a self-conscious process of historical localization. The categories of discourse would be understood as adapted to a specific unit of historical
time. The totalizing aspect would rest on the effort to seize a phenomenon in its interconnectedness; distinctiveness could be established only
in these terms. (It is not inappropriate, here, to recall the valuable work
of the late Georges Gurvitch, ignored with sovereign provinciality in
the English-speaking world, so important in postwar France.[2]) The term
reflection would distinguish sociological thought from what the positivists call protocol statements, or from conceptions of knowledge derived
from simplified ideas about laboratory science. The falsification of hypotheses is not the central task of the social sciences. Their task is the
establishment of categories, of ideas of the sequence of social causation, in which hypotheses may be framed.

I have said that the problem is neither one of ethnocentrism nor
of political partisanship, and by now it is perhaps somewhat clearer
where the difficulty lies. The problem for sociological discourse is to
transcend the intellectual objectifications of the various forms of ideological limitation-objectifications which have to be dealt with in their
own terms as systems of discourse. Further, not all the limitations of
vision and thought in sociology are ideological. Many stem from deficiencies in knowledge, rigor, and imagination. Briefly, the corrective
for deficient sociological discourse is more cogent discourse. In the third
section of this paper, I will attempt to identify some of the contemporary sources of cogency in the social sciences and their implications for

---

[2] Georges Gurvitch, *Déterminismes sociaux et liberté humaine* (Paris: PUF, 1963).

sociology. For the moment, let us continue with this sketch of some of the components of discourse.

The question of ethnocentrism requires attention; it cannot be exorcised lightly. I may begin with the observation that the most resolutely antiethnocentric of contemporary social thinkers is possibly, Lèvi-Strauss.[3] He does, after all, deny any privileged historical status to Western rational thought and argues that, in the sight of nature, all societies are alike. (Lévi-Strauss is a secularized exponent of the thought uttered by Ranke to the effect that all epochs were equal in the sight of God.) Yet it is Lévi-Strauss who claims that the categories imputed by himself to the savage mind are universal, that the structure of human thought in myth is precisely that, human. In other words, the assertion of ethnocentrism implies a conception of a common humanity expressing itself in some of its cultural and social structures. No communication between different groups, no understanding of other cultures would be possible on any other basis. There is a similar problem with respect to antipsychiatry.[4] The attack by Laing and others on the assumptions of customary psychiatric diagnosis presupposes a more encompassing, a truer theory of human nature. The antipsychiatrists on no account renounce the possibility of a theory: they insist that theirs is better.

Warnings about ethnocentrism do have a point, however. Our categories for the construction of ideas of society depend heavily upon Western experience. There is no language of all languages, and our notions of social development bear the imprint of our own. I have referred to the disastrous reliance of sociologists of development on concepts like modernization, which assumed (a) that every place would become like every other and (b) that they would all resemble the United States. It is easier, now, to cast off this idea—not least because the United States bears little resemblance to our colleagues' ideas of it. When we consider events like the Cultural Revolution in China, the Cambodian Revolution, we can conclude that modern social development, indeed, is in question: Max Weber was right to have insisted that cultures could choose to rationalize ritual rather than industrial production. Machine production, in any event, does not predetermine a specific course of social development.

What of the theory of human nature itself? There is no work in sociology in this century (or any other) to compare in originality, profundity, and explanatory power with that of Freud. The death of classical psychoanalysis, as therapeutic technique and as theory, has been

---

[3] Claude Lévi-Strauss, *La Pensée sauvage* (Paris: Plon, 1962), Eng. trans. *The Savage Mind* (Chicago: University of Chicago Press, 1969).

[4] Robert Boyers and Robert Orrill, *R. D. Laing and Anti-Psychiatry* (New York: Harper & Row, 1971).

announced often enough. In the absence of a plausible succession, it remains alive. A perfectly good argument can be made for the position that institutional analysis and inquiry into the biopsychic sources of behavior are different. The difficulty is that analysts of institutions make assumptions about the sources of behavior: it was not so long ago that American functionalist sociology was full of adumbrations of the doctrine of tension reduction (a mechanical derivative of psychoanalytic theory which any conscientious student of Freudian texts would have to repudiate). Our common alternative (found in the work of Parsons, despite his own great interest in psychoanalysis) was the idea that value systems and role prescriptions were capable of mobilizing and fixing a variety of psychological content. I have no doubt that the assertion is true, but it is one of those propositions which can tell us how a system works once it is established, appreciably less about the direction of change. Sociologists still need a theory of human nature, a specific grounding for the classical postulate that humans are political animals or species beings.

Comparative work on personality development was, in some measure, meant to show that the psychoanalytic model had a limited cultural and historical validity. The inquiry encountered two difficulties. The first was (and is) that some sort of psychological explanation had to be offered to replace psychoanalysis, and none was forthcoming. The second was that the limitations did not seem to be so evident: the model held. Now psychohistory has come forward to replace the studies of culture and personality of twenty years ago. I defer an examination of its claims for some pages. For the moment, suffice it to remark that ad hoc theories of human nature (invented for the purposes of each inquiry or theory) confront us with a very large intellectual void.

The intellectual responsibilities of sociology involve us in epistemological discussions which are not the province of philosophers alone. Much of modern sociology proceeds as if the last word on method had been uttered by John Stuart Mill (another set of colleagues attests its devotion to tradition by acting as if the sixth volume of *The Positive Philosophy* were the summit of human thought). Mach has been referred to, and so has Reichenbach. Two simple propositions throw us, however, into disarray. The first is that the methods of the natural sciences do not apply without severe emendation to the social sciences. The second is that the natural sciences themselves are in the midst of an important reassessment of their methodological foundations. Some fields (neuroscience, primate evolution, ethology) look to the social sciences to complete their own lacunae. In the circumstances, a new map of learning has to be drawn—with impermanent frontiers, large extraterritorial enclaves, and uncharted oceans.

Green in Other Gardens

At times, I have the impression that some of our colleagues think that we are the only heirs of the hermetic tradition. Their version, if it may be called that, of our field is of a self-contained theoretic system, with its own methods of gathering empirical data. It is quite true that sociology at its beginnings was concerned with what others left out. The first sociologists, however, thought that important matters had previously been omitted. The contemporary search for distinctiveness is likely to lead us into redundancy or triviality (or both). Many other fields of inquiry deal with social structure and social process, and where they do not, it is often the minimal importance of the phenomena that deters them.

If sociology once dealt with problems neglected elsewhere, it did not neglect the other sorts of inquiry. Many of the major figures in the brief history of sociological thought knew the economics, history, and philosophy of their times. The recent self-containment of sociology may well be responsible for that lack of intellectual substance which is so troubling about our field. Perhaps the time has come to look for a solution to our difficulty or difficulties, if one can be found, beyond the usual academic borders. New ideas, new perspectives, the identification of new problems, may stimulate us to rethink our assumptions and directions. I am uncertain that new findings (insofar as these can be distinguished from new ideas) will do us much good. What the shocks of contemporary history and experience cannot do, scholarly papers are unlikely to accomplish. Alternative structures of thought may, however, influence our perceptions. The preceding section of this paper described some of the problems sociology has to face; this section suggests that there may be answers, if tentative ones, at hand.

The systematic study of politics, in an historical situation in which no institution, no aspect of culture, is shielded from social conflict, is a useful beginning point. Much recent literature on the interpretation of state and society suggests that our ideas of the distinctions between sectors or institutions have to be revised. There was a period, before détente, when Americans and western Europeans expended much conceptual energy on a phenomenon termed *totalitarianism*. Some of us will persist in the belief that differences between societies, with respect to the freedom of political expression and organization, are important matters. It is no less important to recognize that these freedoms may be attenuated, or require redefinition, in a society of pervasive political constraint. The preconditions of totalitarianism may be nearer home than we think.

The growth of public employment (and of unions of public-service workers) makes of the modern state an arena of indirect social conflict.

The services provided by the state are indispensable not only to the citizenry in general but to the controllers of large concentrations of productive property. In taking the benefits of public services, and paying little for them, they are engaged in a form of exploitation no less effective for being indirect. Conflict, however, opposes state to civil servant, civil servant to an amorphous public. Max Weber suggested, to the approval of later liberal epigones, that efforts by groups like the civil servants to make permanent their advantages could so alter market structures as to constitute a reintroduction of an estate society. Perhaps, but it would be no less appropriate to see in this development a displacement of struggles which in an earlier phase of capitalism occurred in the market.

Both processes, the politicization of larger spheres of society and the simultaneous displacement and extension of market struggles, lend urgency to recent attempts to rethink the idea of a public interest. Nineteenth-century sociology, with its insistence on the separation of state and society, may be thought of as an expression of a liberal idea of the public. In the epoch of the industrialization of culture, ideologies and opinions are manufactured. It is difficult to sustain models of social structure which take consensus seriously. The sociology of culture has been thought of as a derivative of the serious task of analyzing social structure. We may now ask if contemporary social structure demands more serious analyses of culture.

The tediousness of the counterculture, its dreadfully hard work at play and its obvious inanities, ought not to obscure the importance of contemporary cultural protest. Dreitzel, in particular, has shown how the fragmentation of contemporary experience has combined with its rationalization to generate counter movements.[5] New forms of politics are, in his view, based on the body, on sexual differences, on unsatisfied religious impulses, on an irreducible hedonism which technobureaucratic society does not deny but imperfectly canalizes. Weber insisted on the primacy of the "metaphysical needs of the human spirit." It should not surprise cultural conservatives that these have made a sensational reappearance.

In another but closely related area, the crisis of the university impels us to rethink the relationship of knowledge to society. Knowledge is an essential component in administration and production. A series of events (some major like the Chinese Cultural Revolution, some relatively minor but significant like the disputes over research organizations and priorities in the United States, France, and the United Kingdom) suggest that the relationship is political.[6] Political analysis in the

---

[5] H. Dreitzel, "On the Crisis of Culture in Industrial Societies." Published in *Beyond the Crisis,* edited by Norman Birnbaum (New York: Oxford University Press, 1977).

[6] Jerome R. Ravetz, *Scientific Knowledge and Its Social Problems* (New York: Oxford

conventional categories does not often rise above description. The work of Habermas, his effort to redefine the Marxist theory of ideology by distinguishing between the categories of work and interaction, opens the way for a critical assessment of the social potential of knowledge. Habermas's effort in this sphere is connected, of course, with his inquiries into the structure and politics of communication.

Some critics have, unreasonably, accused Habermas of liquidating the Marxist tradition by reducing relationships of exploitation and domination to systems of communication. They are unreasonable, because Habermas has attempted the conceptual mastery of a development intrinsic to advanced societies: the internalization of knowledge by the institutions of domination. That, in turn, has its counterpart in the internalization of the fact of domination in our institutions of culture, and in their symbolic products. Certainly, the work of Gorz on the political determination of technical relationships in the division of labor (supported by the work of the American political economist Marglin) provides an empirical justification for Habermas's theoretical concerns.[7] With due allowance for the differences induced by technical development, cultural structures, and political rhetoric, a serious Maoism would take the Starnberg branch of the Frankfurt School seriously. There can be no Cultural Revolution in the West without a new theory of knowledge in society. Habermas's work is political.[8]

We can continue the discussion of new ideas about politics by turning to political economy. The force of inertia in human affairs is very great, and sociologists, like everyone else, underestimate it. The economists continue their work in universities, the private sector, and government—as their conceptual systems crash about our ears, as their refined methods exhibit a sustained incapacity to generate data with either a short-term or a long-term application. At least, this generation of students in sociology will not have to listen to teachers who enjoin upon them the exemplary value of the work of our colleagues in economics. However, the discomfiture of some economists need not be

University Press, 1971); Radovan Richta, *Civilization at the Crossroads* (White Plains, N.Y.: International Arts & Sciences Press, 1969); Jean Jacques Salomon, *Science et politique* (Paris: Seuil, 1970).

[7] André Gorz, "Techniques, techniciens et lutte de classes," *Les Temps Modernes,* August–September 1971.

[8] Jürgen Habermas, *Erkenninis und Interesse* (Frankfurt: Suhrkamp, 1968), Eng. trans. *Knowledge and Human Interests* (Boston: Beacon Press, 1971); *Legitimations-probleme im Spätkapitalismus* (Frankfurt: Suhrkamp, 1973), Eng. trans. *Legitimation Crisis* (Boston: Beacon Press, 1975); *Protestbewegung und Hochschulreform* (Frankfurt: Suhrkamp, 1969); *Technik und Wissenschaft als ''Ideologie''* (Frankfurt: Suhrkamp, 1968); partial Eng. trans. of the two preceeding, *Toward a Rational Society* (Boston: Beacon Press, 1970); *Theorie und Praxis,* 4th ed. (Frankfurt: Suhrkamp, 1971); Eng. trans. *Theory and Practice* (Boston: Beacon Press, 1973).

shared by all. Some did attempt analyses which would include the
political contexts of the market, others insisted on the economy's status as an object of historical thought, others still dealt with the new
world economy, the advanced forms of imperialism. Not all of the
economists in this category are Marxists. (It is entirely unclear that the
hundreds of economists working on problems of capitalism in the state-
socialist regimes were less surprised by the current crisis than their
Western colleagues.) One lesson of recent events is a negative one: no
amount of technical sophistication or methodological refinement will
compensate for erroneous ideas. Many economists, however, had and
have ideas we must consider.[9]

The first such group works on the extension of the market, that is,
on the interpretation of state and economy. Its descriptions of resource
allocation, of the struggle over state policy in areas like fiscal policy,
tax structure, the provision of public services, provide us with a political sociology of modern society which does not limit itself to explicit
political process and ideology. The obvious importance of these studies
for questions of social policy make of them indispensable elements of
a modern sociology of social classes. There is an honorable tradition in
political economy, not all of it Marxist, of attention to the long-term
problems of accumulation and economic structure. Simple examination will suggest how much of the work done by sociologists on stratification rests on changes in occupational and economic structure analyzed by economists. I referred earlier to the industrialization of cultural
production. Sociologists for too long have criticized economists for their
excessive attention to the market, and for their alleged lack of interest
in social factors. Suppose, however, that much of society has become
a market. Certainly, the political economists who have been studying
imperialism have made possible a sociology of world society which
could encompass the interpenetration of internal and external politics,
phenomena like cultural domination and the role of the *compradores*.

We encounter *terra incognita*. Models of profit maximization do not
work when taken as total descriptions of any segment of world society.
Notions of economic politics, of the maintenance of power, seem more
appropriate—particularly when related to the behavior of those who
control large concentrations of productive power. A theoretic synthesis
exceeds our present capacities. Nothing, it is sure, can result from an

---

[9] Samir Amin, *L'Accumulation à l'échelle mondiale*, 2 vols. (Paris: Anthropos, 1970),
Eng. trans. *Accumulation on a World Scale*, 2 vols. (New York: Monthly Review Press,
1974); Paul A. Baran and Paul M. Sweezy, *Monopoly Capital* (New York: Monthly Re-
view Press, 1968); J. K. Galbraith, *Economics and the Public Purpose* (Boston: Houghton
Mifflin, 1973); Ernest Mandel, *Traité d'économie marxiste*, 2 vols. (Paris: Julliard, 1962),
Eng. trans. *Marxist Economic Theory*, 2 vols. (New York: Monthly Review Press, 1969);
François Perroux, *Aliénation et société industrielle* (Paris, Gallimard, 1970).

artificial separation of sociologies of development from analyses of the world market. And a political sociology which assumes that the market is a separate entity cannot be taken seriously. *Summum summarum*, the actual structures of contemporary society do not lend themselves readily to theoretic apprehension. Their underlying unity, if any, has to be won from the data with models that possess some historical saliency.

If it can be said that the past decade has been one of theoretic and methodological confusion in sociology, some of our colleagues in history may have cause for self-satisfaction. The development in several countries of a sophisticated social history has stimulated work in the sociological tradition, and sometimes gone beyond it. There are two customary attitudes to the materials of history in sociology. One is that history supplies a large amount of data, which can be used to test timeless or universal propositions about social behavior. The other is that sociology's task is the ordering of historical sequence, sociological theory systematizing history. When we seriously examine the claims of the historians of the *Annales* group, a third possibility emerges: history elucidates the structures which sociologists study. History, then, is a master discipline—because of its temporal scope and inclusiveness. A large claim, but no larger than recent claims made by sociologists— and one which, in the work of the *Annales* group, may well be true.[10]

The insistence of the *Annales* historians on what Braudel terms *la longue durée* does not ascribe any special property to time. It rests on the observation that some important things in social existence—the development of contexts for specific events, the interaction of several causes to generate a structural effect—do take time. The *Annales* historians, then, study processes of historical accumulation. Their aim is the identification of underlying structures, the differentiation of short-term and long-term cycles, the location of points of discontinuity. Not surprisingly, in their view, what we think of as points of discontinuity often enough are culminations of perfectly regular series.

The *Annales* group has not confined itself to economic history, although its work in that area is striking: the depiction of accumulative cycles, the analysis of the interpenetration of economy, technology, and demographic regulation. Perhaps its most distinctive contribution is the analysis of the combination of spheres: natural and human space, technology and productive organization, economy and social structure, social structure and politics constituting related series. I use the term series rather than structure or system because the group succeeds so well in incorporating temporality in its organization of the data of human activity. One of the concepts employed by the *Annales* group does have a unifying function—that of *mentalités*. "Mind" will not translate

[10]Jacques LeGoff and Pierre Nora, *Faire de l'histoire*, 3 vols. (Paris: Gallimard, 1974).

the term, nor will "ethos," which is closer. *Mentalité* is a cultural system, a set of values, a predisposition to response. In their *mentalités* humans struggle with their environments, interpret their collective existence, appropriate the past and bring it, however unconsciously, to life. A *mentalité* is a totalization of historical constraint and historical possibility. In emphasizing its importance, the *Annales* historians have *not* subscribed to an imprecise voluntarism They have, instead, taken seriously the contemporary interest in the objective constraint exercised by symbolic structures, as analyzed in the fields of aesthetics, comparative religions, psychoanalysis, and structural linguistics. In joining the analysis of these structures to precise accounts of other historical series, the group practices a large social science.

This is an essay and not a treatise; neither is it a *bibliographie raisonée*. I have concentrated on the historians of the *Annales* group; they have a theoretical coherence which makes reference to their work simple. Of course, I could cite other historians, some of them well known to sociologists. Hobsbawm, Rudé, and Thompson have revivified the interpretation of the growth of capitalism.[11] Genovese and his colleagues in the United States, in their exploration of slavery, have obliged us to reconsider the nature of American society.[12] There is a new body of work in Germany on the social origins of Nazism, and in Italy on fascism.[13] Schorske's work on Vienna enables us to speak with more precision of the rationalization of modern Western culture,[14] and Bailyn when dealing with eighteenth-century politics in America tells us much about the migration of societies.[15] The point is not to assimilate these works to a fixed corpus of doctrine in sociology but to see how they change the terms of our discourse.

That is a result we usually expect of comparative studies in culture and society. As I ponder the vast literature on recent politics in the Third World, only a bare minimum of which I have read, I wonder to what extent some of it has the effect of a familiar self-fulfilling prophecy. The interpretation of development beyond the confines of western Europe and North America with models of social analysis abstracted

[11] Eric Hobsbawm, *Industry and Empire* (New York: Pantheon Books, 1968); George Rudé, *The Crowd in History* (New York: John Wiley & Sons, 1964); Edward P. Thompson, *The Making of the English Working Class* (New York: Pantheon Books, 1963).

[12] Eugene Genovese, *Roll, Jordan, Roll: The World the Slaves Made* (New York: Pantheon Books, 1974).

[13] Renzo de Felice, ed., *Il Fascismo* (Bari: Laterza, 1970); Heinrich A. Winkler, *Mittelstand, Demokratie und Nationalsozialismus* (Cologne: Kiepenheuer, 1972).

[14] Carl E. Schorske, "Politics and Patricide in Freud's *Interpretation of Dreams*," *American Historical Review*, LXXVIII (April 1973), 328–347.

[15] Bernard Bailyn, *The Ideological Origins of the American Revolution* (Cambridge: Harvard University Press, 1967).

from our own development is perfectly comprehensible. It may, however, lead us to construct the data in sequences which miss some essential points.

A recent investigation of childhood in Soviet Russia suggested that the spheres of childhood and adulthood were closely connected in that society, and that children very early developed an explicit sense of the primacy of the group.[16] An examination of the history of Eastern Orthodoxy (with its doctrine of the descent of the Holy Spirit upon the entire congregation) will give us some of the sources of this pattern of socialization. No anti-Confucian campaign of rectification of thought in China will convince Sinologists that Maoism does not draw heavily upon Chinese tradition. The systematic onslaught on bureaucracy and hierarchy in Maoism may teach us how traditions are selectively interpreted by new generations in moments of historical discontinuity. It may also teach us how successful revolutions both start anew and reach back into the past. For nearly two generations, some of our colleagues in comparative studies have warned us that not simply our generalizations but our concepts would have to be revised if a truly general sociology were to be developed. We have listened dutifully, but we appear not to have heard. Now, from within the historiography of the West, there is yet another shock. An historian of ideas, Blumenberg, has argued that the idea of secularization (so central to sociological theory) is a residuum of the religious history of the West.[17] If so, the implicit historical sequence assumed by much of our work will have to be revised—but how, and in which direction?

The large interest in structuralism of the past decades has important implications for us, despite the obvious impossibility of equating all of the structuralist ideas to one another with respect to content, method, or scope.[18] Many of the structuralisms attribute a considerable autonomy to symbolic systems. In structuralist logic, this has consequences rather larger than the familiar empirical assertion that symbolic systems direct human action. Structuralist analyses deal precisely with the properties of symbolic systems in their interaction with other aspects of social process. They emphasize an order of constraint, not simply a type of random constraint. It follows that the relationship of social structure to cultural process can proceed only by an examination of the intrinsic organization of culture.

[16] Urie Bronfenbrenner, *Two Worlds of Childhood: U.S. and U.S.S.R.* (New York: Russell Sage Foundation, 1970).

[17] Hans Blumenberg, *Die Legitimität der Neuzeit* (Frankfurt: Suhrkamp, 1966).

[18] Maurice de Gandillac and others, *Entretiens sur les notions de genèse et de structure* (Paris: Mouton, 1965); Jean Piaget, *Le Structuralisme* (Paris: PUF, 1963), Eng. trans. *Structuralism* (New York: Basic Books, 1970); Lucien Sebag, *Marxisme et structuralisme* (Paris: Payot, 1964).

The most obvious instance of this would be in linguistics. Historical linguistics has long been employed as a method of historical investigation. Structural linguistics presents different problems. Chomsky
thinks language is evidence for an intrinsic human reason.[19] His own
radical politics are related to this position, since an intrinsically rational
humanity can construct rational political community. Skepticism about
Chomsky's Cartesianism cannot exclude large questions of the sort he
asks. The structures of language are complex, efficacious, and subtle—
while ordered. Institutions cannot be characterized in the same way,
far from it. Why is humanity capable of so much collective creativity
in a language, and so desperately (even suicidally) impoverished in
other spheres of existence?

The structural study of myth and art may answer more precise
questions about society. The banishment to the symbolic sphere of dis-
appointments and utopias may provide evidence of profound social
conflicts, but it may also fix provisional solutions in an unintended
permanence. Lévi-Strauss's claim to have established not a consonance
but an identity in the structures of social exchange and communication
enables us to examine hitherto obscure realms of human discourse.
Suppose, however, that the laws of combination adumbrated by Lévi-
Strauss are subject to purposeful modification? Let us recall this. When
Marx developed his theory of alienation, of the fragmentation of human substance and the impossibility of human fulfillment, he recurred
to Schiller's theory of aesthetics. Schiller argued that humanity was
never more itself—indeed, only itself—than in art. Aesthetic experience was distinctive because in it the separated powers of a torn humanity were reunited. Most sociologies of art deal with the social conditions of aesthetic production. Suppose we were to ask, under what
conditions can art become life? An inquiry into the possibilities of moving
from art to existence would constitute an exercise in decoding of a
kind ordinary structuralism hardly enjoins upon us. However, that may
be asking a lot: we have hardly begun to appreciate the implications
of the structuralist analysis of culture as it is.[20]

The familiar idea of the objectification of the human spirit in the
formal structures of culture raises, then, the question of the nature of
that human spirit, the nature of human nature. The structuralist response is not all that different from a conventional sociological one.
We never know the spirit, only its expressions—just as we cannot know

[19] Noam Chomsky, *Cartesian Linguistics* (New York: Harper & Row, 1966); *Problems
of Knowledge and Freedom* (New York: Pantheon Books, 1971).

[20] Jean Braudillard, *Pour une Critique de l'économie politique du signe* (Paris: Gallimard, 1972); Umberto Eco, *Opera aperta*, 2nd. ed. (Milan: Bompiani, 1967)); J. P. Faye,
La Critique du langue et son économie (Paris: Galilee, 1973); Frederic Jameson, *Marxism
and Form: Twentieth-Century Dialectical Theories of Literature* (Princeton: Princeton University Press, 1971); Giulio Preti, *Retorica e logica* (Turin: Einaudi, 1968).

a human nature apart from the institutions in which existence occurs. These are satisfactory formulations, with the difficulty that they ignore the legacy of Sigmund Freud. (It is worth remarking that Piaget, who thinks that structuralism as a method expresses a specifically human capacity to construct its world, is reasonably close to psychoanalysis.)

Classical psychoanalysis has a category called "defense by incorporation." Sometimes, sociological theory has provided an instance of that process in its assimilation of psychoanalysis theory. The superego has been depicted as the repository of social norms, the ego as reconciling the conflicting claims of person and role. It would be gratuitous to deny the utility of these observations—but much more is at stake. Psychoanalysis constitutes a theoretical system, not a repository of descriptions of separate aspects of the psyche.

Two major theoretical efforts to integrate psychoanalysis with sociology may be instructive. The first was, and is, the examination of the relationship of Marxism to psychoanalysis.[21] Much of this work was done in Europe in the 1920s and early 1930s; a recent revival of interest in Europe has taken up the discussion. The idea of a repressive society of course was consonant with the revolutionary aims of Marxism—but what were Marxists to make of Freud's belief that a large amount of instinctual renunciation was the price of the achievements of culture? There were other, no less fundamental, difficulties. The metahistorical core of Marxist theory is to be found in the idea of alienation and of the possibility of its transcendence. The analogous element in psychoanalysis is in the process of therapeutic recovery or self-recovery. Yet the recovered self is free—to live in a society characterized by the pervasiveness of alienation. The weight of Freud's metahistory, further—the struggle between Eros and Thanatos—entailed a cyclical and not a progressive interpretation of history. Marcuse and Mitchell have, each in very different ways, historicized our understanding of Freud.[22] Marcuse, in the idea of surplus repression, has examined the consequences of a postscarcity economy. In his view, it would eliminate the social Darwinism of Freud's social theory—and release the liberating potential of psychoanalysis, which would then work for human recovery in a world which could in fact be humanized. Mitchell, by contrast, insists on the extreme usefulness of the psychoanalytic depiction of child socialization and psychosexual development in a society in which the patriarchal family is a residue of centuries of unequal economic relationships. The internalization of these relationships in character development is not, in her view, an artifact of

---

[21] Helmut Dahmer, *Libido und Gesellschaft* (Frankfurt: Suhrkamp, 1973); Wilhelm Reich, *Sex-Pol: Essays 1929–1934* (New York: Random House, 1972).

[22] Herbert Marcuse, *Eros and Civilization* (Boston: Beacon Press, 1955); Juliet Mitchell, *Psychoanalysis and Feminism* (New York: Vintage, 1975).

psychoanalytic theory: the theory, instead, deals with the actual content of history. Mitchell reminds us, additionally, that unconscious psychic function is the form of human existence. The value of both attempts at thinking about psychoanalysis is that historicization, for these two thinkers, is not identical with an external sociologicization: they do not reduce psychoanalysis to a sociology of the family, the better to dismiss unconscious psychic function as an unnecessary theoretic complication.

Neither Marcuse nor Mitchell is usually associated directly with the work of the psychohistorians, but the connection is there. Psychohistory is one of two things. It is an effort to apply psychoanalytic categories to historical data. More important, it is also an effort to revise those categories by combining them, theoretically, with historical inquiry—specifically with inquiry into historical change. The work of Erikson, Keniston, Lifton, Mitscherlich is psychohistorical in this second sense.[23] It goes beyond, therefore, attempts to delineate and depict modal character structures in specific societies. (Academic memory in the social sciences is short. I am aware that contemporary psychohistorians had distinguished predecessors, Mead and Sapir among them.)

What would be the consequences for sociology of taking seriously Erikson's work on identity and his idea of pseudospeciation? The first is more than an application of psychoanalytic ego theory to social process: it identifies not merely objects but subjects of change. The internalization of change, in other words, has to precede a new objectification: if institutions require personalities adapted to them, the converse applies. Erikson's view of humanity's creative capacity may exaggerate it and he may, as a psychoanalytic critique of his work would insist, join ego function to social necessity in a way that erodes analytical precision. He does, however, introduce an historical dimension into social thought where we might least expect it, in psychic function itself. His view of pseudospeciation, further, rests on a theory of sociability which anticipates a global society. It is one of those metahistorical assumptions which calls much else into question. And, while sociologists study death, would they not do well to consider Lifton's assertion that the symbolic struggle against biological necessity is as important a component of psychic existence (if not more so) than the problem of sexuality?

Psychohistory places the psyche at the confluence of biology and

[23] Erik Erikson, *Childhood and Society* (New York: W. W. Norton, 1950); Kenneth Keniston, *Youth and Dissent* (New York: Harcourt Brace Jovanovich, 1971); Robert J. Lifton, *History and Human Survival* (New York: Random House, 1970); Robert J. Lifton and Eric Olsen, eds., *Explorations in Psychohistory: The Wellfleet Papers* (New York: Simon and Schuster, 1975); Alexander Mitscherlich, *Auf dem Weg zur vaterlosen Gesellschaft* (Munich: Piper, 1963), Eng. trans. *Society Without the Father* (New York: Harcourt, Brace & World, 1969).

history. We now learn from our colleagues in biology, ethology, and physical anthropology that what we had thought of as biology, or nature, is subject to history. Humanity had no precise biological determinant: the process of humanization affected biological evolution. I am at a loss to explore the implications of this change in our viewpoint, but the kind of work being done by our colleagues Morin and Moscovici has the promise of recasting many of our ideas of sociability.[24] At the very least, it puts the contemporary ecological discussion in a more serious framework.

Finally, a glance at recent work in the philosophy of science will tell us that not the least of the reification in sociology can be found in the complacent belief that positivistic conceptions of the development and structure of science are still tenable. Kuhn's work on scientific paradigms is important, the work by himself and others on the sources of change in paradigms is more so. With the development of a school of critical science, natural science itself has become the object of the kind of reflective inquiry once dismissed in sociology as a residue of a metaphysical epoch.[25]

One of the questions this raises for us is whether a strict demarcation between a philosophy of science and a sociology of science can be maintained. With his usual acumen, a gift for seizing upon questions whose time has come, Habermas has begun the exploration of the problem. Rather, he has continued it. A precise self-depiction, a sense of the historicity of thought, has characterized much that still lives in the sociological tradition. The assertion of thought's historicity, however, carries with it the obligation to think and think again. A sociology which thinks only about itself, or confines itself to a world of its own objects, is certain to lose its capacity to make significant connection with the movement of thought. A sociology which seeks that connection may, however, question the necessity of its continuing existence.

Some Tentative Conclusions

One of the least appealing aspects of contemporary sociology is its programmatic nature, it perennial announcement of developments to come.

---

[24] Edgar Morin, *Le Paradigme perdu: la nature humaine* (Paris: Seuil, 1973); Edgar Morin and others, *L'Unité de l'homme* (Paris: Seuil, 1974); Serge Moscovici, *Essai sur l'histoire humaine de la nature* (Paris: Flammarion, 1968).

[25] François Jacob, *La Logique du vivant* (Paris: Gallimard, 1970), Eng. trans. *The Logic of Life: The History of Heredity* (New York: Pantheon Books, 1974); Thomas S. Kuhn, *The Structure of Scientific Revolutions* (Chicago: University of Chicago Press, 1962); Imre Lakatos and Alan Musgrave, eds., *Criticism and the Growth of Knowledge* (Cambridge: Cambridge University Press, 1970).

How much is written in the style of that application for a grant in aid of research which declares that, although at the moment nothing is known about the problem, after the research nothing more will need to be known about it! Statements about the direction sociology should take, even if in the form of serious attempts to confront our inner crisis, partake of this disorder, an advanced form of intellectual narcissism. I cannot in all honesty claim to have fully escaped the syndrome. The brevity, as well as the tentativeness, of these conclusions may show that I have at least begun to struggle against it.

It is clear that much of the work which the sociological tradition encompassed is being accomplished in fields other than sociology. That is a tribute to the strength of the tradition—even in the period of its decomposition. It is not, invariably, a tribute to ourselves. Meanwhile, new structures of thought, new types of inquiry, deal with the phenomena of contemporary history peculiar to the postbourgeois epoch. Finally, there are processes of intellectual development, accumulation, and innovation: in the human sciences, most if not all of those are *not* to be found in sociology.

I have suggested that we look elsewhere for ideas and have given some indication of where we might find them. I have not been able to suggest how these ideas can be combined with many of our present concerns, for two reasons. One is that the project, if worthwhile, is intrinsically difficult and can only be proceeded with empirically—not programmatically. The other is that in many areas our intervention would be gratuitous: whole fields of the human sciences are doing perfectly well without us, and we are not needed. Certainly, nothing we can gain from other fields will restore our lost inner unity—more real, in any event, to recollection than in the actual past. The present situation of chaos within sociology, occasionally presented as a benign intellectual pluralism (who, precisely, is deceived by this?), will continue.

Sociologists are clearly unlikely to subscribe in their majority to a single method or doctrine. Marxists and structuralists, in any case, are found in a variety of fields. Sociologists are equally unlikely to accept that the temporality of social structures is their chief interest; in that case they would seek certification as historians. Human nature, if too important to be left to psychologists and psychoanalysts, is not the exclusive province of one field. The economists are doing badly for the moment, but not so badly that they require our assistance. I could lengthen the list, but to what effect?

I would suggest a rather different course. Many of us are primarily interested in society and secondarily in sociology. The analysis of society presents problems, some of them very profound, none of them easy. Many of our contemporaries are doing interesting work on society, much of it quite unclassifiable in the conventional academic categories. Why not join them on the frontiers of thought instead of persisting in the attempt to construct a solipsistic universe of discourse? Sociology may gradually lose it distinctiveness as our efforts combine in a new science of society. That would hardly be a tragedy: the new science would continue that attempt at synthesis and contemporaneity which gave dignity to the sociological tradition. That, however, is a somewhat distant prospect. For the moment, the most effective way to be loyal to the tradition is to accept the consequences of its ending.

• Adapted from a paper delivered at the International Congress of Sociology at Toronto in 1974, this essay will be published at the end of 1975 in a volume edited by Thomas Bottomore titled *Crisis and Contention in Sociology* (Beverly Hills and London: Sage Publications). I wish to acknowledge, with gratitude, support from the John Simon Guggenheim Foundation for my work in social thought.

4

The *Annales* School and Social Theory

Our conference has heard something of a sociological analysis of the diffusion of the work of the *Annales* school. The analysis ought to be worthy of the work of the *Annales* historians when they study the spread of *mentalités;* that is, it ought to begin in concrete data. My own contact with the work of the school began when I was a graduate student in sociology at Harvard University from 1947 to 1952. George Homans had begun his career as a historical sociologist, and he insisted to anyone who cared to listen that they ignored the work of the *Annales* group at their peril. Not many listened. The reading of graduate students in sociology at Harvard those days was not broad, since it was the view that that tradition of social thought had reached its culmination—if not perfection itself—in the work of our distinguished teacher, Talcott Parsons. Pious footnotes, in principle, could be added to the canon. That other and very different approaches might be of value was not an idea that many entertained. Those of us who were not devoid of a residue of human skepticism, however, did not think it disloyal to Professor Parsons to read more widely. After all, if Parsons himself had stuck to the classical economics of his epoch, he would never have been led to Max Weber. In any event, it was also from reading then-contemporary French sociologists like the late Georges Friedmann (an editor of *Annales* for a time) and Georges Gurvitch that I learned of the tradition of *Annales* and its presence in French social science. Meanwhile, the historian Bernard Bailyn was a fellow student, and he and I talked about his critique of Braudel's book on the Mediterranean. Others at Harvard referred to the work of the school. I taught in a general social science course under the political scientist Samuel Beer. He had studied medieval institutions at Harvard and Oxford, and looked with disfavor on teaching assistants who did not know Marc Bloch. My own doctoral work on the German Reformation led me, of course, to Lucien Febvre. I'd say, however, that what fascinated me and others about the *Annales* school was that it offered a historically grounded study of society to those of us who found ourselves in a scholarly environment with two prominent characteristics. The first was that the study of society was seen in distortedly systematic terms, ahistorically—a revival of Comte which dared not utter his name. The other was that the study of history itself often proceeded from provincial postulates, from the self-congratulation of the ideologues of the new American Empire. Instinctively, we saw in the work of the *Annales* group an alternative, at once methodological and political.

I later had the good fortune to spend a long period in Europe. It was through the British social historians, and above all Eric Hobsbawm and the group around *Past and Present,* that my appreciation of the *Annales* school was deepened. The *Past and Present* group was divided between those who can be termed the Anglo-Marxists and the others, but it was surely united in the conviction that the direction of its work made it the British counterpart of the *Annales* group. London, where I taught, was not far from Paris. I made the acquaintance of a number of French sociologists like Henri Desroche, Edgar Morin, and Alain Touraine, all of whom were connected with the VIe *Section* of the Ecole Pratique des Hautes Etudes. Many of my contemporaries in Britain shared my conviction that whatever important might be happening in the social sciences was likely to be centered at that extraordinary institution and recorded, sooner rather than later, in *Annales.* I therefore account the *Annales* school a critical influence in my own continuing education.

So much for intellectual autobiography. It is not irrelevant to my theme, which is the contribution of the *Annales* school to social theory. I use the term, social theory, rather than sociology because I doubt whether sociology in the form in which it has been taught for the past generation can justify its existence. Its existence, no doubt, can be explained—but that is not justification. The line of descent in sociology from Comte to Durkheim entails a number of presuppositions. One is that society evolved in linear, indeed unilinear fashion. Another is that the structures of society were sufficiently visible to be isolated for purposes of analysis—isolated, indeed, from the flow of history. We could say that in this view of sociology, it was a metahistory, since the elements of history were those social structures apprehended by sociology. From these ideas to the view that the progress of human thought culminated in the self-description which was sociology was a short step. That obsessive self-congratulation on having discovered something new which characterizes just those sociologists who utter banalities has philosophical roots—even if they are unaware of them.

In different philosophical form, some of these ideas also informed German sociology. Durkheim had encountered Toennies' work when a student in Germany. He stated in the tradition of Saint-Simon and Comte what the Germans took from Herder, Hegel, and von Stein. The Germans were concerned with the emergence of a secularized society. They asked which beliefs and values had been substituted, which ones could be substituted, for religion. They were also concerned with the emergence of a distinctly industrial society, in its capitalist form. Toennies' distinction between *Gemeinschaft* and *Gesellschaft* was a theory of social evolution. In a more historicist idiom than French thought, it nevertheless promulgated the very sequence of evolution for which Comte and Durkheim claimed scientific warrant. The view of politics found in both French and German sociology was quite similar. Society had primacy over the state. Politics was influenced by the development of a uniform and rational culture which transcended the divisions of class and the remnants of tradition.

If this account of the presuppositions of academic sociology is correct, whatever the influences of sociology upon the founders of the *Annales* school, their theoretic assumptions were different. Consider the case of Max Weber.

Weber certainly did not depart dramatically from Toennies (nor did he differ markedly from Saint-Simon and Comte, who along with Marx, anticipated the analysis of the Protestant ethic) in his view of the evolution of the West. However, his description of the process of rationalization in Western society had specific historical limits. There was a general cultural process Weber termed rationalization, but he invariably examined it within historical contexts whose particular characteristics he stressed. Rationalization always occurred, for Weber, in an historically unique society, under unique cultural conditions. Weber was so far from a belief in a generalizing social theory that we can say that his ancestor was Ranke, with his belief that all epochs were equal in the sight of God. For Weber, historical epochs and societies were unique configurations. The method of *Verstehen* was a method of value analysis, a mode of seizing a *mentalité*. It was not simply an ancillary technique to be used with others (like quantitative analysis) in the establishment of ahistoric generalizations about all social structures. Weber, then, renounced the development of a total social theory which could be applied to historical data. He ended as he began, a generalizing or theoretic historian. The curious ambivalence, that alternation between affinity and antagonism, which has marked the dialogue between Marxists and those who took Weber as their paragon, bespeaks this quality in Weber's work.

The very first issue of *Annales* carried an appreciation of Max Weber by Maurice Halbwachs, then a colleague of Bloch and Febvre at Strasbourg. Bloch referred, often enough, to Durkheim. He cited Fustel de Coulanges to the effect that history was not the collection of events from the past, but the science of human societies. The plural, in the usage Bloch gave to it, is significant. Of course, Bloch (as any sensitive historian) analyzed the historical stratification of society, the ways in which its institutions contained layers from the past. Durkheim did show considerable awareness of this, in his work on religion. Bloch also insisted on the necessity of comparing different types of social structure, again, a theme from Durkheim. Nevertheless, when we consider the theoretic implications of Bloch's own work, *Annales'* initial tribute to Weber assumes rather more significance than the repeated references to Durkheim. If we examine the theoretic structure of Bloch's analysis of feudal society, many of the general notions advanced by Durkheim dissolve. Surely, feudal society can be understood *inter alia* in terms of *anomie,* symbolic integration, social cohesion, and the array of concepts which can be derived more or less faithfully from Durkheim's work. The difficulty is that every society can be described in these terms. Moreover, if we take an assertion as apparently straightforward as Durkheim's methodological precept that social facts are defined by constraint and exteriority, it too crumbles under the weight of social and symbolic complexity in medieval society. In medieval culture, meanings generated structures—as least for long periods. Durkheim's belief that structures generate meanings, in the light of any reading of medieval society, seems arbitrary. Bloch's analysis of the complexities of medieval culture and society offers us an opportunity to experiment with a variety of social theories. Most of all, however, it defines an historically unique and relatively self-contained social universe. It would be too much to say that feudal society had its own laws. It would also be too much to say that its inner working verifies the working of laws established by the kind of sociology entailed by Durkheim's program. The problem we now face is: does historical work of the kind done by Bloch postpone until some later date, when much of it will have been accumulated, the verification of sociological laws? Alternatively, does it render suspect the notion of a science of societies, precisely because of their historically specific properties? The very notion of the accumulation of data presupposes the equivalence of the categories under which the data are subsumed. That is, it presupposes a refined development of an abstract science of societies—the very end the accumulation is supposed to serve. The usual way to escape this dilemma is to posit a continuous alternation between empirical and theoretical work, a gradual refinement of theory, a sharpened focus for empirical analysis.

The recent reconstruction of the history and philosophy of natural science allows considerable doubt as to whether the natural sciences ever developed in this way. Moreover, as with all ideas which seek to reconcile what may be irreconcilable, the notion of a higher unity of empirical and theoretical work in the historical social sciences is far easier to promulgate than to concretize. Choices have to be made, and these are not only choices as to the allocation of energy and time. One or another framework to be used in inquiry has to be chosen, and the framework itself severely limits if it does not entirely dictate the questions to be asked and the sorts of answers which can be given.

I have said something about the methodological presuppositions of early sociology. What about the next generation of sociologists, those whose work dates from the First World War? We must consider them in order to appreciate the kinds of social theory at the disposal of the first generation of *Annales* historians. The sociologists whom we consider were by no means uniform in their thought. One relatively new tendency, which has since come to dominate much of academic sociology, was the positivist detachment of sociology from its original philosophical and historical bases. A search for the elements of social action and the laws of their combination superseded the analysis of structures and sequences. History was viewed, by these positivists, as a source of data for timeless or universal propositions—devoid of specification for given historical contexts. At the same time, the substratum of sociology altered. Whatever their differences, the first generation of academic sociologists took the actual historical development of the West as their point of departure. The ideas developed to explain that development, detached from historical inquiry, were now used for purposes of analysis which claimed to be universal. In fact, a political substratum had replaced an historical one. The politics in question were specific. Sociology became an administrative or technocratic discipline. In the case of the Chicago school of sociology, the development of a technical discipline was justified by a recourse to a program of social reform. Just as the *Verein für Sozialpolitik* (or the *Evangelische Sozialkongress*) in Weber's time sponsored inquiry with a reformist end in view, the Chicago school's investigations of the city, of ethnic groups, of social pathology had political purposes. The initial association of American sociology with a variant of middle class reformism, however, was a particular case. Sociologists declared themselves competent to supply reliable (and valid) data to the administrative agencies of society. The substratum of a technocratic politics was perfectly compatible with a theory of social knowledge ostensibly devoid of values, or of any metahistorical pathos whatsoever.

Metahistorical pathos is now ours in surfeit. In reaction to the combination of positivistic method and technocratic bias, some English-speaking sociologists (and social scientists, generally) have recently been receptive to "Critical Theory." "Critical Theory," as pursued by many, has promulgated a utopia, a notion of the self-transcendence of humanity. "Critical Sociology," which began in the work of the Frankfurt School, was itself a response to a specific historical situation. The defeat of the German working class movement became the occasion for the effort to rethink Marxism, to add a cultural and psychoanalytic dimension to its view of structural conflict. Those dimensions, in the thought of the Frankfurt School, were historically specific. They were described as the destruction of *bourgeois* culture, the industrialization of cultural production, the problems of socialization in the *bourgeois* family under conditions of late capitalism. The very phrase, late capitalism, suggested a historical sequence. "Critical Theory" in some of its contemporary forms has abandoned these specific points of reference in favor of an entirely generalized discourse. In that discourse, terms like alienation have become—if anything—less precise than in their original Marxist usage.

This ahistorical deformation of the Marxist tradition has been accompanied by a scholastic treatment of Max Weber which also seeks the impossible—emptying his legacy of history. In the work of the phenomenologists who follow Schutz, the structures of human history are reduced to a form of intentionality. (It is not fair, however, to tax Schutz with the simplifications of his epigones—and his students Berger and Luckman cannot be charged with neglecting history.) The name of Merleau-Ponty, too, will remind us that a systematic analysis of historicity and a phenomenological analysis of human consciousness are consonant. The vulgar phenomenologists make of history a gigantic construct, one place amongst others for humanity to find its essence. A phenomenological sociology, in its commonplace form, pushes past history to affirm the existence of metahistorical structures. There is also a positivist line of descent from Max Weber. It is the one, when all is said and done, followed by Talcott Parsons. There, historical structures are dissolved into their supposedly universal elements. Positivists and metahistorians, whatever their intellectual and political antecedents, each looked to the future—if in rather different terms. For the positivists, the future was the future of social science, the derivations of general laws from a series of painstaking empirical inquiries. Ernest Gellner once remarked that great discoveries in substantive ethics were always to be found on the next page of philosophical treatises. The verification of general sociological laws always awaits the completion of the next large empirical inquiry. For the metahistorians, a human essence incorporated in a finished model of society was to be found in the future. That future waited upon either a general transformation of society, or a successful conquest of the intellectual frontier by a phenomenological method which would reduce all antitheses to accidents, consequences of imperfect perceptions.

The metahistorians and the positivists, then, each refused history. The separation of social theory from historical analysis made of social theory an academic speciality amongst other specialities, a perpetual commentary upon the substantive work of others. Its justification was found in philosophical and political concepts, not in the progressive illumination of historical process. It is not impossibly difficult to understand the extreme intellectual tensions which caused this flight from history (often enough, disguised as some form of mastery of it). Knowledge of history does not encourage a belief in a distinctive realm of theoretic discourse about society. History can be understood as a succession of structures, each with distinctive characteristics, indeed with distinctive laws of internal function. On this assumption, the tasks of historical analysis and theoretic discourse are the same: establishing the distinctiveness of separate epochs, indicating the main lines of development within each, identifying the regularities specific to each, and positing the central elements of processes of change within each. The language of theory and the language of history become one. If no ahistorical categories are acknowledged, every theoretic statement is a historical generalization. Rather than searching for universal categories, we seek to enlarge our capacity to perform specific analyses. The difficulty is that we have to stay within the limits of the epochs and structures we know, or can know. It is a difficulty because it seems to leave us unprepared to deal with surprises, with new developments, the emergence of new structures.

At this point, the *Annales* school comes to our assistance. More precisely, the confluence of the *Annales* school with Marxism, mentioned earlier by Eric Hobsbawm as it applied to British historiography, has a larger significance. The problem facing social theory in the light of the work of the *Annales* is not given by the autonomous movement of discourse. It is given by problems which arise in the historical consciousness itself, which demand statement and formalization. What is termed the crisis in social theory is an extension or refraction of a general problem in the social sciences or human sciences. Recently, Thomas Bottomore—the British sociologist who is well acquainted with French thought and the work of the *Annales*—edited a book entitled *Contention and Crisis in Sociology*. It is the record of a symposium at the last International Sociological Congress (Toronto, 1974). There were seven participants: Bottomore, an Indian, an Italian, a Pole, a Soviet scholar, a Spaniard, and myself. Each argued that there was indeed a crisis in sociology, and in particular in social theory. Each proceeded to describe a rather different crisis. Social theory taken in its traditional form, abstractly, has suffered from fragmentation—and from entropy.

It has lost intellectual energy. The *Annales* school, if its work is understood aright, has made possible a recasting of our understanding of social theory, a revivification of social theory. It reminds us that social theory can become once again an ancillary, a derivative, or an instrument of historical understanding. I use these terms with a considerable awareness of their imprecision, but that imprecision can in turn be circumscribed.

Let us distinguish between complete and tentative formalization in social theory. For all its brilliance and fecundity, the system set forth by Lévi-Strauss in *La pensée sauvage* strikes me as tentative. Lévi-Strauss claims that he has found (really, invented) the elements of human communication. The claim is premature. The system given us by Lévi-Strauss entails a return to the construction of a model of society which becomes more elegant and economical as it becomes more remote from the complexity of specific historical structures. The model contains the putative elements of all social structures, but using them does not bring us closer to knowledge of a given historical totality. That knowledge recedes, a we subsume the concrete historical phenomenon under a form of discourse which relates the elements to one another. Alternatively, it recedes in favor of a very empirical description which defers the task of theoretical analysis. Some of the newer generation of *Annales* historians suppose that the key to historical analysis lies in the development of a hyper-structuralism, that historical analysis is really just another form of discourse, which can win dignity only by attaining awareness of its status as discourse. The inevitable dissolution of the historical object is the price we pay for reaching its inner structure. Indeed, we dissolve it because we know that it has no inner structure apart from our own construction of it—and construction is a matter of discourse, not entirely dissimilar to play. The notion of *Annales* as a journal, a school, in which all the human sciences collaborate, appears to provide organizational support for this theoretic idea. The idea, however, rests on the assumption that a continuous change of perspective, the successive application of different models of society and the psyche, is now the only way to interpret history. That assumption implies, of course, that we experience a multiplicity of perspectives (in our historical situation) simultaneously. Rather than choosing amongst them, we recur to a neutral system of ordering—delaying to the indefinite future any other synthesis. The view is certainly persuasive on many grounds, but it expresses a drastic renunciation of the intentions of the *Annales'* first and second generations. In the language of this paper, we can say that in the guise of a new positivism, it restores to the interpretation of history a new metahistorical pathos.

In a recent issue of the *Journal of Social History,* the Genoveses criticized the *Annales* school on rather different grounds. One was that the work of the *Annales* (and of M. Braudel himself) was systematically apolitical. It did not deal with domination as a defining and pervasive concept of social hierarchy. Another was that it ignored production, and especially relationships of domination organized in production. Finally, the *Annales* school was charged with ignoring the social antagonisms entailed in the transformation of nature, with ignoring that major process itself. These charges make good polemical copy, but I do not think they are sustainable. They do have the advantage of enabling us to think again about the relationship of the *Annales* historians to Marxism, to an historically-conceived social theory. An examination of the problem may bring us closer to the nature of the contribution of *Annales* to social theory in general.

Can the *Annales* historians be taxed, fairly, with ignoring domination? It is much more accurate to describe them as situating systems of domination in context. Their contextual analysis at times points to the obstacles to the exercise of power, at time to the historically specific forms in which it is exercised. The work of the *Annales* historians is, at the least, compatible or consonant with much of the Marxist canon. Consider the Marx of *Capital,* of *The Eighteenth Brumaire of Louis Napoleon,* of the powerful and subtle methodological essay in the *Grundrisse.* It is true that the *Annales* historians do not focus on power. Neither do they reify a concept which (as the sad history of the discipline of political science shows) too often encompasses everything—and nothing. They do not consider power an undifferentiated relationship, but they examine power in its institutional context, and they do not hesitate to consider the ideological aspects of domination. This is far from an evasion of the problem of domination but does entail a potentially productive detachment from some of the usual ways of dealing with the problem. Our colleague from Leiden has characterized the entire twentieth century as one in which the state apparatus, power relations, dominate the entire social system. If so, the ways in which power is exercised in the cultural industry, through the educational system, in production, are not simply modes of state power. Rather, these ancillary networks diffuse domination throughout the industrial societies (and not only these). The work of the *Annales* historians (including some of the work on *mentalité*) makes it easier for us to understand these phenomena, which are sometimes opaque. The assertion that domination is omnipresent, after all, does not imply that it is omnipresent in the same way.

The work of the *Annales* group on *mentalités* is far from concluded, and there are clearly differing emphases, differing lines of intellectual development, within it. The *Annales* historians, however, do not reify the notion of *mentalité.* They do not posit value-systems which emanate from nowhere in particular to influence the historical process. They study the interconnection of *mentalité* with the texture of culture, with the organization of society—and often enough identify those contradictions and *lacunae* in *mentalités* which enable us to analyze these systems, in Marxist terms, as ideologies.

That the *Annales* historians pay a large amount of attention to nature, and to its modification by human effort in social forms, seems obvious. We could even say that some of the earlier *Annales* work on the social development of the natural (and technical) environment anticipated the modern ecological discussion. From Lucien Febvre on the earth to Barry Commoner on eco-systems is not an impossibly long leap.

Let us turn to the idea of historical time series, of seriality. The interest of Marxists in the points at which relations of quantity become relations of quality leads them to look for systematic dicontinuity, systematic rupture, in time series. Notions of discontinuity and rupture depend, of course, upon notions of continuity and comparability. A standardized time series implies continuity and comparability. Is it true to tax the *Annales* historians with obsessive concentration on unbroken serality? Some series in history are unbroken, or relatively so, and knowledge of them is a precondition of the development of the capacity to identify discontinuities. Even the tracing of certain time series across the boundaries of different historical formations may allow us to think more sharply about the differences at issue. I'd prefer to say that the emphasis on time series by certain *Annales* historians is ambiguous. It can lead to a denial of rupture; it can also lead to a more sophisticated analysis of discontinuity. I am aware that we incur the danger of categorizing historians, in this instance, as technicians amassing data for later theoretical treatment. Is this not a danger courted by some *Annales* historians, themselves?

Differences of interpretative intention, differences of generation, mark a school whose unifying characteristic is a search for a method. The method is itself not a technical problem, but a question of the intention motivating technique. The *Annales* historians intend to construct a total history, a history of the inner inter-connectedness of cultures and societies. Their own work rarely falters in this one essential respect: *Annales* historians do not hesitate to move from data like time series to the implications of the data. The implications, for *Annales* historians, are usually measured by the contribution of the data to the construction of an image of the society.

What separates the *Annales* historians (or a good many of them) from Marxists is a dimension of political consciousness. No Marxist scholar is unaware that Marxist analysis, ultimately, has had a political aim: the analysis was and is supposed to heighten the capacity of humans to transform their social circumstances. In fact, a considerable amount of valuable Marxist scholarship is relatively detached or insulated from the political aims of Marxism. Put in another way, we can say that it sublimates those aims. The *Annales* historians seem to have

substituted for this a general, indeed voracious, human curiosity and
sympathy—but it is not a replacement for or an equivalent of a Marxist
political consciousness. A study of the politics of the *Annales* historians,
of the ideological and political careers of the successive *Annales* generations, would be rewarding. For the moment, we can say that the confluence of the *Annales* school and Marxism is to be found in several
aspects of method: the idea of a historical formation as a totality, the
assumption that the totality has several levels—not all of them immediately accessible to analysis, the belief that certain essential social processes are discernible only through temporal sequences.

Marx himself said that he wished to determine the laws of motion
of capitalism. The Newtonian phrase suggests that Marxism itself may
be historically relativized. If Marxism is the study of the laws of capitalism, it conceptual structure and methods may not be applicable to
other social formations. Lukács, from within the Marxist tradition, advanced the possibility that a future socialist society would have other
laws. Most critics of Marxism look not ahead, but backward (or side-
ward), arguing that social formations other than capitalism are indeed
organized differently. The relativization of Marxism would involve an
intellectual task more delicate, and more difficult, than declaring that
Marxism does not apply across large areas of history. It would require
specification of the ways in which it does not apply, the description of
alternative models of domination and exploitation, of different functions for ideology. In these respects, the relative closeness of the *Annales* historians to Marxism gives them the status of *frères ennemis*—
and, not quite paradoxically, of allies.

Finally, then, we come to some of the specific contributions of the
Annales school to theoretic discussion, contributions which may help
sociology in its most urgent task, self-liquidation. The study of *mentalités* does not present us with cultural values (or ideologies) taken as
self-contained systems. It presents us with the study of cultural values
as actualized in high and popular culture, in religious system and profane belief, in gesture, routine, and ritual. The idea of *mentalité* as exemplified in the work of the *Annales* historians, enables us to study the
texture of human consciousness, its organization, in relationship to the
multiple systems of constraint in which consciousness is embedded.
We can understand *mentalités* as responses to constraint, and as challenges to it. The study of *mentalités* has the therapeutic effect of all true
anthropology, making us aware that our own categories are limited
and bound to our own time and place.

The sub-title of the journal *Annales* includes the term *Economies*.
The plural is important. The *Annales* school depicts economic systems
as resulting from the struggle between certain values and historical
constraints. These values are not engendered by an autonomous sphere
of culture—or, once engendered by it, immediately have to leave that

sphere. Economic values adapt to the social relations of production, influence the rate of development of those relations (and, at the limit, their possibilities of development) and are finally superseded by other values when the relations of production change. The conception of economic institutions promulgated by the *Annales* school (particularly its earlier figures, to be sure) insists on the social nature of the relations of production. It avoids generalizing excessively from one model or type of production. More strikingly, it avoids the presupposition that a production system is necessarily integrated in a society, and it opens the way for an analysis of what the Marxists term contradiction.

The ecological analyses of the *Annales* historians enable us to understand systems of social communication in terms of the continuity, density, and fluidity of social structures. The contrast with the formalized theory of social communication of a thinker like Lévi-Strauss is striking. The concrete analysis of the *Annales* school enables us to understand a political datum of some importance, namely, the power to command. If we consider matters like the dismal performance of most command economies, economically and politically, we can see that their systems of transmission for commands are defective. Indeed, it may be that no lengthy system of transmission for commands can be effective. Contemporary efforts at decentralization, participatory democracy in economy and state, assume added weight in the light of the implicit social and historical generalization of the political economy of the *Annales* School.

The most important single contribution of the *Annales* historians to social theory is a very general one. They have promulgated a more complex, more differentiated, vision of history as a replacement of the nineteenth-century historical generalizations which were fundamental to social thought at the end of that century. The work of the *Annales* school requires social theorists (and not least, sociologists) to produce models of society which will include the dimension of time—models which, in Marc Bloch's terms, treat the present as only the most recent segment of the past. In theoretical discourse, it is no longer possible to advance timeless propositions. The temporal sequence in which the propositions are supposed to be true will have to be specified. The many historical levels of the phenomena under examination will have to be delineated, and the chains of causation of varying degrees of historical force will have to be established. Social theory, thought of in this way, approaches a general science of history. It would also cast off the legacy of its own past, an outmoded model of historical progression, and a political philosophy tied to the belief that capitalism was the final form of human society. (Weber was genius enough to see that both were dubious.)

The newer *Annales* generation, meanwhile, appears to be looking for a terrain above or beyond politics on which to situate itself—whilst cultivating structuralist discourse on society. The effort is unlikely to succeed, since social theory itself will now be dividing into two components. One is theoretic reflection on history. The other is theoretic political discourse, that is, systematic reflection on a future political community. A social theory distinct from the study of history, and from political philosophy, will disappear. Modern history's structures and rhythms are very different from those which led to the rise of a modern social theory (institutionalized for a time in academic sociology, but only for a time). The contribution of the *Annales* school is a major one. It has obliged us to rethink our most basic assumptions.

Postscript. Classical sociology sought to apprehend the unique historical structure of bourgeois society (Hegel surely derived the term from Ferguson's "civil society"). Classical sociology also sought to promulgate universal laws of society. But no sooner had the classical sociologists stated their program than it became, should have become, apparent, but didn't—we now have the wisdom of hindsight—that only they could fulfill it. And they could only fulfill it in that historical moment. Even, I think, Max Weber, who derided at times—something we weren't quite taught at Harvard—the making of a special sociological theory or special sociology, was aware of this historical fatality or historical limit. So I think both processes would have to occur, a reorganization of the scope and the objects of social science. This is not the same thing, I think, as the autonomous development of a new discourse by human sciences, which realize that they are only epistemes. I think it is a much more profound social and cultural process, and at the same time, as a refraction of that, the development of new categories of theoretic discourse, categories which would certainly not be the exclusive property of sociology, or of some entity called social theory but which would be part of the general heritage or apparatus of social science—I can't quite find the right word. It would be part of the assumptions and consciousness of persons working in what we might have thought of a while ago as separate disciplines, but which we now see to be converging—not converging in some gigantic, new, and automatic synthesis, but converging on new objects of inquiry, because the old ones are being commonly eroded.

Let me try to put the problem in a somewhat different way. What are the contemporary social and cultural impulsions to the making of theory? That is to say, what problems, social or historical problems in their concrete impact upon ourselves, seem to demand answers? The first is the problem of resistance, resistance to what we could call global centralization or the centralization of power, economic and cultural production in the ostensibly competing state-systems which constitute the world-system. The foci of resistance are surely not only political movements, guerrilla actions, or alternative models of society however important they may be. There are other kinds of resistance. They are found in the demand for a political recognition of the pluralization of world society. Another demand is the demand for a new type of technology or a new mastery of technology sometimes called intermediate technology. The vocabulary and indeed the arguments vary, but it is clear that a new relation to nature and a new relation to technique will have somehow to be developed. There is also the notion of limits, or of the adumbration or the pursuit of new limits, to human nature, either wider or narrower, than we have hitherto thought necessary. There is also the recasting of, among other things, the social and cultural foundations of psychoanalytic theory. Finally, in this sphere of knowledge, there is the critical theory of knowledge that is associated with the work of thinkers like Kuhn, but also of others, which considers knowledge as in itself a constituent not simply of consciousness and of the process of gathering more knowledge, but of domination. Now it seems to me that if we take these impulsions, or these loosely related problems which I stated in a most imperfect way, as the beginning points for contemporary theoretic reflection, the *Annales* historians have done, not as well as anybody, but more than most people, in giving us some kinds of answers about the evolution of our own society, which might enable us to find elements for, on the one hand, a new view of social development, and, on the other, despite their explicit renunciation of politics, a new notion of human community.

II

MARXISM AND AFTER

The papers in Part I dwelt upon our intellectual situation in very broad terms. The essays now before us ask if anything is left of Marxism—and, in any case, what can be learned from that nineteenth-century doctrine as the twentieth century draws to its close. The essays were written, of course, under the dark memory of Stalinism and the stultifying oppressiveness of the post-Stalinist Communist regimes. They were also products of the Western Marxism of the postwar decades. The Marxism at issue was not only the Marxism of class conflict but the Marxism of generalized domination. Its fundament was not historical materialism as the basis of a science of society but the spiritual critique of existence found in the theory of alienation. The section includes, then, an effort to contrast Marx's theory of human nature, his insistence that alienation would be overcome, with Freud's ambivalent pedagogy. Freud's project was in part a demand for the re-education of the human race and in part an injunction to renunciation of high hopes for improvement—a contradiction which found exquisite expression in the last paragraph of *Civilization and Its Discontents*. In the discussion, I was adamantly enough attached to the legacy of the Enlightenment to claim that it enjoined upon us a selective appropriation of the notions of transformation of human nature in Marx and Freud. The ensuing metatheory of human potential would set the direction of psychological and social inquiry, by emphasizing the creative possibilities of a search for a new common life. Politics would be understood as a struggle to attain values and not merely to defend interests. Having said that, I promptly demonstrated sympathy for Freud's ambivalence by itemizing the many contemporary processes which bespoke a pervasive repetition compulsion, a nearly insurmountable tendency to domination. Nearly insurmountable, I insisted, was not totally insurmountable: transformation remained possible. Is the essay just a reminder of the permanent force of utopia? If so the permanency of utopia is itself a problem which demands explication.

The metahistorical belief in the possibility of human self-transcendence is an element in Marxism (and in the Enlightenment tradition, generally) which can be understood as religious. Marx himself held that religion was a consequence of alienation—and so, alienation once overcome, would disappear. An inquiry into the Marxist theory of religion, then, can tell us much about the entire structure of Marxism. Drawing upon a body of scholarship often driven by questions about Marxism, the essay on religion points to the fact that it has had critical and even revolutionary social consequences. It certainly has not been un-equivocally quietistic. Looking back, we now see that Marx was in every respect a contemporary of Darwin, Mill, and Spencer in their skepticism about religion. (Darwin, no Social Darwinist himself, did express perplexity at what did and could contribute to a higher human morality.) The persistence of religion at the very least suggests that its supersession is not imminent under any circumstances. The new aspects of our historical experience, like fundamentalism's resurgence, are in fact very old ones. We are about as advanced in this matter as Feuerbach and (possibly wiser) we have to consider seriously whether Marxism in many of its variants was a secular religion. "Beyond Marx in the Sociology of Religions?" of course asks if and how Weber went beyond Marx. I concluded that their views were not as totally dissonant or opposed as many insist. Weber examined religions in their total social contexts, and his approach may now strike us as rather similar to that of the later Marxists—who substituted ideas of totality for sharp distinctions between a material base and an ideological superstructure. In any event, Weber's own metatheory of human existence holds that the "metaphysical needs of the human spirit" may be expressed in a limitless plurality of value universes. In the circumstances, we can hardly think of an actual or possible human community—only of endless spiritual warfare. What separated Marx from Weber was not, then, that the one was "materialist" and the other "idealist" but that the one thought humanity could come to peace with itself and the other did not. If common language has some meaning, Marx was the more religious of the two.

The very brief final essay on Marx after the Marxist epoch was part of a discussion with colleagues from Rome (Father Jean-Yves Calvez had been the Jesuit Assistant General in charge of Europe at the Jesuit Curia) and Jerusalem (Professor Shlomo Avineri, a distinguished student of modern political and social thought). I will claim a certain amount of prescience for the essay, which anticipated some of the elements of the Central European and even Soviet revolt against the post-Stalinist regimes. These were a libertarian sensibility, an insistence on participation, a belief in citizenship. Marx was clearly well ahead of himself when he declared that the French Revolution having created citizens, the time had come to create human beings. We should be satisfied (in the Western democracies as well) were we to arrive at the conditions of the practice of citizenship. That we have not done so is the consequence of another set of phenomena touched upon in the essay, the new cultural powers of capitalism. Some sort of transcendence is, again, on the historical agenda—and the project, however indistinct, leaves open the question of whether the post-Marxist epoch may in the end turn out to resemble a pre-Marxist one, like the period immediately before and just after the French Revolution.

5

Beyond Marx in the Sociology of Religion?

I   Introduction

I have attached a question mark to the title—and for a number of reasons. In what sense may we, intellectual descendants of Marxism whether or not we claim to be attached to the Marxist tradition, go beyond Marxism with respect to the sociological analysis of religion? In the original Marxist *corpus*, a view of historical progress implied that religion and irreligion would both disappear with the self-creation of a new humanity. Clearly, as disabused descendants not alone of Marx-

* I am grateful to the John Simon Guggenheim Memorial Foundation for a Fellowship which has given me the leisure to complete this paper and to the Fondazione Giovanni Agnelli, Torino, for its hospitality during the writing of it. An earlier version of the paper was delivered at the 1969 Annual Meeting of the Society for the Scientific Study of Religion, and a summary of this version was presented to the Eleventh Conference of the Conference Internationale de Sociologie Religieuse at Opatija, Yugoslavia, in September 1971.

I should also wish to record my indebtedness to two colleagues and friends who work on similar problems. Three years of association with Professor Lewis Mudge of the Department of Religion at Amherst College, including a seminar we undertook together, have taught me much. My readers will have no difficulty, further, in recognizing the influence on my thought exerted by Henri Desroche. The English-speaking public may count itself fortunate that it now has two works by Desroche available in translation (1971, 1972).

ism but of the entire nineteenth century, we at the moment entertain few hopes for that self-creation. The revolutionary means expected to realize a new humanity have usually, when applied, re-created old servitudes in new forms: for a transcendant God has been substituted what Hobbes termed the mortal God, the state—or its antagonist, the movement or party. In societies which have experienced revolution, and in those which have not, new types of alienation have superseded or supplemented alienation arising from the labor process. It would be absurd to speak of a supersession of religion, even if we can verify the attenuation and transformation of some of its inherited structures and sentiments.[1] Briefly, we confront no renewed or liberated humanity. The old gods may not be entirely with us, but neither have the new Adam and the new Eve appeared. In this sense we cannot go beyond Marx in the sociology of religion, but we have to go around the master in the search for other modes of analysis, new types of vision.

A second meaning of going beyond Marx, then, may attach to the familiar notion of secular progress in science—in this case, in social science.[2] In this account of things the privileged mode of interaction between historical experience and the human mind is codification. That codification proceeds by a formalized process of trial and error, seeks to explicate the essential elements and internal relationships of enduring or recurrent structures, and so brings to social phenomena the sharpness of vision developed in the natural sciences. Going beyond Marx in this sense would entail the substitution for the Marxist theory of religion of a superior one, superior not alone or even primarily because it deals with new phenomena, but because it deals differently with old phenomena. The last point is important because it marks a distinction between a Marxist-inspired revision of Marxism (on account of new historical experience) and a rejection or severe emendation of Marxism on a basis which claims to be scientific. Going beyond Marx in this last sense would entail a rupture with the Marxist epistemology, which holds that human purpose and value are inextricably bound to our notions of social process. In this view only the fusion of human purpose with historical experience can provide an adequate basis for knowledge.

The choice of a beginning point for this essay, then, implies a philosophical option. We may take the standpoint of conventional social science (which, to be sure, appears less conventional and monolithic the closer one examines it) and adumbrate a criticism of Marxism

---

[1] See Caporale and Grumelli (1971). This book contains the contributions to the Vatican Conference on the sociology of religion, valuable in their own right, and indicative of the current discussion of secularisation. See also the Introduction to the anthology edited by Lenzer and me (1969).

[2] The current discussion of method in the social sciences may be described as intense. See MacIntyre (1970), Friedrichs (1970), Gouldner (1970), Birnbaum (1971).

which rests on the progress of sociology. Alternatively, we may attempt to incorporate the legacy of this progress in a new historical vision which, like Marxism, fuses purpose and analysis. A splendid project, the latter, but rather vast for the briefer compass of this paper; the more so as, the Marxist anthropology fragmented, it is difficult to elaborate another one for our immediate requirements. Let us say frankly that this paper is a minor part of a search for a new vision like the Marxist one in scope. It will accordingly manifest the jaggedness and the contradictoriness of all such efforts, but perhaps this may be compensated for by a certain metaphysical openness. At any rate, we shall move from within the Marxist system to its boundaries and then outside these in the effort to find a new historical-philosophical location from which to examine the sociology of religion.

II The Marxist Sociology of Religion

The Original Theory

The exegesis of the original Marxist texts and of their historical sources seems to know no end. We are in possession of a very considerable critical and historical literature (most of it the work of scholars not living under Marxist regimes, whatever their own philosophical or political opinions).[3] Interestingly, some of this work has been accomplished by theologians: we may cite the work both of the German Protestants associated with the Marxismusstudien[4] of the German Protestant church and of the learned monks of several orders in Paris (Calvez 1956, de Lubac 1969). These scholarly efforts have not been without political meaning: the German Protestant effort to recapture the critical part of the German philosophical inheritance has been a component in the loosening of the cultural and political rigidity (and, let it be said, the crushing boredom) of the "restoration" of German social structure after 1945. The French Catholic encounter with Marxism has been part of that movement of renewal and innovation in French Catholicism which took dramatic form in episodes like *les prêtres contestataires* and their forerunners, the *Prêtres ouvriers* (Petrie 1956), but it also influenced the former Papal Nuncio in Paris, Cardinal Roncalli, who became Pope John. The secular participants in this scholarly effort have had other organizational and doctrinal concerns: many were

[3] A recent international conspectus is provided by the International Social Science Council (1969). This was the UNESCO Conference of May, 1968, on the same theme—convened as the French student-worker revolt was breaking out. See also the valuable symposium cited by Lobkowicz (1967).

[4] Studienkommission der Evangelische-Kirche Deutschlands, *Marxismusstudien*, Vols. I–V (Tübingen: Möhr, 1954–59).

disappointed or dissident socialists engaged in a search for a new humanistic fundament for a Marxist politics which had become bureaucratized or tyrannical. Still others have been concerned with the problem of the end of philosophy, with the Marxist effort to effect a philosophical transcendence of a reflective view of the world by developing a new type of human *praxis*.

If the literature of exegesis and criticism is considerable, so is the intensity of scholarly dispute contained in it. The relationship of the earlier to the later writings of Marx, the role and continuity of Hegelian components in his thought, and the weight to be assigned to human reflection in the Marxist conception of *praxis* are among the questions at issue. This is not the place to review these controversies, but we may say that the relationship of "material" to "ideal" factors in the Marxist analysis now appears to be much more subtle and complex than in schematic representations of an unequivocal and unilinear determination of "superstructure" by a material "base." We are entitled to conclude that the Marxist theory of religion has to be conceived of in the light of these newer inquiries into the original texts. Indeed, the matter is made simple by the fact that much of the interpretation has turned about the writings of Marx and Engels on religion.

For our purposes two major themes emerge from these writings. The first concerns the Marxist critique of the critical philosophers of the early nineteenth century. The second is the Marxist analysis of human alienation. Let us consider each in turn. I have termed Marx's immediate predecessors in philosophy critical and for good reason. Marx did not singlehandedly overturn an idealist metaphysics, much less develop his own system in a single leap of the metaphysical imagination. What he and Engels did was to utilize the intentions and contradictions of their predecessors to develop a new system (Löwith 1964a). Hegel voiced considerable respect for the historical function of religion in general and Christianity in particular, but he contributed no little to its relativization in describing it as one form among many of the manifestations of spirit. The Hegelian theologians Bruno Bauer and Friedrich David Strauss took Hegel at his word and examined Christianity in its context. The one concluded that the Gospels were the inventions of their apostolic authors, seeking self-understanding, the other, that Christian belief entailed a mythicization of human experience. All three were accused of inconsistency by Ludwig Feuerbach. The spirit, he held, was upon examination a manifestation not of itself but of human self-consciousness. The mythic object of deification in religion, and especially in Christianity, was humanity itself. The destruction of the Hegelian notion of the spirit, the reinterpretation of the work of the biblical scholars to uncover the human aspirations at the root of the Christian Gospels, were the preconditions for a new humanistic philosophy. German philosophy, Marx and Engels declared, had to go through a brook of fire (a play on the name of their colleague, Feuerbach) in order to be purified. Their conception of purification, however, rapidly took a more stringent emphasis.

Originally enthused by the young Hegelians' attack on the obscurity and abstractedness of Hegel's conception of spirit, delighted by their effort to make concrete the religious tradition of the West in universal human characteristics, Marx and Engels at first embraced the new philosophical anthropology (Easton and Guddat 1967). Their own dissatisfaction with it was a consequence of their realization, in their own terms, that it was a doctrine of humanity not much less abstract, no less remote from the concrete, than Hegel's notion of spirit. In the place of an abstract spirit the young Hegelians had set an abstract humanity. They had replaced the worship of God by a religion of humanity. And, to solve the concrete problems of a society stricken by exploitation and poverty, convulsed by industrialization, dominated by political tyranny, they could offer only the work of "critical critics"—philosophical discourse without reference to tangible historical realities.

Feuerbach, Marx and Engels declared, had depicted a humanity alienated from itself because it was subject to the creations of its own mind—to religious images of itself. Feuerbach's solution for this subjugation was to correct the images, to restore to or endow humanity with its own highest attributes. These, however, remained ideal, mental or spiritual creations with a humanistic content but still remote from the suffering of humanity in its concrete setting. Humankind needed religious imagery because it could not confront its own reality, but that reality was obscured by abstract humanistic conceptions in a manner not distinct from the workings of religion. The question was a different one: Why did humanity need religious or philosophical idealization? The initial answer could be found only in the misery and degradation of humanity's concrete conditions of existence, and we do well to remind ourselves that Marx and Engels (professing intellectuals) regarded a certain form of religious adherence as a higher but no less definite form of degradation than material exploitation or political subjugation. The Marxist search for the sources of religion and the Marxist effort to end religion were henceforth to be concentrated on the question of humanity's self-inflicted imprisonment in its own world—on the problem of alienation. Before considering the notion of alienation in greater detail, however, we must turn to another of the sources for the Marxist theory of religion: the notion of a secular community as a successor to the kingdom of heaven.

Marx and Engels took their view of society from three sources—German philosophy, what has been termed French socialism but what is better described as early French social thought, and British political economy. Marx himself has noted ironically on the ways in which the laws of the market—as described in British political economy—curiously parodied the inscrutable workings of the Calvinist God. His conceptions of religion, however, may well owe much to Robert Owen's (1963) utopian view of a cooperative, nay, harmonious, human community. Owen's "New Moral World" was to be the result of a Christian critique of capitalism's destruction of human dignity and community. It paralleled themes found in some of the early French utopians and in the German social-religious thinker, Weiteling. The common element in these writings was the notion of a humanity come into possession of its religious heritage by realizing in new social forms the religious vision of community. Marx, of course, denied that humanity required a religious legitimation for its search for a true community: he dismissed the utopians as empty moralizers, again guilty of applying an abstract criterion to historical concreteness. Yet his own view of religion was immensely clarified by his encounter with these utopian Christians and post-Christian utopians. In one respect they demonstrated the close connection between religious ideals and a defective social reality: In a response to earthly misery which sought to heal the split in the actual human community by creating on earth a community hitherto reserved for heaven. In another respect they did provide Marx with elements he could transmute into his own version of eschatology: they insisted, in terms rather different from those of Aristotle, on Aristotle's definition of man as a political or communal being. Marx envisaged the self-realization of humanity as the creation of a new or true community. This was to develop from human need and through extreme conflict; it was to be produced, briefly, by the intolerability of its absence, by the self-destruction of its negation, the class society. Marx held that his morality was immanent in the historical process itself and, therefore, free of theological content. It was freed of theological content, however, by his transcribing theological terms into profane or secular ones.

A similar process, if with a somewhat different content, occurred with Saint-Simon's (1964) idea of a new community. Saint-Simon did not hesitate to use the term "the New Christianity," to describe his social ethic and political program. There were near-comical elements in it, as in the suggestion that the Papal Curia be replaced by a "Council of Newton." As did his disciple Comte, however, Saint-Simon admired the hierarchical order and spiritual discipline of medieval society (or what they thought was such). The notion of a secularized equivalent of Christianity serving to unite society—an equivalent to be constituted of positivistic doctrine—was drawn from the social theology of the Restoration. The thinkers of the Restoration hoped for a return to a society dominated by church and throne; Saint-Simon and Comte thought this impossible but were anxious to find new institutional supports for order. Marx's own revulsion for this sort of thought was very great, attached as he was to the tradition of the Enlightenment. Yet it was precisely Saint-Simon's program, which proposed to reconcile order and technological progress, which illuminated both the conservative functions of historical Christianity in Europe and the authoritarian bias of some of Christianity's critics. Saint-Simon's sociology of religion, which proposed to use a scientific equivalent for it to domesticate society, was in itself a caricature of the Enlightenment doctrine that institutional religion was a device for subjugating humanity. It would be absurd to deny the possibility that early Marxist texts can be found to substantiate the view that for Marx and Engels, communism was a "religion of mankind." As their critique of religion, and ideology, developed, however, they arrived at the position that a true religion of humanity was humanity itself, in its practice. That, however, required a liberated humanity, not one held together by a new or proto-religion, even it if spoke the language of science.

The Marxist sociology of religion, then, is inseparable from the radical humanism of Marx and Engels. That humanism opposed a true humanity to an inauthentic, or injured and subjugated one and propounded a general doctrine of the human condition in the analysis of alienation. The analysis was and remains a remarkable philosophical achievement. The Enlightenment, from which Marx and Engels drew so much, had opposed an authentic human nature to inauthentic or tyrannical institutions. The tyranny destroyed, human nature could flower. The achievement of Marx and Engels was, not least, the historicization of the antithesis. The real problem of history, they found, lay in the interiorization of tyranny by the species, in its systematic deformation by and in its own historical structures. They opposed a potentially fulfilled humanity to an actually degraded one. Recent scholarship has shown how the notion of alienation drew upon the Hegelian legacy, upon romantic esthetics (the young Marx wrote poetry and even in his most polemical and abstract moments remained a great German prose stylist), and upon the pedagogic and psychological theory of the French Enlightenment.

Two principal components constitute the elements of the theory of alienation. The first refers to human practice (or, as put in the original texts, *praxis*). Hegel had developed at length the notion of the exteriorization of the spirit. He had also, a point seized upon by Marx and Engels, described the human form of that exteriorization: the historical development of labor, particularly in bourgeois society. The key to human nature, Marx and Engels held, was to be found in human *praxis*, and there was no more important *praxis* than labor. Labor was, further, not merely a means of self-reproduction for the individual: it was a mode of self-reproduction for the species, and the relations of work were the fundamental relations of all sociability. The second component of the theory of alienation, then, was the notion of sociability, perhaps best characterized as the notion of community. Human beings were constricted, denied their full development, because certain historical forms of the labor process inevitably resulted in false or distorted communities. In these the relationships of labor or production were relationships of subjugation and not of fraternity. Moreover, the products of human labor—under the advanced historical circumstances of Marx's time—in effect assumed a life of their own, and ruled over their producers. Humans related to one another through these products, or through buying and selling them, and not directly. True community, a direct relationship of humans to one another, had no chance to develop.

The elements of the theory of alienation are, then, human self-exteriorization in labor and the denial of the human community in the relations of labor. The mechanism by which these elements produced alienation was the division of labor. At bottom of the idea of self-exteriorization lay, certainly, a notion of human substance, of human wholeness. In the division of labor that wholeness was denied or, more specifically, fragmented. Humans produced to meet their needs but did so indirectly. The market mediated their relationships and placed the many, who had nothing to exchange but their labor power, at the disposal of the few, who controlled the means of production. It is important to note that for Marx and Engels, it was not private property (in the sense of ownership of the productive apparatus) which produced alienation, but alienation, in the form of the division of labor, which eventuated in private property. In a labor-divided society market forms of relationships inevitably developed once the forces of production had attained a certain degree of complexity. Bourgeois society was the market society par excellence, and it had driven the division of labor to its extreme point. Previous societies, like feudal Europe, had known the division of labor and, of course, exploitation. In these, however, production and exchange relationships were invariably combined with other, human relationships. Where, as in bourgeois society, production and exchange existed for and by themselves, the alienation of men from one another, and from their own possibilities of wholeness, was maximal.

The notions of wholeness and community which underlay the theory of alienation were used, then, to develop a negative account of human history. History was the record of humanity's failure to achieve fully human status. The Marxist account of history has, indeed, been described by Marx himself as, in effect, a prehistory: humanity can begin when alienation is overcome. It is in this context that we can insert the Marxist theory of religion: religion is a spiritual response to a condition of alienation. The Marxist theory of religion, however, was much more specific. It ascribed the religious forms of alienation to the specific forms of production, labor relationship, and relationship to nature found in the successive stages of human history. Perhaps we may put the matter in another way: in making concrete a general theory of religion as produced by human insufficiency, Marxism recorded the specific alienation of the several stages of history.

The precise mode by which religion was produced was a replica of the prevailing mode of production in human society.[5] In particular, Marx and Engels held, the division of labor had immensely significant consequences for spiritual and intellectual labor. Under very primitive conditions individuals and the societies to which they belonged them-selves produced their own spiritual worlds—systems of codification and interpretation of experience. Where the society was closely and im-mediately dependent upon nature, natural religions developed. With the growth of the forces of production and the introduction of the division of labor, religious specialists appeared who concentrated on the production of systems of belief. These were important, nay, indis-pensable social functions; and if history records a progression toward a market system in commodities, it does not do so in the sphere of the spirit. What was produced, by whom, and for whom were matters of jealous interest to those in power in labor divided societies. The gen-eral Marxist proposition that those who owned the means of produc-tion also owned the means of intellectual (or ideological) production was particularly true with respect to religion. Natural religions were transformed into state religions, and these, in turn, with the increasing density of the cultural tradition, into religions legitimated by (as well as legitimating) the state. With the consolidation of larger societies, polytheisms based on fusions of regional subsocieties (each with its gods) gave way to monotheism, proclaiming a strong and uniform moral discipline.

It may be objected that this does not sound particularly "critical" at all, but rather like conventional nineteenth-century accounts of the evolution of religion, of the sort we might find in the works of Taylor or Spencer. Just so. Marx and Engels were part of one of the first generations to profit from the new archaeological and philological in-quiries into the history of religion. Their account of the facts and se-quence of religious history, then, is different in no significant respect from that of their learned contemporaries. What did distinguish their work was the interpretative context in which it was placed, their ac-count of the inner structure of religion and its relationship to society. Perhaps we may look at the matter in another way. For Marx and Engels the production of religious systems was part of the general pro-cess of the production of ideology: indeed, through most of human

[5] To avoid burdening the test with citation after citation, it will be understood that I give a general sketch of the theory. See Niebuhr's introduction to Marx and Engels (1964), for a useful introduction to the texts.

history religion was not alone the privileged but the exclusive mode of intellectual and spiritual discourse. As a mode of ideology religion shared its most general characteristic. Ideology was not, as is sometimes believed, a false account of the human condition or social situation. Rather, it is a partial one, determined by the imperfect development of humanity. We may say that ideology was the truth of a false condition, and this, by extension, included religion. Marx and Engels had an acute sense of the spiritual dimensions of human existence, as well as considerable knowledge of the Western religious tradition. Religious interpretations of the human condition were necessary, in their view, precisely because of the misery and degradation of that condition. Religion, as a derivative of alienation, could not be attacked frontally: when alienation was overcome, religion itself would dissolve. There was, however, a precondition to the political organization of the attack on alienation—or, rather, its causes—and this was a condition of (relative) enlightenment. Some parts of humanity, at least, had to be free of the sort of ideological domination contained in religion. This is the meaning of the famous remark at the beginning of Marx's "Contribution to the Critique of Hegel's Philosophy of Right": "For Germany, the criticism of religion is in the main complete, and criticism of religion is the premise of all criticism" (Marx and Engels 1964: 41).

Let us ignore, for the moment, the ambiguities of the position (how may some attain insight into a world still alienated?) and consider yet other dimensions of the Marxist theory.

The impulses which produced religion were, for Marx and Engels, profoundly human: a demand at once for dignity and consolation, for explanation and moral coherence. Religion was a response to peoples' homelessness in the world, an effort to construct an imaginary home— a moral universe in which humanity could find repose—and an ideal image of itself. It is clear that this account of religion is far from a moral denigration of it; moral revulsion attached to the conditions which produced religion. Indeed, in his work *The German Peasants' War* (which remains a masterpiece of historical interpretation of the entire German Reformation), Engels declared that in religious epochs even critical and revolutionary thought had to find religious expression (Marx and Engels 1964: 96 ff.). Further, in his writings on early Christianity Engels likened its beginnings to the (then contemporary) beginnings of socialism among the European workers—as a spiritual movement for social dignity. With Marx, he was conscious of the progression of religious thought from tribalism to universalism, no doubt, a legacy of the Hegelian historical interpretation of the history of religion as a mode of the history of human self-consciousness and human development. Precisely that progression accounted for the original Marxist rejection of German classical philosophy: like the religious tradition from which it derived, it created a world of images and concepts remote from the actual structures of human reality. If philosophy in its abstract form was the legitimate successor of theology, all the more reason to concentrate the emancipatory activities of reason on the similarities between religion and philosophy (similarities contained in the general Marxist analysis of ideology, which encompassed both).

Moreover, concrete political consequences followed from the analysis of religion. The demand for religious emancipation, for freedom of religion from state control, was according to Marx simply a demand that people be free to enslave themselves. The freedom of religion guaranteed in the Declaration of the Rights of Man, and in the several American state constitutions, did not emancipate people: it made some of them citizens, perhaps, but not yet free people. Indeed, the bourgeois revolution, as it proceeded from seventeenth-century England to eighteenth-century France and the United States, ostensibly opened new possibilities for humanity while actually consolidating a new servitude. That revolution made the market the central institution of society and introduced, in effect, new types of religion. Christianity with what Marx termed "its cultus of abstract man" (Marx and Engels 1964: 135), particularly in its bourgeois and Protestant forms, was a precondition for the development of the abstract and universal market relations (with money as a common denominator) of capitalism. These relations having been introduced, a curious regression occurred: a new type of fetishism appeared—the fetishism of commodities—quite unlike the fetishism of the primitives who were bound to nature. Bound to the market, people conceived of themselves as dominated by the products of their labor, commodities. They did not see that they had created this world and that (granted the proper historical conditions) they could undo it and create a humane universe. By a curious paradox the apogee of the development of new human powers, in the new productive apparatus of industrial capitalism, substituted for the religious conceptions of the past new phantasmagoria—the reified world of commodity production. Humans, at the point in their history when they were most remote from that total dependence upon nature which characterized the primitive stages of human development, were the opposite of sovereign. They were also remote, however, from an element of primitive existence which Marx and Engels valued rather strongly—integration in a community. They confronted a world they had made, unaware that they had done so, isolated from one another, fragmented and crippled in their common humanity. The replacement of theology by bourgeois political economy by no means signified that the sources of alienation were gone. The human needs to which religion was a response were as poignant, their satisfaction apparently as impossible, as ever.

It was at this point that the radical humanism of Marx and Engels proposed a transcendence of religion. The reconquest of humanity by itself demanded, first of all, a process of self-recognition. Humanity had to recognize the fact and the inner structure of its bondage. It had to eschew religious and metaphysical solutions to its difficulties and learn to see itself as it was. Therein, however, lay hope: a humanity thrown back upon its own resources could realize its own potential. This reduction of historical experience to a human essence, found in the process of labor, had a rigorous metaphysical derivative of an antimetaphysical kind. People had to see themselves as practical beings, had to develop their capacities for autonomous activity free of the fears rigidified in religion and free of the terrible limits set by the bourgeois social order. No narrow (or even larger) utilitarianism was implied by this doctrine. It was not so much that people were to be freed to follow their interests, but that they were to free themselves—qualitatively—to follow new interests. As they did so, Feuerbach's project of a religion of humanity would dissolve: in possession of themselves, people would not feel compelled to worship an idealized image of themselves.

The philosophical and historical assumptions of the Marxist theory of religion, then, are inseparable from the theory of alienation. In the original Marxist texts the assumptions were stated more often than not. Nevertheless, we may phrase the Marxist sociology of religion in a somewhat different, possibly more concrete way. The components of this version of the doctrine are three: the development of the division of spiritual labor, the structure of the religious situation in the first half of the nineteenth century, and the problem of concrete transcendence.

The division of spiritual labor has proceeded, according to Marxism, *pari passu* with the division of material labor. In the original human community, the community had a direct relationship to nature: this was part of humanity's early and unfragmented apprehension of its own existence. As the productive forces grew, internal relationships of domination and exploitation developed in the once unitary human community. A particular and specialized spiritual production became necessary to legitimate the new division of labor, to explain it, and to assuage the fears and inchoate desires it evoked. That spiritual production took the most diverse forms—priests attending a polytheistic pantheon, caesaro-papist monarchs, charismatic churches, and heretical sects. In general, to the stages of the division of labor there corresponded phases in the division of spiritual labor and its product. The entire scheme is saved from excessive schematism by two elements frequently unappreciated by Marxism's critics.

The first is the Marxist appreciation of religious diversity and conflict attributed, of course, to differentiation and conflict in the society. Did not Engels attribute the rise of Christianity to the spiritual needs of the Roman Empire's proletariat, to the death of the pagan gods (Marx and Engels 1964: 316 ff.)? The phrase "spiritual needs" gives us the second element in the theory. Human history, for Marx and Engels, is not alone the history of production and of the class struggles inextri-

cably bound to production relationships. It is also the history of the
spirit—if of the human spirit struggling against blindness, despair, and
its own limitations. Marx, it should be recalled, was acutely aware of
changes in the history of the spirit of the sort contained in the Reformation. Of the latter, he said that Luther had turned priests into laymen by converting laymen into priests, by internalizing what had been
ecclesiastical discipline (Marx and Engels 1964: 51). His own anticipation of the modern analysis of the Protestant ethic was connected
with a larger theme in his sociology of religion. The emergence and
(temporary) consolidation of bourgeois society introduced a new form
of (distorted) spirituality. What had been Protestantism became an
egoism the more ruthless for the absence of any other historical possibilities of human relationship. Marx likened the workings of the market to the inscrutable decisions of the Calvinist God, but the doctrine
of the fetishism of commodities implied a regression from monotheism
to a more primitive spirituality. The ambiguity, the incompletion of
historical development was indeed another theme in the Marxist sociology of religion. Monotheism was, for instance, depicted as the product of a higher, more developed civilization with a more dense and
universal set of cultural contacts and, of course, production relations.
Yet out of monotheism the thinkers of new epoch derived their metaphysical notions: to these, people were subjugated as surely as if they
worshipped old gods.

It is at this point that we may turn to the Marxist analysis of the
religious situation in its own period. The subordination of people to
the market created not alone intolerable material deprivation, but severe spiritual suffering. In the resultant crisis some of the relationships
of spiritual domination were becoming visible—not least, the uses of
the churches as ancillary political organs. The Constantinization of
Christianity, Marx and Engels implied, was a continuing process. They
denied, however, that there was absolute utility to the demand for
religious emancipation. This demand, which insisted on the separation
of church and state, in reality called for the spiritual reproduction of
market relationships. Just as people on the market were forced to sell
their labor power in systems of exchange which they did not create, so
people on the spiritual market would be cast into psychological dependence upon a supernatural order for want of the ability to perceive the
natural and social order. Marx adduced the example of the United States,
where the church was entirely separated from the state and where the
separate churches flourished in a way unmatched in Europe. Germany
(and other societies in Europe, like Italy and Russia) were no doubt
historically backward: there, the struggle against religion and the
churches was a preliminary to the real struggle against the conditions
which made religion necessary. Where, however, capitalist production
relations were developed in their full form, political atheism had to

give way to unalloyed communism. Here again, Marx and Engels made use of the ambiguity of historical forms: they likened the beginnings of the socialist movement among the working class to the beginnings of Christianity (Marx and Engels 1964: 316). There are, indisputably, passages in the writings which give credence to the view that Marx and Engels thought of communism as a religion of humanity or as a successor to the historical religions. The proletariat, after all, was assigned the role of a surrogate for all of humanity. Humanity could regain itself only when the proletariat, as its most injured part, assumed the task of revolution—a mode of universal historical redemption. Yet the end of religion, in the Marxist theory, is perhaps best understood as part of the problem of concrete transcendence, to which we now turn.

The revolution anticipated by Marx was to bring about not alone a change in social relationships, but a spiritual change as well. Humanity would abandon the gods, because it would no longer need these: instead, it would learn to live with itself. In the place of the multiple spiritual alienations of its previous existence, humanity would live wholly—in a new *praxis*. This may be termed a concrete transcendence, because it would come (or was supposed to come) from an organic continuation of revolutionary activity. By revolting against the conditions of alienation, people would begin the process of ending alienation. The progression from one world to another, then, from the realm of necessity to the realm of freedom, was to be concrete. People required not theological images of the universe, nor yet their metaphysical derivatives: they had to meet the concrete tasks of their history. Did this imply, for internal structure of Marxist theory, a recourse to scientific modes of thought as the exclusive model for the apprehension of reality? Is there not an undertone, or a component, of pragmatic utilitarianism in these aspects of Marxism? Perhaps, but we do well to recall that Marx himself mocked the narrow utilitarianism of Bentham as philistine. Equally, despite the relative infrequency and lack of development of Marx's ideas on science, he did not regard science as an exclusively utilitarian pursuit. Rather, it was a development of humanity's highest powers, an expression of the struggle against inert nature, but also a realization of the human unity with a higher nature, which encompassed the human potential. The connection between science and *praxis* meant that science for Marx was not strictly cognitive: it was, rather a mode of social existence. What we think of as social science, then, was part of a general development of human power which also found expression in the rise of the natural sciences (what Marx [1953: 479] once called the scientific power). The opposition between religion and science, then, was for Marx not alone the familiar one of the antithesis of falsehood and truth. It was, rather, the opposition of an inauthentic—however necessary—stage in human development to an authentic one. Within what Marx designated as human prehistory, religions and the beliefs attached to them were more or less true. Bourgeois ideology, to draw an analogy from the more general aspects of Marxist theory, was in face a truer statement about society than its predecessor—the organicist theory of the early modern period—because it came closer to the essential relationships which constituted society. The progression from metaphysics to metacriticism, as theology decomposed, was equally an approach to truth: out of the theoretical humanism of the metacritics, the radical humanism of *praxis* could develop.

It would be absurd to deny the secularized religious content of the Marxist system as a whole: an extensive literature has drawn the analogy, at times with profundity (Blumenberg 1966, Löwith 1964b). A secularized religious content, however, remains secularized: the Marxist categories require, for our purpose, not transformation back into their supposed religious sources, but examination in their own terms. Before proceeding to that examination, we might well consider the treatment of religion in Marxist theory after Marx.

The Marxists After Marx

We may begin with Engels, despite his own role as Marx's early collaborator. His own pietistic background made Engels especially sensitive to the religious dimensions of human existence, and his knowledge of the history of religions was not small. Engels's modification of the Marxist theory of religion had two aspects not unrelated to the general utilization of the theory found in his writings on a number of subjects. He did have a tendency, despite the religious sensitivity (what Max Weber might have termed religious musicality) he manifested, to describe religion at times as a direct expression of class interests. How the interests of a class may be identified, whether and under what conditions classes become aware of their interests, questions of the division of spiritual labor within given classes—these are matters which have long troubled students of the Marxists texts. The key to this emendation of Marxism is to be found in the word "direct" as applied to the expression of these interests: the burden of Marx's argument was that the situation of a class necessarily produced a situation of alienation, which in turn generated religion. That the specific forms and content of a historical religion were deeply influenced by the historical situation and social location of a class is, of course, a proposition Marxism shares with any number of other views of religion. The notion of religion as directly derived from class interests, in its reductionist form, is not compatible with the central tenets of the original Marxist analysis. Marx and Engels both were aware, of course, that at time religion was used or interpreted by classes high and low in terms consonant with their interests: this assertion is, however, not one about the origins of religion. The second tendency in Engels's thought stems from his assimilation of Darwinism. At times, he seemed to favor a doctrine of the natural selection of religions in situations of historical competition. The factors affecting natural selection, on this account, would be those at work in the general Marxist depiction of social process. We may note that this general depiction was, for all of its evolutionary and even naturalistic content, pre-Darwinian. People interacted with nature, but human labor, human society, and the human spirit were qualitatively distinct from nature. In the circumstances no mechanical causation of historical process was possible. History was a succession of structures, each with its own internal laws. A specific historical structure, given the general human propensity to develop religions, set limits to the religious systems that could live within it. This doctrine, whatever else it may be, is far from social Darwinism.

Perhaps I have made too much of these emendations of Engels. Let it be said at this point that he was at one with Marx in supposing that, within any historical structure, ideology (including, of course, religion) was not a mechanical derivative of production relations. In any given historical process, particularly in the short run, ideologies (including religions) had some autonomy. This is another way of saying that religion was an important historical force, not despite, but because of, its role as and expression of human alienation. The ambiguities in Engels's treatment of religion, however, were to lead to a certain crudification in the work of his successors, Kautsky (1910) and Bernstein (1895). There, religion was depicted as a reflection of class interests, as a direct means of class domination. The distinction (found in practice if not in theory in the original Marxist writings) between religion and ideology was erased: nothing of the substance of human spirituality was left in these analyses. Two curiously disparate reasons may be given for this development. These German Socialist thinkers (and politicians) took up positivism as a method. They proclaimed an almost total identification between the methods of the natural sciences and those of the social sciences. This is not the place to elaborate on the view that this frequently (as in some contemporary sociological studies of religion) leads to a position external to religion. By "external to religion," I mean a certain tendency to reduce religious structures to their observable contexts, to refuse a direct apprehension of religious consciousness, to treat it as solely epiphenomenal. This position is quite comprehensible when we connect it with the late nineteenth-century view that Marxism was a positive science, not a philosophical anthropology. On this view alternative interpretations of social existence were not just that: they were codification of error, radically different from and discontinuous with Marxism. The second reason for the positivistic insensitivity to religion in this version of Marxism is paradoxical. If

Marxism were a science, if all other notions were in error, then Marxism's predictions as to the human future (a revolutionary utopia) had, somehow, to be verified mechanically and inevitably. No political movement can long maintain itself with a doctrine of inevitable triumph, however useful this may be for the purposes of converting those outside it and for maintaining the morale of those within it. Bernstein, in particular, met this problem by recourse to a Kantian morality. Socialism would come about because it ought to come about, not as a development of humanity's highest potential, but as an expression of humanity's actual moral characteristics. The element of qualitative and historical transformation was excluded; a static notion of humanity was introduced. In this setting, too, religion seemed at best arbitrary, at worst irrelevant or obscurantist—an element in history embarrassing to explain and most conveniently dispatched by treating it as a factor in prehistory. Kant's own interpretation of religion was rather different, but it was disregarded.

From Bernstein and Kautsky a line may be traced downward to Lenin (1947). Lenin's genius clearly resided in spheres other than the interpretation of culture or epistemology. The religion he knew best was the caesero-papism of Czarist Russia. The theory of knowledge he advanced was one in which human thought was a reflection of the world. In the circumstances he dealt with religion as a pure and simple mystification. Lenin's views on religion marked, to some degree, a low point in the history of modern Marxist thought. We may say that it has taken decades for the official Marxist movement associated with Soviet communism to recover from the canonization of Lenin (which was followed, to be sure, by the domination of the movement by a former student of orthodox theology, Stalin). Current work in the Soviet Union and in the other state socialist regimes is increasingly vital and sophisticated: as it has yet to take definitive theoretical form, it will be dealt with in the section on the current sociology of religion.

Much of the most striking work on religion in the Marxist tradition has been historical with a deepening or an emendation of the Marxist theory as a by-product. We may therefore reserve, equally, for subsequent treatment the writings of thinkers like Borkenau, Goldmann, and Kolakowski. Two twentieth-century Marxist theorists, however, merit our attention now. Lukacs (1971) did almost no work on religion as such. However, his insistence on the philosophical components of Marxism—and, in particular, on the utility of concepts like *reification*—has contributed to the renaissance, more recently, of a serious Marxist philosophical anthropology. In his work the concept of reification is central; with it, the way has been opened to a critical consideration of religious ideas (and institutions) as reified sets of symbols. The way has also been opened to those inside the religious tradition for a purifying critique of the accretions attaching to their own tradition. With the use of the concept of reification, some religious thinkers have gone so far as to distinguish between authentic and inauthentic religion. Lukacs has also contributed a notion of revolutionary *praxis* as a dialectical leap into a human future as yet to be made. This had, clearly, reinforced the secularized eschatological elements inside Marxism. At the same time, it has provided a somewhat more rigorous theoretical framework for the Marxist notion of human development and contributed in this way to a possible specification of the distinction between Marxism and religion. It must be said that Lukacs's work on these themes, in his *History and Class Consciousness*, was repudiated by Communist orthodoxy (and, alas, by Lukacs himself). In no account did Lukacs move on to consider religious phenomena explicitly. In his subsequent work on aesthetics, in which he attempts to ground esthetic experience in an idea of a humanity at once ideal and possible, his use of religion is exceedingly fragmentary and unsystematic, even shallow.

The personal religious inheritance of a thinker is important. Lukacs was Jewish and, not surprisingly, developed an aesthetics with a heavy emphasis on the moral responsibility of the artist. Antonio Gramsci (1966), the second original Marxist we have to consider and the founder of the Italian Communist party, came, of course, from a culture steeped in Catholicism. The assimilation of Gramsci's thought to modern Marxism, to modern thought as a whole, is only now beginning. Gramsci insisted on the necessity of a Marxist analysis of culture and on the peculiarities of the Italian national culture. He conceived of the Roman Catholic church, historically, as rooted in the populace, as promulgating a doctrine complex, even subtle, for the intellectuals, but simple and comprehensive for the rest of the nation. What he admired in this process was its organic quality, its genuine synthesis of elements directly related to the activities and aspirations of a people. He derided the manipulative and political Catholicism which opposed Italian anticlericalism and socialism, but, in doing so, he in effect appealed to a more organic, more historically effective, version of religion. He did so in reflecting on the spiritual tasks before those who would organize a revolutionary, laicist party in Italy. Gramsci's Marxism is remarkable for its awareness of the educative tasks of a revolutionary party and in this respect is a concrete advance over what was programmatic in Marx himself—the modes by which humanity was to liberate itself from religion. Gramsci's most interesting work on religion is also fragmentary, and much of it was written in a fascist prison: its full development remains a task for his successors. We may note that his insistence on the educative tasks of a revolutionary movement has had considerable influence on Italy: the Italian Communist party has, in fact, doubled its vote (from circa 14 to circa 28 percent) since the end of the Second World War. The late Palmiro Togliatti, Gramsci's successor as leader of the party, in his celebrated "Political Testament," reminded the party that it had to take a differentiated and sympathetic view of religion (cited in Garaudy 1968: 118). This was more than a gesture at political coexistence with Italian Catholicism: it was an attempt to win again for political Marxism the theoretic legacy of the struggle against alienation. In the Togliatti "Testament," indeed, religion emerges as a potential force against alienation, as the possible bearer of humanity's aspirations along with socialism.

We are already anticipating the section on the Marxist-Christian dialogue. One of the striking results of the theoretical advances in Marxism achieved by Lukacs and Gramsci is the way in which these have been absorbed not by the socialist movement alone but by the oppositional party within Christendom. The critique of its ossification, of its remoteness from human aspiration, owes something to the doctrine of reification. The demand that the churches break their alliance with ruling elites and contribute to the practical education of subject populations draws, to some degree, upon Gramsci's reflection on Catholicism. For the moment, we may conclude that these advances in Marxism go some way beyond the original texts without radically transcending them or profoundly altering the original Marxist perspective. They constitute, then (a phenomenon observed more than once in the history of religions), a recovery of the past as well as an uncertain move into the future.

III   The Theoretical Critique of the Marxist Sociology of Religion

Introduction

The theoretical critique of the Marxist sociology of religion has two components. The first is straightforward enough—the development of other analytical assumptions, of different ideas about the relationship of religion and society. The second seems equally straightforward— direct criticism of Marxism, its emendation and refutation. The two are, of course, inseparably related: a critique of Marxism must always rest on its own theoretic foundations. More difficult still, the systems opposing Marxism usually share some assumptions with it. Indeed, they often have been influenced by Marxism and have incorporated some of its notions. We have to deal as well with inversions and reversals: the party of order, in early nineteenth-century sociology, insisted that only religion could hold society together and sought to buttress tottering thrones with refurbished altars. The critical party, to use Saint-Simon's terms, reversed the argument, and held that the elimination of religion was a precondition of social and political change. Moreover, the development of sociology at times seemed to verify the

Marxist theses on ideology (and their underlying notions about alienation). Those thinkers who adduced permanent characteristics of society were, often enough, eternalizing transitory historical phenomena—objectifying, in Marxist terms, structures actually created by people. Finally, sociologies of religion inevitably bear traces of the religious traditions within which, if only by opposition, they develop. We cannot, briefly, oppose to Marxism a uniform sociological critique: we have to turn, instead, to a multiplicity of sociologies of religion.

The Sociology of Religion in German Sociology

The encounter of German sociology with Marxism has always been direct. Not alone did Marx and Engels write (and think) in German: the German Social Democratic party represented a Marxist political and spiritual presence in German society. Moreover, the close relationship of German academic philosophy to German Protestant theology, the political role of the established Lutheran church, the *Kulturakampf* which set Catholics and Protestants against each other in the late nineteenth century, the very great impact on German culture of Darwinism all contributed to making religion a continuing problem for German social theory. It would be an absurdity to begin by stating that the non-Marxist Germans assigned primacy or even autonomy to spiritual factors in history. They did see religion (and ideas, generally) as constitutive of social reality, a proposition which is not entirely incompatible with Marxism, depending upon the larger framework in which the constitutive process is set. They were fully aware of the deep-rootedness of religious ideas in social process, not least Weber, whose sociology of religion at times loaned precision and verification to Marxist hypotheses. One major and enduring difference between German sociology and Marxism, however, will be found in philosophical anthropology. The Germans were historicists, but the way in which people made their history were for them rather different than that described in the Marxist canon.

Toennies may be termed the founder of modern German sociology: his influence on Weber, for instance, has been under-estimated. In one sense his *Gemeinschaft und Gesellschaft* (1964) may be thought of as an effort to find as many academic circumlocutions as possible for the phrase, "capitalist commodity production," which was not much in favor in the German universities at the end of the nineteenth century. Toennies was, indeed, a Social Democrat. His interpretation of human spiritual history, however, had a nostalgic, indeed romantic, cast. Industrialism in its capitalist form had torn apart the integument of human society, had replaced organic relationships with artificial ones, had generated a new and not necessarily more profound sensibility. The entire analysis of his work, in a descriptive sense, resembles nothing so much as an amplification of the characterization of bourgeois society found in the *Communist Manifesto,* where that society is taxed with having made profane everything held sacred by previous generations. Toennies clearly believed that only an organically united—and therefore authenitic—community could develop conceptions of sacredness. Associative societies manifested rationalized modes of thought, discrete and individualized modes of feeling, a severance of the ties of people to nature and the human past embodied in religious tradition. Toennies provided no very systematic explanation of the transformation, even if he ascribed it to the emergence of market capitalism and its products—industrialization and urbanization. Indeed, even Toennie's description of a modern social mentality is just that—a description—and not a total explanation.

Toennies, then, interpreted religion (and the religious changes which, by the time he published his work in 1887, had already led to a large degree of secularization) as part of a total historical process. His critique of Marx was implicit in the implication that alienation was not a universal human condition but that it was a specifically modern disorder. Further, his analysis of modern society suggested very strongly that existence in it was possible without either God or human liberation. Put in another way, we may say that he interpreted history as having direction but not purpose. Toennie's work was part of a general German response to national social transformation. A philosophical response to this experience, with important consequences for sociology, was Dilthey's (1962) work.

Dilthey, as a philosopher of culture, proposed to answer the question, "How was historical knowledge possible?" by constructing a theory of history entire. Knowledge was possible because as knowers we intuited the human essence underlying historical flux. Yet flux was the form of history, in which, Dilthey here in effect paraphased Ranke, all epochs were equal in the sight of God. History was a succession of human value structures, modes of sensibility, knowledge, and judgment. The history of religion, in this view, was a partial aspect of a broader history. Insertion in a broader context, however, did not mean the analytical reduction of religion to other social factors. Indeed, religion as a privileged mode of crystallization of the human value structure merited our attention precisely as a way of seizing the peculiarity of a society or an epoch. Here was, in effect, a bourgeois humanistic response to the areligious humanism of the radicals and the conservative religiosity of the antihumanists. Religion could not be interpreted as a form of alienation, because there was no appeal for Dilthey from an actual to a potential humanity. Neither, however, could it be interpreted on its own terms, as a supreme and unique value universe. It was, on the contrary, the specific form taken by humanity in a given epoch. Something of the tension, nay ambiguity, of this position was transmitted by Dilthey to Weber.

The view that Weber's work on religion constituted a final and "scientific" falsification of Marxism is exceedingly difficult to sustain.[6] The Marxism Weber knew best was apparently—particularly with respect to the analysis of ideology and religion—the somewhat mechanical and positivistic doctrine of the German Social Democrats. Weber's fundamental differences with Marxism resided as much in the sphere of philosophical assumption and method as in the historical analysis of social structures. At first glance, it would seem that with respect to assumption and method the difference is enormous. The method of *Verstehen* involved the intuitive apprehension of the meanings imparted to social life by a divided humanity. Its division lay precisely in the plurality of value universe it constructed, the apparent axes about which Weber himself constructed his image of society. In fact, in his concrete historical analyses, the assumption of the construction of a human value universe was subordinated to the immediate exigencies of causal discourse, an element of ambiguity in Weber which makes the interpretation of his legacy so difficult.

There is a demonic anthropology in Weber, in which the choice of values by humanity is utterly arbitrary (and so leads to a Darwinian or, rather, Hobbesian struggle among bearers of different values). This Weber combined with a pervasive belief in what he termed the metaphysical needs of the human spirit, which constituted the perennial psychological basis of religious experience. His theory of religion, however, did something other than combine universal human religious need with particular historical content arbitrary with respect to humanity, if lawful with respect to the specific conditions of existence of a historical group. Weber had an uncanny, almost perverse, grasp of the religious consequences of religious beliefs in this respect, not entirely unlike Marx. The historical process of rationalization, in which the transcendent elements were driven out of Western society, was for Weber a direct consequence of the Western religious traditions going back, before Latin Christianity, to the Old Testament. The similarities between Weber's description of rationalization and the Marxist concept of alienation have been noted, and for the moment we need only suggest three. The omnipresence of a means-end calculus meant that a certain kind of technical rationality pervaded all human relationships, a parallel to the conversion in Marxism of all human relations to market relations. The bureaucratic structures necessary to a rationalized society had an objective existence of their own. Finally, the destruction of transcendence

---

[6] See the debate on Max Weber at the German Sociological Association's celebration of his centenary (Stammer 1965).

in rationalization also entailed the extirpation of previously glimpsed possibilities of human wholeness. This last seemed reasonably close to the notion of the denial of human wholeness contained in the idea of market-derived alienation. However, Weber envisaged no transcendence of rationalization, or, at any rate, none that could have intrinsically more moral and human value. He saw no authentic human possibility that could arise after the destruction of religious transcendence: the disenchantment of the world was final, and efforts to deny it were illusory and futile. Marx supposed that humanity's spiritual longings would be fulfilled by its own spiritual maturation. Weber's historical pessimism allowed him to believe only that the precious metal of the spirit would be converted to dross by history.

It is quite true that for Weber ideas, and above all religious ideas, were historic forces; but it is equally true that in this account of history, these ideas spend themselves. Protestantism, that fusion of inwardness and of rigorous ascetic discipline, ended in the banality of acquisitiveness, the philistinism of bureaucratic subjugation, the deep reflectiveness of caste ritual. The metaphysical splendors of Taoism allowed a profane system of family and emperor worship to regulate Chinese life. The prophecies of Israel have indeed been fulfilled—as Weber thought they might—in a small state with an army and (several) universities. Weber's unique contribution to the sociology of religion may consist of his depiction of the resistances encountered by the spirit, which eventually shaped and even subdued it. The analogy with Marxism is clear, but so is the difference. Weber supposed, in effect, that the products of the religious imagination of humanity would themselves fail in their original intention and so, in turn, generate new explosions of faith. Weber's colleague, Troeltsch (1956), contributed to this depiction of history in his account of the changing relations of church, sect, and mysticism in the history of Christianity. We may put the matter in extremely schematic form and say that for Marx, the spirituality distorted in production took religious form but that, for Weber, the spirituality authentically invested in religion was distorted by the relations of production.

These are clearly questions of metahistory. They should not obscure the very considerable contribution made by Weber to the analysis of the social context of religion. We may analyse his contribution in terms of the rubrics class, culture, and politics. In his essay on *The Protestant Ethic and the Spirit of Capitalism,* Weber (1930) was unequivocal: Calvinism, for all of its effects on Western social structure, had a class basis in the interests, culture, and aspirations of the petty and middle bourgeoisie. He largely ignored, as Borkenau was to point out later, the problem of the Calvinism of the nobility. The analysis of the class basis of Protestantism—and its forerunners among the later medieval sectarian movements—was deepened in the subsequent essay

"Classes, Estates, Religion" in *The Sociology of Religion* (Weber 1963). There, the urban and mercantile-productive style of life of the bourgeoisie was depicted as an indispensable element in what was to become the Protestant rationalization of Christianity. In his treatment of the world religions, without exception Weber gave precise accounts of the location of religiosity in the stratification system. The psychological mechanisms by which religion was produced in these circumstances were, clearly, intuited by Weber without his specifying these. The notion of "elective affinity" had its role here, and the affinity was between the type of spirituality and religious duty emphasized by a religion and the concrete imperatives of existence of particular social groups. To the intellectuals (at first, in priestly form) feel the task of elaborating these affinities into coherent systems of belief. Not the least important aspect of Weber's sociology of religion is its emphasis on the role of religious specialists. Their emergence was the occasion for the introduction of a new possibility of stratification in not alone religious organizations, but in entire societies: the capture or appropriation of exclusive rights of access to divine wisdom of charisma by intellectuals clearly was an element in the struggle for power. In general, Weber saw the political uses of religion as dependent upon alliances between political and spiritual elites for the purpose of sacrilizing domination. (There is a direct connection to his analysis of bureaucratization, where secular versions of esoteric doctrine and practice are in the possession of a new type of intellectual.) Let us recall Weber's celebrated dictum that the negatively privileged fashion religions which legitimate what they will become, whereas the privileged elaborate doctrines which emphasize their being. Weber, at any rate, posited no absolute distinctions between religion and the rest of humanity's works. Assertions of his insistence on the autonomy of religion in society, therefore, do not seem to be unequivocally well-founded. There are, however, two senses in which he may be said to have gone beyond Marx. The first is in his profoundly pessimistic renunciation of hope for a transcendence of alienation, and that precisely at those points in his work at which Weber insisted on the human content of religion, on its dealienating function. The second is in his extremely detailed and careful specification of the social sources, institutionalization, and historical consequences of the world religions. Here, a good deal of Weber's work can be appreciated as an unintended tribute to Marx.

I have already said that Weber's analysis of the bureaucratic intellectuals evinces striking similarities to his view of the general role of the custodians of arcane doctrine. His predilection for treating aspects of secular existence as continuations or equivalents of religious phenomena is even more evident in his writings on the modern cultural situation. The interest of the intellectuals is aesthetics (divorced from any moral or social purpose) and sexuality, he thought, were searches for substitute realms of the spirit. His analysis of the Socialist movement itself was not free of religious or ecclesiastical analogies, although he was careful not to deal with socialism *in extenso* as a secularized religious movement. Indeed, despite, or because of, his despair he did approach Marx on one point. The search for substitute realms of the spirit, the superficial similarities between modern bureaucrats and ancient priests did not lead him to posit a unilinear descent or equivalence between religion and nonreligion. He was sardonic about those who supposed that a religion fit for a rationalized society could be conjured out of the historical air: the time for belief, he held, had gone.

With Weber, the theoretical epoch in German sociology did not close. The twin caesurae of the Nazi triumph in 1933 and the postwar restoration of pre-1933 German social structure have impeded, however, the continuation of an original German contribution to social thought. For whatever reasons, the most original and internationally influential of recent German schools of sociology, the Frankfurt school, has given remarkably little attention to religion. From the dense mass of German sociological treatments of religion which have succeeded Weber, I select two for summary treatment. Mannheim (1952) is thought of, sometimes, as a successor to the Marxists. His theoretical debt to their work (and in particular to Lukacs) is obvious. What is less obvious is that his own depiction of religious movements, in *Ideology and Utopia*, used typological procedures and was, therefore, a retreat from the historicism of both Marx and Weber. The religious modes of apprehending reality including chiliasm, seem to erupt from the substratum of history or succeed one another when abstractly conceived and classified conditions obtain. Briefly, Mannheim removed historical direction from his analysis and worked with a supposedly universal sociology. Was his interest in phenomenology responsible? I am at a loss to answer, but the phenomenological influences on sociology may point in another direction. The phenomenologists insist on the human construction of reality (Schutz 1967, Berger and Luckmann 1966, Luckmann 1967). Transposed to the analysis of religion, this would oblige us to interpret religious systems as the imposition of meaning upon the world. The empirical elements of this position were developed by Weber: their theoretical utilization in the sociology of religion might promise an extension of Marxism in quite unanticipated ways. In this account of the sociology of religion, the struggle against alienation is universal and perennial. There is, as yet, nothing in the method which enables us to distinguish between systems of meaning which contribute to maintaining alienation and those which constitute authentic efforts to humanize the universe. The use of the term "authentic" suggests, once again, that we have moved into realms not usually associated with sociology. Whether we have moved beyond Marx is, however, a different question.

Durkheim and a French Critique of Marxism

If Durkheim (1964) and his school, with their very great influence on the sociological analysis of religion, had simply propounded the thesis that religion was a mode of social integration, there would be little difficulty in dealing with them. We could remark that for Marx, at definite epochs (in fact, for most of the history of humanity), religion was equally that. If Durkheim had simply opposed to a society un-aware, unconscious of its processes a model of sociological knowledge functioning as a technique for the mastery of history, again, we could note a considerable consonance with Marxism. The concrete religious studies of Durkheim's students—Mauss (1968) on the primitives, Gra-net (1957) on the Chinese—and their wider influence (on, for in-stance, Febvre's [1932] studies of religious belief in the Renaissance and Marc Bloch's [1961a, b] medieval historiography) pose, in their concreteness, no overwhelming problem.

These establish close connections between religious forms and the rest of social organization, uncover identical meanings in each. This is different from the Marxist tradition (which insists on the transforma-tion of concrete social existence in religion), but we could simply note the difference.

The difference of meaning, however, between the Marxist sociol-ogy of religion and the Durkheimians is far greater. In his recent In-augural Lecture at the Collège de France, Raymond Aron (1971) (whom it is difficult to tax with excessive sympathy for Marxism) observed that he always found it difficult to accept the Durkheimians' curious disinclination to deal with social conflict. Durkehim's sociology, and in particular his sociology of religion, is a consensualist doctrine in a very specific sense. Today we employ the term "consensus" to desig-nate an ultimate (or at least important) element of agreement about values in society. Durkheim certainly thought that this was present in society or, at least, described its absence as pathological. However, he made use, fundamentally, of Saint-Simon's concept of consensus: a description of the self-constitutive process of society, of the structural consonance of its parts. The intention of Durkheim's sociology was consensual in the sense that sociology was meant to identify and ad-umbrate the consonance. Further, it was supposed to offer, peda-gogically, the society an occasion for self-reflection, or more precisely, self-recognition. The functions of sociology as an instrument of edu-cation (we might today term it a policy science or the supreme policy science) derived from its capacity to instruct people about two things: the constraints which bound them and the moral character of these constraints.

From this point of view, the striking thing about Durkheim's so-ciology of religion is that he portrays religion as having essentially the same tasks. It is true that religion operates with conceptions of the sacred, with realms of the spirit remote from scientific analysis. The source of religious beliefs and sentiments, the object of worship, however, is society itself. Religious symbolism transforms human dependence upon society into a different set of meanings. The sociology of religion is, in effect, a venture in interpretation employing symbolic rationality to establish the underlying rationality of social control. Marx proposed that religion be transcended as part of a process of transcending a given and oppressive state of society. Durkheim proposed that religion be understood so that the true source of morality (and personal integration) could be known.

In this reading, Durkheim must be thought of *(horribile dictu)* as a "conservative." We face a contradiction. Durkheim's own views of socialism were extremely critical, as he did not see class conflict as the supreme mode of access to a just society. Yet he was unequivocally reformist in his politics and, indeed, saw one of sociology's chief tasks precisely in its potential as an agency of social intelligence. There is no reason to suppose that a thinker must be consistent to be valuable, but we cannot dismiss the contradiction as simply that. Two aspects of Durkheim's sociology of religion may make it less of one than it initially appears.

The first aspect, paradoxically, is its attention to the suprarational, spontaneous, even Dionysiac elements in religion. In those moments when societies become aware of the sacred, in which routine is transformed, societies attain the truth about themselves. Moreover, they create (more accurately, re-create) themselves. Religion, then, may be a force for the transformation of a social order, for the propagation of a new set of ideas and sentiments. Durkheim (1960: 609-11) described the French Revolution as abortive but voiced his hopes for other transformations. Where, however, would these ideas and sentiments come from? The second component of interest in Durkheim's sociology of religion at this point is its evolutionary character. Durkheim is sometimes read as a sociologist who propagated, or sought to do so, invariant laws of social process. He did not, however, always follow his own *Rules of Sociological Method* (1938). There remained in his work an image of social development derived from the evolutionary rationalism of Saint-Simon and Comte. Religion, as the crucible in which social categories were formed, was the predecessor of science. If science, however, was a set of social categories, and if society was able at times to remake its categories, then religion was not exclusively an expression of humanity's passive dependence upon a (static) society. It was, rather, an anticipation of freedom.

Perhaps so, but this libertarian interpretation of Durkheim encounters a major difficulty. Nowhere does Durkheim define or envisage a humanity apart from its concrete social forms. At no place does he oppose a vision of humanity transformed to his image of a humanity identical with its own transient structures. Like Marx, he may have anticipated a postreligious future; unlike Marx, he hardly grounded this philosophically. The creation and re-creation of society in religion was not, according to Durkheim, a mere reflection of its previous existence. The specificity of religion resided precisely in its creative capacity, in it making of society out of dispersed and atomized activities. We may say that Marx anticipated the development of this supreme human capacity precisely with the disappearance of the obscurantist, dehumanizing, functions of religion. Durkheim held that the capacity was perennial, and that if religion was to be replaced as a repository of the sacredness of society's awareness of itself, its functions would have to be assumed by science. Not only, then, the absence of a doctrine of alienation distinguished the two thinkers; their conception of transcendence differed radically as well. For Durkheim, society was always intentionally created; for Marx, intention had as yet to come. The two thinkers poke strikingly different languages; upon inspection, the profound differences between them are more impressive than the ones immediately obvious. Did Durkheim go beyond Marx? We can assert that only from within the premises of Durkheim's system.

Structuralism, Religion, Marxism

No recent method has been more discussed than structuralism and none with so little uniformity of terms. Structuralism may be thought of as the unexceptionable doctrine that behind the empirical flux of history, there are relatively enduring forms. It may be conceived as of as a method which points to these forms and which cuts across some of the conventional boundaries of our traditions of social thought. We have had at least one version of Marxist structuralism (Althusser 1970) and yet another of Freudian structuralism (Lacan 1966)—both indubitably Parisian in accent. The spread of the discussion owes much to the fact that almost any discussion of structure will touch on perennial problems of method and substance in the social sciences: the relations of reality to appearance, of the one to the many, of process to form, of history to event, and of the mind to its object. For our purposes, we would do well to concentrate on structuralism as developed by Lévi-Strauss (1966) and his collaborators (Sebag 1964), a structuralism which in effect deals with the relationship of mind to society. The intellectual itinerary of Lévi-Strauss, from philosophy to social anthropology and back again, has been remarked upon often enough. Lévi-Strauss has indeed promulgated a theory of the universal characteristics of mind, or at the very least has engaged in an intensive search for one. Unlike his predecessors in the history of philosophy, Lévi-Strauss has not taken the view that professors of philosophy, by introspection and ratiocination, may discover in their own heads principles of mind visible only obscurely in the rest of humanity. Rather, his emphasis on arcane and esoteric data drawn from the interstices of modern societies and from its primitive predecessor and contemporary societies exemplifies one of his basic contentions: the unity of humanity is a spiritual unity. One initial point is clear: for all of his human sympathy, for all of his respect for the integrity of cultures often dismissed in the pejorative use of the term "savage," Lévi-Strauss sees them as the repositories of a cognitive reason. Spiritual yearning, terror, notions of transformation and transcendence are certainly far from absent in his work. Yet for him religious phenomena are interesting precisely insofar as they constitute hidden cognitive systems. When we ask, therefore, what distinguishes structuralism from Marxism, it is the latter with which we must credit a more systematic appreciation of the emotive (rather than the denotative) component of religion.

Myths, religions, utopias, and social philosophies—all are systems of messages, languages by which a historically fragmented humanity explains nature and history to itself. The task of a sociology of religion, in the first instance, resembles that of cryptography: behind the specific imagery, content, and emphasis of the single language, sociology can and must discover a conceptual system. The particular conceptual system, further, operates with universal modes: antitheses, equivalences, rules for transformation. The whole constitutes a prescription for a universal grammar or decoding system. Once the operation of decoding is achieved—at least for one language—how may it be related to its setting?

It is at this point that the antithesis of Marxism and structuralism becomes clearer. In one way, no systematic relationship to a setting is possible for a religion (or any other human language): it is the language, the symbolic system, which is the central constitutive element of the setting. Structuralism, here, has important links to the French tradition elaborated by Durkheim and the Durkheimians (Mauss was, indeed, Lévi-Strauss's teacher). An arbitrary or conceptual separation of social structure from its spiritual processes is possible in structuralism but the conceptual separation rests on a premise, precisely, of separation. The systems of meaning contained in the coded vehicles of the spirit may be used by social forces external to these, but the meaning remains independent.

Structuralism, then, confronts the Marxist theory of ideology with two rather different arguments. The first insists that the human world is given order by the languages of the spirit: the distinction between ideology and *praxis* disappears. The second argument maintains the distinction but insists that it is total: the spheres interact blindly, but there can be no transfer of meaning. Indeed, there is no universal human meaning; myth, religion, philosophy are composed of universal elements but select and combine these in ways which are arbitrary from the viewpoint of a universal meaning. The notion of total human self-realization or the transcendence of alienation is incompatible with this argument. Indeed, for Lévi-Strauss and his colleagues, we may say that alienation (or something very like it) occurs precisely when a group is deprived of its particular system of meaning. (They partake of a general contemporary tendency, which we find equally in the works of so unsystematic a thinker as Fanon.)

Curiously, Lévi-Strauss himself has insisted on his affinity with Marxism. He locates this in his emphasis on processes of exchange. Groups exchange (products and messages) internally with other groups and with nature. Their systems of meaning are codifications of that process, indeed, they give it structure and direction. In the sense that Marxism supposes that people create their own environment, this is compatible with Marxism; but what else could Marxism or any other sociology in fact suppose? Structuralism denies direction in history, insists on history as a plurality of competing value universes, and treats the notion of transcending alienation as itself another myth. In any terms it has gone beyond Marxism; the real question is whether it has gone beyond many of our traditional conceptions of humanity itself.

Psychoanalysis, Marxism, and Religion

The similar intentions of Marxism and psychoanalysis have often been discussed. Each was a derivative of the Enlightenment. Each sought to replace irrationality and domination with reason and liberation. If we take into account their obvious differences of conceptual structure and object, may we see the two systems as complementary? The project is not unequivocal. First, we have to deal with profound differences of philosophic assumption. Marx remained a Hegelian and the later synthesis in his work of conceptions of the dialectic with data processed in an empirical-positivistic way (above all, in his political economy) is incomplete. Freud was a student of the German university generation marked by the Darwinian controversy: he employed the strict and naturalistic conceptions of causality of a laboratory physiologist. It is quite true that his transposition of these to the spheres of psychology and history posed great difficulties; we may say that he followed a trajectory which reversed that of Marx from empiricism to metahistory. The briefest examination of the theory of religion in Freud will pose some of these difficulties.[7]

In fortunate cases, Freud held, psychoanalysis could cure (in the

---

[7] See of course Paul Pruyser's extended essay on Freud in *Beyond the Classics in the Sociology of Religion,* Charles Y. Glock and Phillip Hammond, eds. (New York: Harper and Row, 1973).

sense of replacing one unconscious structure by another) neurosis. Yet, when he designated religion as "universal obsessional neurosis of mankind," he seemed to imply that the cure, if any, lay in the future. We may understand his theory of religion in three steps. The first concerns the beginnings of the psychohistory of humanity entire. Religion originated in a complex of rituals and beliefs which transposed onto a symbolic plane the original Oedipical act, the slaying of the primal father. Symbolic transposition enabled humanity to internalize the guilt resulting from this act, and, no less important, to develop internal psychic structures which made possible an irreducible minimum of social cohesion. The second plane entails the psychohistory of individuals, who, in effect, recapitulated in their psychic development the history of the human race. The noted (or notorious) equivalence of primitivism and infancy has its place here: primitive peoples lived all their lives in psychocultural structures which were (at least for a good deal of the time) transcended with the development of civilization. The third step is the latter: the progress of civilization entailed the repression of infantile belief, but it also entailed its continuation in the sublimated or socialized form of institutionalized religious tradition. Moreover, civilization was not unambiguous: it continued and even heightened repression, but the development of the human ego in science gave humanity a chance to understand itself and so to escape or at lease minimize repression. Like so many nineteenth-century thinkers, Freud seemed to work with the evolutionary antithesis, religion-science, and, of course, he understood psychoanalysis as science.

Two conspicuous differences with Marxism emerge. Freud worked to a time scale which was much slower than the Marxist one, as well as with a humanity much more resistant to change, immensely recalcitrant to recognize its own highest interests and powers. Equally important, Freud denied (at times, quite explicitly) that institutional change could in and of itself create the preconditions for a triumph of reason. The repetition compulsion alone would re-create, in the individual psyche, the infantile conditions which generated religion. The task of reeducating humanity was just that, but it was a task which had to be entrusted (for the foreseeable future) to a small elite of the enlightened or the thoroughly analyzed. Further, the battle would have to be repeated in each generation. If new educational methods, new familial relationships, could minimize the incidence of neurosis, they could by no means eliminate the danger. A liberated humanity was a chimerical notion, a humanity slowly made aware of the necessity for a perennial struggle against the unconscious was not; but even this seemed infinitely difficult to attain.

There is another, starker way of posing the question. Freud ascribed a very different content and structure to human desolation than did Marx: their notions of alienation, superficially similar, are structurally diverse. Freud held that the transposition of the struggle against alienation (in his terms, neurosis) had to move from a generalized critique of religion to a specific attack on the psychic structures which generated religion. Again, the resemblance to Marx's critique of Feuerbach is superficial. The psychic structures which generated religion could not be changed; but they could be understood, and humanity could be taught to live without religious consolation or discipline. Freud hoped—with no very great conviction—that this could be true of humanity entire: for the foreseeable future, the only revolution he could envisage was one carried by a small elite. The concrete transcendence envisaged by psychoanalysis, then, had a dimension of sobriety, even resignation, as well as one of liberation. The radical elements of cultural criticism in Freud, as well as the specific analysis of religious systems, were carried further by some Freudians: these are best dealt with under the next general rubric of the paper.

IV Historical Critiques of the Marxist Sociology of Religion

Should I have termed this section an empirical-historical critique of the Marxist sociology of religion? It is common enough to classify studies of religion in three ways: comparative, empirical, and historical. The briefest of reflections will suggest that the generic rubric is historical: all of these studied are focused on phenomena apprehended in their historicity at a given time. If "empirical" is taken to mean quantitative studies, there is no reason why quantitative methods—rudimentary or complex—cannot be applied to historical or comparative data. (I at one point [Birnbaum 1959] enumerated the socioeconomic characteristics of the Zurich elite in Zwingli's time, the better to deal with the relationship of capitalism and nascent Protestantism in that society.) The term "historical" seems appropriate, both on general epistemological grounds and for reasons specific to Marxist theory, which above all claims to be one grounded in history.

If one thing needs saying, let it be said now. The literature on the relationship of religion to society is immense, and most of it has implications for the Marxist theory. Troeltsch once remarked that he had been criticized for not using primary sources to write his great book on the social doctrines of Christianity, but that had he done so, he would hardly have progressed beyond Saint Paul. This is not a Troeltsch-like effort, in either quantity or, alas, quality: it is, rather, a work of reflection. What I propose to do is not to survey the literature (which, now, would require the efforts of a well-endowed consortium of gifted scholars), but to set down a set of personal conclusions about it.

The Industrial Societies of the West

Three very general propositions may be derived from the Marxist texts with respect to the development of religion in the industrial societies of the West. I restrict these propositions to the West because (a) we confront, here, capitalist production relations and (b) we confront, equally, a specific version of the Judaeo-Christian tradition. These three are the following. With the development of capitalism and the profanation of all relationships religion must undergo an internal transformation: the notion of the fetishism of commodities refracts a more complex reality, in which total visions of transcendence give way to fragmented irrationalities. We may (even if Marx did not) describe these as substitute or inauthentic religions. Second, as important social groups—and above all, the working class—become aware of their real historical position and interest, they will free themselves of religious belief: in its early (authentic) or late (inauthentic) forms. Third, as power and property are threatened by organized socialism, the functions of the official churches as spiritual police agencies will become more compulsive and more evident.

What has, in fact, happened? Of a generalized decline in religious belief and sentiment with respect to the transcendent doctrines of the Judaeo-Christian tradition there can be little doubt. This decline has been most marked in areas of society most affected by the industrialization process. The evidence as to its causes, however, points in rather contrasting directions. One cause of the decline in belief seems to lie in the rise of technical-instrumental modes of mastering nature and society: disbelief among the more highly educated, the more technicized, groups of society is quite high. Another source seems to be the fragmentation, verging on destruction, of certain communal institutions—region, local community, extended family. We are more certain of the fact of decline in belief, even of its proximate sources, than we are about the phenomena which have replaced or succeeded belief.

A conceptual difficulty intrudes at this point. I have said that Marx employed, in a manner only half-explicit, a conception of inauthentic religion. It is surely possible that a superficial continuity in religious belief and practice for modern population groups conceals profound inner discontinuities. For obvious reasons, generalized studies of the inner structure and spiritual organization (if that is the term) of modern religious beliefs are sparse. It is easier to ascertain rates of decline in ecclesiastical participation, to compute answers to questionnaire inquiries about particular beliefs, than to make judgments about the whole. Pin's (1956) study in Lyon and Lenski's (1961) work in Detroit attempt to conceptualize the quality of piety in each case; Luckmann's interpretation of an "invisible religion" is another, more global effort of this kind. The German historian of ideas Blumenberg (1966) has suggested, in a book which must shake most sociologists of religion, that our operating assumptions about a unilinear process of seculari- zation bear profound traces of theological thought. There is no easy way out of this difficulty, but just as the Marxist theory fuses evalua- tive and cognitive categories, responses to it (on one level, at least) tend to do the same. We can say with some conviction that the struc- ture of industrial society, its fragmentation of roles in particular, makes a religious interpretation of it as a totality exceedingly difficult for those who live in it: the areas in which transcendence seems possible are ever more tightly constricted, if available at all.

Substitutes for transcendence (in its previous forms) are not diffi- cult to hypothesize: nationalisms, regionalisms, and other compulsive forms of communalism constitute one genre, although it must be said that the self-defense or self-consciousness of a community, however attenuated or even distorted, is not necessarily a substitute religion. The end of the fusion between these communalisms and religion may, indeed, have invested them with energies once attached to religion. The same may be said of the modern cults of acquisitiveness and sex- uality, both conspicuous in Weber's sociology of *ersatz* religiosity. An- other path of inquiry would bring us to the jagged, inorganic, and intrinsically senseless universe of mass culture: a world of antisymbols. Upon reflection, we could say (with Adorno 1947) that this universe is marked by dreadful immanence. Repeating the surface of daily ex- istence in industrial society, it embodies and legitimates its pervasive irrationality.

It is clear that efforts to verify or falsify the Marxist hypotheses on religion in industrial society entail interpretations of the data which go beyond a purely empirical plane to interpretations which may or may not be consistent with Marxism but which are equally global. A secular decline in the pervasiveness of religious belief (as well as of ecclesias- tical control) is easy enough to establish. A causal analysis involves us in a historical time series which is not empirically verifiable by any one inquiry, however plausible it may appear. We can say that the decline of a belief in transcendence has left a vacuum, into which any number of contenders for the succession have rushed. We can say, equally, that the fragmentation of existence in industrial society makes any inter- pretation of the social totality difficult and that interpretations of a re- ligious kind are especially difficult for those immersed in the technical- instrumental sectors of the society. The ascriptions of the multiple ir- rationalities in the culture of industrial society to capitalist forms of exchange is possible, but, rather than a verification of the Marxist the- sis, it would constitute yet another application of it.

Perhaps more light may be shed on the theory when we consider the religion of the industrial working class (Isambert 1961). Where that class has been organized in Socialist parties, these are frequently

antireligious or areligious. This, however, may be due to an external
association between the *ecclesiae* and those with power and property.
It may be due, equally, to the inheritance by the Socialist movement
of a bourgeois tradition of anticlericalism and militant rationality (in
Italy, the regions with the highest Communist votes are those with a
long-term tradition of struggle against the papacy). That there has been
a pronounced decline in the religious adherence of the industrial working
class in general since the beginnings of industrialization is obvious.
Some other tendencies, however, complicate the analysis.

There is evidence to suggest that Socialist movements may have
directly religious components. The role of the Methodist churches and
of Methodist leaders in British socialism has been conspicuous. Left
Catholicism is not merely the work of intellectuals: it has had, and has,
solid working-class support. I do not refer here to the varieties of cor-
porativist anticapitalist doctrine found in Catholicism, but to unmistakably Socialist Catholic groupings aiming not at the modification of capitalism but at its supersession. In Christian Socialist movements (which
have to be distinguished from Christian social movements, which have
very different political aims), the transition from religious notions of
community to profane utopias is exceedingly visible. It may be said
that in the recent transformation of the Catholic trade union in France
and similar developments in Italy (in both countries, these unions are
often more militant, less compromising, than the Communist-led ones)
suggests that the transition for some is now complete on an ideological
level. Further, we have to account for the fact that whatever the attitudes of adult male members of the working class, the women until
recently have manifested more attachment to religion and to the
churches.

Perhaps, however, the primary difficulty with the Marxist thesis
on the supersession of religion in the proletariat is this (Birnbaum 1969:
106–166). A self-conscious proletarian attempt to overthrow capitalism with the aid of a coherent revolutionary doctrine has not been a
consistent feature of the history of industrial society. Instead, the Socialist movements (and their trade union components) have often subsided into a politics which we may term reformist. Further, an ideological division of labor in the movement has assigned doctrine to the
intellectuals, the laborious tasks of organization (and combat) to the
workers. In some societies (Wilhelmian Germany and to some degree
modern France and Italy) the working-class movement has itself constituted a counterchurch. Additionally, the working-class struggle to
acquire bourgeois culture (with all that this implies) has meant that a
genuinely working-class culture with a postreligious component has
not developed. The cultural and social integration of industrial societies, as haphazard as it is, has worked against the emergence of such
a culture. Interestingly, the foremost of the Latin Marxists, Antonio

Gramsci, saw the development of such a culture—and, in particular, a critical view of religion—as an essential task for a revolutionary party in Italy. In short, the historical conditions for a test of this aspect of the Marxist theory have as yet to be realized. The theory has a self-confirming mechanism built into it: if the proletariat should accept its role, its Prometheanism would indeed superseded religion. For the moment, no part of Western humanity is Promethean. Whether or not the new Prometheus speaks Chinese, I cannot say.

The Marxist hypotheses on the churches as spiritual police agencies are somewhat easier to deal with. In part of industrial society the churches have identified with values (and with elites) we may term preindustrial. Here, the struggle against the churches, against integralism, has united an enlightened bourgeoisie and the Socialist movement. What was true of the Lutheran state church in Germany, or of Latin Catholicism, has not been true in societies with more ecclesiastical pluralism. There, a virtual stratification of the churches has occurred, such that churches of the dispossessed have been as prominent as the churches of the propertied. It is true that in the United States the main-line Protestant churches, in particular, have reinforced aspects of the national ethic which facilitated public attachment to a capitalist economy. These same churches, however, have repeatedly been the foci of ideological conflict overflowing from other sectors of the society. Meanwhile, clerical integralism in the Latin societies has been challenged from within the Catholic churches themselves. In an epoch of global contestation, these have not been immune. We can say, in conclusion, that the churches have ceased to act unequivocally as spiritual policy agencies at the same time as they have ceased to serve as spiritual centers for society as a whole. The desperate efforts of ecclesiastical elites and of theologians (not the same parties, by any means) to adapt or modernize the churches suggest that long-term historical processes are working against them. It is difficult, however, to see either the opposition of a spiritually liberated working class or the churches' attachment to exploiting classes as the sole, or even primary, cause of the decline in the power and influence of the churches.

Studies of Religion in Pre-industrial Europe

The number of such studies is, of course, enormous and many have been undertaken by historians (and a very few sociologists) aware of the implications of Marxist theory for their work. It may be suggestive, however, to see what resources are at our disposal in this vast field. We may begin with studies of heretical and Christian revolutionary movements (Werner 1956, Williams 1962). These have been explored in considerable variety and depth, from the early Middle Ages to the Reformation. Do any general conclusions emerge from data often esoteric in nature? (The study of medieval sects, obviously, calls for detailed knowledge of church history, theology, and social history and is made more difficult by the fact that, the sects having frequently been historical losers, their history has been recorded by the victors, their enemies). One negative result seems clear: we cannot assert that the heretical movements introjected different kinds of theological—both material and ethical—reasoning into the medieval cosmos. LeGoff's (1957) studies suggest that the intellectually innovative scholastics were aware of their own artisanal status in the medieval division of labor without their invariably promulgating explicit heresies.

logians were indispensable to the Christian interpretation of popular discontent. Another conclusion suggests itself: where these movements were unequivocally movements of the oppressed, they often were urban in character involving the artisanate or the early urban proletariat. The peculiar quality of urban social relationships was a certain distance from the immersion in nature of rural society: this, apparently, encouraged critical reflection in the cities.

Max Weber attributed the origins of Protestantism to the concrete experience of urban production, the rational and visible connection between work and its results. He saw this as, in effect, demystifying. Weber's hypothesis is not contradicted by the historical literature; it is also perfectly compatible with Marxist notions on the emergence of profane thought. Are we entitled, however, to introduce a notion of historical progression (from religious belief to critical-causal social explanation) into the more obscure reaches of Western social history? Perhaps, but we would do better for the moment to say that urban heretical movements introjected different kinds of theological—both material and ethical—reasoning into the medieval cosmos. LeGoff's (1957) studies suggest that the intellectually innovative scholastics were aware of their own artisanal status in the medieval division of labor without their invariably promulgating explicit heresies.

Heresy and revolution, then, were sometimes fused, sometimes distinct in the medieval period. The analysis of the social composition of the groups which espoused heresies without a prominent revolutionary component is, however, instructive. We find, to transpose a term from Marxism, multiple alienations. Oppressed or exploited regions, elites in situations of dislocation, women: these were some of the bearers of heresies. Moreover, in their theological content and ethical consequences, heresies almost always provided for alternative paths of life, new forms of social relationship. No doubt, analysis can trace the situations of spiritual alienation at the root of heresies to deeper changes in the medieval structure of production. These movements within a sacred society, however, raise a very general question. If we confront alienations within a total religious alienation, are we asserting something permanent—relatively irreducible—about the conflicts induced in humanity by its social nature? If we interpret heresies—revolutionary or not—as efforts to master alienation, do we not open a perspective in which the Marxist notion may be generalized? I shall return to this question later, but perhaps the distance between ourselves and the medieval period allows us to see this problem more clearly.

Let us turn to an area of inquiry which is a *locus classicus* of the discussion of the Marxist theory: the relationships of Protestantism to capitalism. Weber qualified his own researches, it will be recalled, by insisting on the necessity of complementary studies of the influence of social process on religion. Further, in his later works, he came much closer to ascribing some of the characteristics of Protestantism to a preformed style of life dependent upon a particular set of early bourgeois production relations. The literature, again, is enormous. I shall select two inquiries undertaken from a Marxist point of view. The first is the late Franz Borkenau's (1934; also Birnbaum and Lenzer 1969:282–91) general study of the emergence of a modern mentality. Methodologically, Borkenau rejects a crude theory of religion and thought, generally, as a reflection of the relationships of production. What is at issue, Borkenau holds, is the total position of a group within a changing historical structure. He depicts Calvinism not alone in its urban setting but as a religion of the gentry, of displaced and threatened nobles; as in France and Scotland. His mode of analysis begins with the concrete social tasks presented by an environment to a group and proceeds to consider its spiritual resources for mastering these. Borkenau insists that Calvinism was not as central to Western spiritual development as Weber thought and establishes a rather different genealogy for both theoretical and bourgeois political economy and the practical morality of the nascent European capitalist class. For our purposes, what is important is the promulgation of a method of analysis sufficiently supple to account for the internal structure of a long-term historical process. Borkenau shows, in effect, that the antithesis of material or spiritual causation needs to be recast in terms allowing for the specification of the components of a long-term process.

A more recent Marxist effort to combine theory with historical analysis focuses on the French seventeenth-century Jansenists, Catholic equivalents, in effect, of the bearers of a Calvinist morality. Goldmann's (1955) study of *The Hidden God* makes use of a central device, the notion of a vision of the world. The vision of a world peculiar to a group expresses its aspirations, sufferings, and existential grammar. By concentrating in great detail on the inner differences among the Jansenists, their relationships to society and the state, Goldmann also arrives at the conclusion that their religion was a response to a threat. He identifies its bearers as a declining state nobility. We may note that in both cases the social alienation described by these Marxist scholars was experienced by elites—if elites in a situation of decline. We may also note that the recourse to specific historical studies has an important methodological consequence for the testing of the Marxist hypotheses: these, insofar as they are instruments of inquiry, are built into the data. What is remarkable about the contributions of Borkenau and Goldmann is the degree of precise specification they are able to supply as to the objects and limits of their examination of history. That they have cast considerable illumination on Western religious history, there can be no doubt. The synthesis of studies of this kind into a convincing critique or replacement for the Marxist historical hypotheses remains for the future. We may note, once again, a tendency for generalization of the notion of alienation, this time accomplished by the analysis of groups not always directly involved in production.

Religion in the State Socialist Regimes

A very obvious interest attaches to the study of religion in the state Socialist countries (see Klohr 1967, Birnbaum 1971:162–80). Two questions in particular concern us. How far have these societies gone toward overcoming what they officially and formally conceive of as alienation in its religious form? Second, how do sociologists in these societies conceive of the survival of religion in their societies? It is easy enough to say that the first question exceeds the limits of this paper, but upon an answer to it turns our estimate of the disalienating potential of at least one version of Marxism. An answer is, in any case, rendered difficult by the fact that open inquiry into religious phenomena in these societies was difficult, almost impossible, in the Stalinist period. It has now resumed, with rhythms and results which vary from country to country.

In general, in examining religion in these societies, we have to distinguish between a role that can be termed oppositional and a role which can be designated as normal. (I hesitate to use the term, but hesitate even more to use the term "perennial.") Religion and, in particular, the churches have assumed oppositional roles in these societies as the loci of beliefs and values (and communities) not integrated in the new political consensus. The relationship between the Orthodox church and the Soviet regime is now one of coexistence, but we may recollect that matters were far more antagonistic in the early years of the Russian Revolution. In countries like Poland and the German Democratic Republic, the Catholic and Protestant churches, respectively, have at times seemed to serve as countercommunities, even counternations. These phenomena are important enough, but on a Marxist basis they may be disposed of in a manner which is more or less straightforward. The Revolution in Russia did break the cultural fabric, it was intended to do so, and it was inevitable that a portion of the population—frequently, those who were most remote from urban society and culture in any case—should group itself about cultural values of a more traditional kind. To the objection that the peasantry, in particular, was one of the beneficiaries of the Revolution, it could be said that economic benefits and cultural traumas frequently coincide. The Revolutions in Poland and the German Democratic Republic were, as the Communists in these countries will freely admit, largely brought in by a foreign army. In the circumstances social resistance to the new regime coalesced with national resistance. Nothing, or almost nothing, follows for our long-term evaluation of the disalienating potential of the state socialist regimes except for the banal observation that if Rome was not built in a day neither has Communism been constructed so quickly.

Suppose, however, that we take a rather different approach. Marx once discounted the separation of church and state, declaring that it would not lead to a diminution of the social role of religion as long as the production relations which gave rise to capitalist forms of alienation persisted. The state socialist regimes have entered a period of relative official neutrality with respect to religion. Production relations in the state socialist regimes are clearly not capitalist ones: what have been the consequences of allowing the citizens of these countries something very like freedom of religious (or irreligious) choice?

It is here that we have to use the work of our colleagues from the state socialist societies. Perhaps it would be useful to distinguish between data from the Soviet Union, which has had a Marxist regime for fifty-four years, and the other countries, which have had Marxist regimes for only about half of that time. In the Soviet Union our colleagues' data suggests that a decline in religious affiliation is closely correlated with urbanization. Not dissimilar findings come from the other societies, although the inquiries I have seen do not use urbanization as a global indicator of social change but refer, instead, to integration in new sectors of the labor force, new residential communities—in short, marked discontinuities with previous forms of existence. These findings seem to parallel our data from other societies. Let us recollect that the Communist vote in Italy has doubled since the end of the last war, not alone on account of vigorous political efforts but because of the industrialization and laicization of Italian society. On the face of it, the data from the state socialist regimes, recorded by sociological inquiry, do not show that a revolution was the necessary precondition for the decline in religious belief and in the influence of the churches.

It should not be thought that our colleagues from these societies are simple-minded, or single-minded, adherents of the thesis that complete disalienation has occurred in principle in their nations. They are well aware of contradictions between reality and its propagandistic

representation and of the fact that profound social changes are historical phenomena: they take time. For obvious reasons, our colleagues
have hardly attacked another set of hypotheses. The nationalization of
capital in the state socialist societies has not altered the facts (whether
ineradicable or not) of domination and exploitation in these societies.
Its modes have changed, the processes remain. Above all, the division
of labor and relationships of domination within it are intact: whatever
theoretical discussions are in progress in these societies on the fusion
of manual and intellectual labor, practical progress in this respect does
not seem very rapid. (The Chinese case comes to mind: the Cultural
Revolution has claimed that it has made progress towards the fusion.
I am unable in these pages to judge the claim or to consider its obvious
implications for the spiritual history of humanity. The remark of a
nineteenth-century sceptic about Christianity comes to mind: "Interesting," he said, "if true.") In the circumstances Marxist theory requires us to look for a considerable remnant of alienation in these
societies. If alienation there is, religion or something like it must (on
Marxist hypotheses) follow. We are forced to consider the hypothesis
that Marxism itself, in its official or Constantine form, serves as a successor to religion in ways not anticipated nor wished for by Marx himself. There are indications that at some point in the near future, our
colleagues may be able to explore this hypothesis. For the moment it
remains a hypothesis.

The World Beyond Western Europe and North America

Most of the population of the world lives in the nonindustrial or in-
completely industrialized societies located beyond Western Europe and
America. These societies manifest an astonishing variety of religious
tradition. Some (as in Latin America) have transplanted European religions, others, syncretic fusions of European traditions with their own,
yet others are embedded in different, often older (and no less profound) religious systems. Their entire religious history is, of course, a
field for the exploration of Marxist hypotheses; it covers a good deal
of the spiritual history of humanity entire. We do well to remember,
however, that the Marxist theory of religion concerns primarily its
supersession in the industrial West. Marx supposed that culture contact, imperialism, and industrialization would destroy other traditions
and had, in any event, attitudes of a distinctly nineteenth-century kind
toward these traditions, which he thought of as obscure and even bar-
barian.

It can be argued that one of the most successful applications to
these societies of an aspect of the Marxist theory has been accomplished by Weber. His studies of China, India, and Ancient Judaism do
not simply reverse the usual Marxist modes of analysis. Rather, they

concentrate on property and production relations and their political correlates, and they treat religious organizations and symbolic structures as developments within the limits set by these material factors. True enough, Weber evokes the cases in which, having developed in what we may think of as a material basis, these religious factors themselves set limits to future material development. The interpretation, at this point, is so large that it leaves the territory of social history for that of the philosophy of history. To the notion of a progressive alienation in history, Weber opposes his own conception of a plurality of value universes existing, as it were, solipsistically. And to the notion of humanity as creating itself through labor (and labor's concretization in production relations), he opposes the idea of humanity creating its universe by interpreting the problems of work and society. Marx and Engels did write of the interaction of production relations and other factors in history, but clearly Weber goes beyond this point to assert the occasional primacy of religion in the total historical process.

More recent inquiries touch upon the Marxist legacy at many points (Balandier 1955, Wertheim 1965). An entire series of studies on the millennial movements of primitive peoples supplies us with data of an astonishingly similarity to work on the Middle Ages. In these movements religious conceptions (revitalized and sometimes syncretically fused with new elements from without) legitimate protest and revolution at conditions of exploitation and domination by alien peoples. It is interesting that a distinguished French student of Islam, and of the third world generally (Bercque 1964), has written of the "Dépossession du Monde." In his view colonialism and imperialism inflict alienation upon the cultures and peoples who are victims of Western society and who must, in turn, struggle to repossess their world. That struggle, however, often takes religious forms. One Marxist analysis would note the positive consequence of colonialism and imperialism: the forcible incorporation of backward peoples in the world market and, potentially at least, a new world culture. Another component of Marxism, however, would have to deal with the utilization of religion, an earlier form of alienation, against a later form.

The breadth and depth of the materials at hand, the richness of scholarship on the religions of the world and their social contexts, would require a separate analysis. While the beginnings of Marxist studies on these problems may be noted, the comparison of religions in different historical settings entails a conceptual grammar and raises philosophic problems, which may not be soluble in Marxist terms; is the self-contained world system of Confucianism a transcendent religion or a social ethic? Further comparison may turn that upon Marxism itself. Is the notion of progressive direction in history itself a component of the Western religious tradition, even in its Marxist form? The historical transcendence of Marxism itself was envisaged by Lukacs as an inevitable result of revolution, which would bring about a new society functioning according to different structural principles. Suppose that a comparative view results not in a transcendence of Marxism but in exposing its historical relativity? We have already heard that history is a Western myth. If so, Marxism itself is part of it.

Psychoanalytic Studies of Religion

A good many practicing psychoanalysts have observed that the symptomatology of their patients has changed over the past decades. The disorders treated by the earlier generation of analysts seem to have become less prominent, and a generalized malaise—character disorder, as it is sometimes called—has become evident. Part of this observation may be due to changes in psychoanalytic technique and theory. Part, however, is no doubt due to real historical changes in the mileu from which both analysts and patients are drawn. This constitutes justification enough for treating psychoanalytic studies of religion as historical studies. We are unable to observe the process by which humanity becomes disalienated, since none of the historical conditions for that have occurred. Psychoanalysis, however, may, with all regard for the conceptual distinctions between psychoanalysis and Marxism, allow us to see the internal mechanisms of alienation at work in real people.

Case studies of individuals with religious beliefs or members of religious organizations are available but these, for our purposes, have two drawbacks. The cases are drawn, inevitably, from a society in which secularization has occurred. The choice of religious belief, therefore, as an expression of the personality rather than, let us say, an exclusively scientific career may or may not tell us anything about the movement of the social whole. Second, these clinical studies inevitably (and properly, from the viewpoint of their own logic and aim) do not treat systematically of the relationship of individual to context.

We too have a literature of what may be termed clinical extrapolation, in which psychoanalytic concepts are used to explore the social role of religion. Erich Fromm's (1951, 1963, 1966) work in this area is interesting, not least for its own inner evolution. Fromm began by dealing with changes in family structure as precipitates of larger social changes (in production relations and authority systems). These changes in turn induced new patterns of psychological conflict in new generations, and these, again, found expression or stabilization in the symbolic sphere of religion. This, in turn, served as a system of reinforcement for social controls by defining reality in ways which precluded its concrete or political transcendence. Fromm's subsequent work on the Reformation implied a somewhat different approach in that it depicted a society (the nascent bourgeois society) unable to control the inner conflicts of humanity. Indeed, the terrible God of Calvinism generated more anxiety than the religion could assuage. Put in the language of a mode of sociological analysis, a functional response to a market society became dysfunctional. Fromm also developed, to be sure, a conception of modal or typical character in a society—social character, which was constructed to perform the tasks imposed upon it. What Fromm had done to this point was to show the mechanisms (family structure and character formation) by which social conflicts were transformed into individual ones. Further, and most importantly, he held that these conflicts were systematic deformations of human potential, caused by society's need for social character of a compliant kind. It is not too much to assert that he sought and found conceptual equations for transforming the Marxist doctrine of alienation in religion into psychoanalytic vocabulary. Strikingly, after having established a progressive characterological deformation—accomplished in part by a religion—Fromm returned to a search for a universal human essence expressed in religion. He renounced, in other words, the notion that religion was an unequivocal sphere of alienation. Instead, he now saw it as the historical repository of a humanity denied expression in ordinary social routine, above all, in the social routine of a society without God. The utilization of psychoanalysis by anthropologists— Roheim (1969) among the orthodox Freudians, Kluckhohn (1962) Kardiner and Linton (1949), and Mead (1967, 1969) among these with less rigorously classical Freudian views—has added new dimensions to our understanding of primitive systems of production and exchange. The addition of a new dimension of understanding, however, does not necessarily constitute a modification of Marxist analysis. In particular, most of these studies are set in short-term historical contexts. Where, as in the case of Mead's return to the South Pacific or the retrospective analysis conducted by Linton and the psychoanalyst Kardiner of change in a primitive society, a historical direction is considered, we can, in effect, see the transformation of the old gods. Mead's work on the assimilation of a simulacrum of modern culture by primitives is particularly instructive. The most we can say, however, is that new alienations seem to replace older ones. Alternatively, we have to recognize that these inquiries were not directed to verification or falsification of Marxist hypotheses: they may be combined with these, or they may be used to assert a pluralization of historical experience.

It is curious that Erikson's (1958, 1963, 1969) studies take us deeper. Curious, not because of their obvious quality, but because Erikson began on the terrain of psychoanalysis and worked both outward and inward to history. His turn outward required studies of the social organization and social history of the groups and individuals he analyzed: these gave the demands of reality on the psyche, the materials it had to master to keep a tenuous equilibrium. His turn inward enabled him to put the psyche in historical perspective. Not alone did humans confront an external or fixed reality in the form of an enveloping social history. They converted the elements of that history into modes of activity, into the remaking of history. Erikson uses the Freudian notion of conflict between culture and nature, history and the psyche, to demonstrate the humanization of history. In his work neurosis ceases to figure as historical accident or wound: it becomes the mode in which individuals integrate themselves, poorly or well, with tradition. Moreover, it becomes an area in which tradition is transformed. The term "dialectical" is much abused these days and I do not think it has appeared more than once or twice before in this essay. Let it be said that Erikson apprehends the relationship between historical movement and character as dialectical, as interpenetrating. With respect to religion, it is significant that his interest is in religious innovation, religious movements, such as in Luther's recasting of medieval Christianity, or Gandhi's interpretation of Hinduism. The social role of religion entails the opening of new possibilities of human development and experiences, as well as the fixation or stabilization of inherited relationships. Erikson once reported on a conversation he had had with a primitive psychotherapist, whom he obviously treated as a respected colleague: the struggle against alienation, for Erikson, involves psychoanalysis as one of its historical forms but is not new. Erikson avoids the notion of progressive direction in history, partly, to be sure, to avoid flattering his twentieth-century contemporaries, of whom his opinion is not excessively high. The elements of sociocultural criticism in his work, then, are frequently implicit. His depiction of the universality of neurosis, or, more exactly in his terms, of characterological conflict, is in fact not a promulgation of a universal fatality. Just because those conflicts occur in historically specific forms, the possibility for their ultimate supersession is given. In that sense, Erikson's detailed historical and clinical work, his almost ascetic eschewal of larger political or social commentary, gives a radical cutting edge to his version of psychoanalysis. The history of humanity as a history of multiple alienations is not, in the end, entirely incompatible with the Marxist vision. Recall the title of the book, *Gandhi's Truth:* the truth in religion can be found in the universal aspirations it presents in culturally concretized form. Without intending to do so, Erikson may have taken us back to Feuerbach but this time, with the inner psychic structure of religion identified with the universal structure of the psyche.

Erikson's interpretation of the Freudian tradition, then, assigns to the ego a function analogous to the role of work in the Marxist account of human history. The work of the psyche transforms nature and history into a new, if impermanent, synthesis. To be sure, an analysis of this kind is not only present in the writings of Freud, but it pervades them: it remained for Erikson to draw conclusions and approach character as a historical phenomenon. Freud supposed that the struggle against religion had to become universal, if men were to understand their conflicts. Erikson views the struggle against religion (which includes, in his view, the search in some epochs for truer religions) as but one of the several forms of enlightenment. I have already said that Fromm, who began from Marxist positions, in the end found rather positive functions in religion. Are we experiencing—and not alone in psychoanalysis—a "resacralization" of Western thought?

V   Conclusions

The Dialogue

I have before me a bibliography of the Marxist-Christian dialogue (Van der Bent 1969), which has hundreds of titles and is, according to those who compiled it, incomplete. The dialogue, as it now stands, has three elements. The first is an effort at understanding among intellectuals— Marxists on one hand, theologians on the other. A Marxist reconsideration of religion or, at least, of simple interpretations of religion and its social role, has been accompanied by a theological revaluation of radical humanism. The Marxists have found humanist elements in religion, and the theologians have returned the compliment: they have found transcendent elements in Marxism. Where, in fact, no such mutual recognition has taken place, the very discussion of fundamentally different positions has enabled each to be seen in somewhat new perspective by its protagonists.

The second aspect of the dialogue is an official one. The Marxist regimes and Marxist parties have sought some *modus vivendi* with Christian interlocutors. In countries like Poland and the German Democratic Republic, the churches have been powerful and autonomous forces not always well-disposed to the regime: the process of *rapprochement* has had obvious theoretical consequences. In the Latin Catholic countries (France, Italy, and Spain), the Marxist parties have recently spared no effort to find common ground with some, at least, of their Christian countrymen. In Chile, it may be recalled, Christian Democratic parliamentary votes helped to select President Allende, and a small Catholic Socialist party forms part of his government. The establishment by the Vatican of a secretariat for relations with nonbelievers and multiple contacts between the Vatican and the Marxist regimes are part of this tendency. It may be objected that some at least, of the official relations between Marxism and Christianity are anything but spiritual: they have to do with the relations between two worldly powers.

That is precisely what bothers the third set of participants in the dialogue. These are the proponents of *contestation* in the churches, the trade unions, the universities, and near (but usually no longer in) the main-line Marxist parties. The youth revolt has manifested striking similarities of spiritual structure wherever it has broken out. A considerable anti-nomianism, an insistence on a return to the sources of the movements or institutions in question, a demand for and the practice of experiments in institutions, and, above all, the conviction that ideas have to be lived to be valid: these are its components. Young priests using Marxist political ideas, Marxist students seeking a life of apostolic spiritual purity in new communal forms, attest, each in their fashion, the new sort of dialogue.

I write here of a movement of thought and action so contemporary that it may be described as a mood or temper. Its ultimate consequences for the Marxist sociology of religion are still unclear. For the present, we may state the following. The philosophical-theological dialogue has led to a profound reconsideration of the possibilities of transcendence. The Christians have been induced to reexamine their own tradition, and some have given transcendence a far more concrete and earthly definition as a result. It is of note that one of the most influential Protestant theological works of recent years, Jürgen Moltmann's *Theology of Hope* (1969) bears the influence of the work of Ernst Bloch. Bloch, an independent Marxist, is himself Jewish and has a new interpretation of the Old Testament. In his view, its revolutionary elements were falsified by priestly and royal scribes. Bloch (1968) has recently declared that only a believer can be an atheist, and only an atheist can be a believer. In his version of the dialogue, religion is a record of humanity's perennial struggle for self-transcendence.

The official dialogue takes up themes contained in the discussion between theologians and Marxists but with pronouncedly different accents. A period of coexistence—indeed, of collaboration—between Marxism and Christianity, for an indefinite period means a renunciation of some of the more stringent Marxist positions. If the path to a more human future leads not through religion but can be taken only with those of a religious spirituality, clearly radical humanism has been severely attenuated. The precondition of revolution (or even of structural reform, which is all the Western Communists now seek, that proving difficult enough) is no longer the transcendence of religion. It is, rather, a more modest mutual recognition of our common humanity; more modest, perhaps, but no less unusual in its historical implications. This, again, is too conservative for those in the forefront of the youth revolt (a generic term for the entire movement of *contestation* in the West). The recognition of a common humanity strikes them as too much like a resignation to an old humanity. A humanity remade is what they seek. Their indifference to the struggle against religion as such, their utilization of religious tradition, has a very different basis than the official dialogue. In the youth revolt transcendence cannot take the form of a Marxist radical humanism, since this was too theoretical. A new form of practice is needed to supersede ideology and anti-ideology, religion and atheism. We seem back at Marx's own beginning point.

Reflections

I do not propose to give a theoretical summary of a theoretical essay. The word "essay" originally meant just that, a tentative effort to state a problem. For tentativeness and statement, I make no apologies. The Marxist sociology of religion is a finished and self-contained metatheory. A metatheory is a critique of historical existence, whereas a theory is a set of propositions about a movement within history. On the basis of the metatheoretical doctrine of religion as alienation, Marx and Engels uttered a set of propositions about religion in history, chiefly Western history. I have said that the examination of the truth or falsity of single propositions cannot falsify the metatheory. It infuses the theory, and were we to abandon the metatheory, our theoretical grammar would be different, our theoretical propositions constructed of different elements. That much said, we may still ask if the weight of the evidence about the Marxist doctrine suggests points at which a reevaluation of it may begin. The philosopher Hans Blumenberg, in a remarkable recent book, has suggested that the very notion of secularism is a legacy of religious thought. The book is required reading for sociologists of religion, since if we take it seriously, our present conceptual apparatus dissolves. We are, Blumenberg suggests, still the prisoners of theological concepts, still looking for the reenactment of a divine drama on earth. He has taken up anew a theme prominent in Marxism with its demand for a radical humanism which would transcend both religion and atheism. The historical evidence, however, is that radical humanism of this sort comes hard. Not alone is Western society still pervaded by institutions and beliefs from its religious past, but secularization (I use the term for want of a better one) requires newer, if less sublime and less authentic gods. The fetishism of commodities, the reification of power, the poor consolations of a desperate hedonism are as prominent in the state socialist regimes as elsewhere. The attenuation of religion does not mean its transcendence. The absence of God by no means entails the presence of a humanity more mature, much less fulfilled.

The precise status of scientific-instrumental thought in Marxist theory still requires adumbration. There was a sense in which Marx opposed science to religion. Religion was the science of a false human condition, science was the practical expression of a mature humanity true to itself. Modern science and technology, whatever their potential, can hardly be seen as a true human practice in Promethean terms. The scientists and technicians hardly control the products of their own labor, which are expropriated by other social elites for purposes having to do with the mastery of people, not in the interest of a mastery of nature for all humanity. Should the scientists and technicians combine with the more educated and skilled sectors of the contemporary labor force to constitute a new revolutionary vanguard, they would rewrite the role of surrogate for humanity entire ascribed by Marx to the industrial proletariat. Indeed, for most of humanity (consider the peoples of the third world and a goodly section of the population in the industrial West) science and technology are modern forms of magic. An instrument of liberation, as Marx conceived of it, has become a new form of alienation.

Withal, we have to conclude that the Marxist hope of a total transcendence of alienation seems out of reach. Humanity without religion is no more human than humanity with it. Religion has been succeeded by multiple alienations, different in structure, not all that different (in the Marxist sense) in their consequences. The idea of a progressive direction in history, the Enlightenment's legacy to Marx, is difficult to sustain. No wonder, then, that Marxists and Christians have become reconciled: each seeks a kingdom not of this world (that the reconciliation is in part the work of Jewish intellectuals, working the derivatives of their traditions of commentary on eschatology, is a reminder of a component in Marx's own work). The humanizing function of religion, from our historical viewpoint, now seems a theme in the Marxist sociology of religion which has more than nostalgic functions. Humanity, for the time being, has not gone beyond the Marxist sociology of religion. Indeed, it has hardly arrived at Marx's own beginning point (Blumenberg 1966).

Bibliography

Adorno, T. W., and Horkheimer, Marx. 1947. *Dialektik der Aufklärung.* Amsterdam: Querido.

Althusser, L. 1970. *For Marx.* New York: Pantheon.

Aron, Raymond. 1971. De la condition historique de la sociologie. *Informations sur les Sciences Sociales,* Vol. 10, no. 1.

Balandier, G. 1955. *La Sociologie actuelle de l'Afrique Noire.* Paris: Presses Universitaires de France.

Berque, J. 1964. *Le Dépossession du monde.* Paris: Seuill.

Bernstein, Edward. 1895. *Die Vorläufer des Neueren Sozialismus.* Stuttgart: Dietz.

Berger, Peter L. 1967. *The Sacred Canopy.* Garden City, N.Y.: Doubleday.

———, and Luckmann, Thomas. 1966. *The Social Construction of Reality.* Garden City, N.Y.: Doubleday.

Birnbaum, Norman. 1959. The Zwinglian Reformation in Zurich. *Archives de Sociologie des Religions,* No. 2 (1957). 1969. *The Crisis of Industrial Society.* New York: Oxford. 1971. *Toward a Critical Sociology.* New York: Oxford.
———, and Lenzer, Gertrud. 1969. *Sociology and Religion.* Englewood Cliffs, N.J.: Prentice-Hall.
Bloch, E. 1968. *Atheismus im Christentum.* Frankfurt: Suhrkamp.
Bloch, Marc. 1961a. *Feudal Society.* Chicago: University of Chicago Press. 1961b. *Les Rois thaumaturges.* Paris: A Colin.
Blumenberg, Hans. 1966. *Die Legitimität der Neuzeit.* Frankfurt: Suhrkamp.
Borkenau, Franz. 1934. *Die Übergang vom Feudalen zum Bürgerlichen Weltbild.* Paris: Alcan.
Calvez, Jean Yves. 1956. *La Pensée de Karl Marx.* Paris: Editions du Seuil.
Caporale, Rocco, and Antonio Grumelli, eds. 1971. *The Culture of Unbelief.* Berkeley and Los Angeles: University of California Press.
Desroche, Henri. 1949. *Signification du marxisme.* Paris: Editions Ouvrieres. 1962. *Marxisme et religions.* Paris: Presses Universitaries Francaises. 1965. *Socialismes et sociologie religieuse.* Paris: Editions Cujas. 1968. *Dieux des hommes, dictionnaire des messies, messianismes et millenarismes de l'ére chretienne.* Paris: Editions Mouton. 1971. *The Shakers.* Amherst, Mass.: University of Massachusetts Press. 1972. *Sociology of Religions.* Amherst, Mass.: University of Massachusetts Press.
Dilthey, W. 1962. *Pattern and Meaning in History: Thoughts on History and Society.* New York: Harper & Row.
Durkheim, E. 1938. *The Rules of Sociological Method.* Trans. S. A. Soloway and J. H. Mueller, ed. G. E. G. Callin. Chicago: University of Chicago Press. 1960. *Les Formes elementaires de la vie religieuse.* Paris: Presses Universitaires Francaises: 609–11. 1964. *The Elementary Forms of the Religious Life.* London: George Allen and Unwin.
Easton, Lloyd D., and Guddat, Kurt. 1967. *Writings of the Young Marx on Philosophy and Society.* Garden City, N.Y.: Doubleday.
Engels, Friedrich. 1966. *The Peasant War in Germany.* New York: New World.
Erikson, E. 1958. *Young Man Luther.* New York: Norton. 1963. *Childhood and Society.* New York: Norton. 1969. *Gandhi's Truth.* New York: Norton.
Febvre, Lucien. 1942. *Le Probleme de l'incroyance au xvi siècle, La religion de Rabelais.* Paris: Michel.
Friedrichs, Robert. 1970. *A Sociology of Sociology.* New York: The Free Press.
Fromm, Erich. 1951. *The Forgotten Language: An Introduction to the Understanding of Dreams, Fairy Tales and Myths.* New York: Holt, Rinehart and Winston. 1963. *The Dogma of Christ and Other Essays on Religion, Psychology and Culture.* New York: Holt, Rinehart and Winston. 1966. *Escape from Freedom.* New York: Holt, Rinehart and Winston.
Garaudy, R. 1968. *From Anathema to Dialogue.* New York: Vintage.
Goldmann, Lucien. 1955. *Le Dieu caché.* Paris: Gallimard.
Gouldner, Alvin W. 1970. *The Coming Crisis of Western Sociology.* New York: Basic Books, Inc.
Gramsci, A. 1966. *Il Materialismo Storico.* Torino: Einaudi. 1966. *Il Risorgimento.* Torino: Einauldi.
Granet, Marcel. 1957. *Chinese Civilisation.* London: Routledge and Kegan Paul.

International Social Science Council. 1969. *Marx and Contemporary Scientific Thought*. Paris and The Hague: Mouton.

Isambert, F. A. 1961. *Christianisme et classe ouvrière*. Paris: Casterman.

Kardiner, A. et al. 1959. *The Psychological Frontiers of Society*. New York: Columbia University Press.

Kardiner, A., and Linton R. 1949. *The Individual and His Society*. New York: Columbia University Press.

Kautsky, Karl. 1910. *The Class Struggle*. Chicago: C. H. Kerr.

Klohr, O. 1967. *Religionssoziologie, Internationales Forschungsbericht*, Jena.

Kluckhohn, Clyde. 1962. *Navaho Witchcraft*. Boston: Beacon Press.

Lacan, Jacques. 1966. *Ecrits*. Paris: Editions du Seuil.

LeGoff, Jacques. 1957. *Les Intellectuells aux moyen-age*. Paris: Seuil.

Lenin, V. I. 1947. *Materialism and Empiro-Criticism, Critical Comments on a Reactionary Philosophy*. Moscow: Foreign Languages Publishing House.

Lenski, G. 1961. *The Religious Factor*. Garden City, N.Y.: Doubleday.

Lévi-Strauss, C. 1966. *The Savage Mind*. Chicago: The University of Chicago Press.

Lichtheim, G. 1964. *Marxism, an Historical and Critical Study*. London: Routledge and Kegan Paul.

Lobkowiez, Nikolaus. 1967. *Marx and the Western World*. Notre Dame, Ind.: University of Notre Dame Press.

Lowith, K. 1964a. *From Hegel to Nietzsche: The Revolution in 19th Century Thought*. New York: Holt, Rinehart and Winston. 1964b. *Meaning in History*. Chicago: University of Chicago Press.

de Lubac, Henri. 1965. *La Drame de l'humanisme athée*. Paris: Union Générale d'Editions.

Luckmann, Thomas. 1966. *The Invisible Religion*. New York: Macmillan.

Lukacs, G. 1971. *History and Class Consciousness*. Cambridge, Mass.: Massachusetts Institute of Technology Press.

MacIntyre, Alasdair, and Emmet, Dorothy, eds. 1970. *Sociological Theory and Philosophical Analysis*. New York: Macmillan.

Mannheim, K. 1952. *Ideology and Utopia: An Introduction to the Sociology of Knowledge*. New York: Harcourt Brace Jovanovich.

Marx, Karl. 1953. *Grundrisse der Kritik der Politischen Oekonomie*. Berlin: Dietz.

————, and Engels, Friedrich. 1964. *On Religion*. With an Introduction by Reinhold Niebuhr. New York: Schocken.

Mauss, M. 1968. *Sociologie et anthropologie*. Paris: Presses Universitaires Francaises.

Mead, Margaret. 1967. *Male and Female*. New York: Morrow. 1969. *Inquiry into the Question of Cultural Stability in Polynesia*. New York: A.M.S. Press.

Moltmann, Jürgen. 1967. *Theology of Hope*. New York: Harper & Row. 1969. *Religion, Revolution and the Future*. New York: Scribners.

Owen, Robert. 1963. *A New View of Society*. London: Dent.

Petrie, John. 1956. *The Worker Priests*. London: Routledge and Kegan Paul.

Pin, Emile. 1956. *Pratique religieuse et classes sociales dans une paroisse urbaine*, Paris: Editions Spes.

Roheim, G. 1969. *Psychoanalysis and Anthropology*. New York: International Universities Press.

Saint-Simon, M. C. 1964. *Social Organization, the Science of Man and Other Writings*. New York: Harper & Row.

Schutz, Alfred. 1967. *The Phenomenology of the Social World.* Evanston, Ill.: Northwestern University Press.

Sebag, L. 1964. *Marxisme et structuralisme.* Paris: Payot.

Stammer, O., ed. 1965. *Max Weber und die Soziologie Heute.* Tübingen: Möhr (Siebeck).

Toennies, F. 1964. *Community and Society.* East Lansing, Mich.: Michigan State University Press.

Troeltsch, Ernst. 1956. *The Social Teachings of the Christian Churches.* New York: Macmillan.

Van der Bent, A. 1969. *The Christian Marxist Dialogue.* Geneva: World Council of Churches.

Weber, Max. 1930. *The Protestant Ethic and the Spirit of Capitalism.* Trans. Talcott Parsons. London: George Allen and Unwin. 1963. *The Sociology of Religion.* Trans. Ephraim Fischoff. Boston: Beacon Press.

Werner, Ernst. 1956. *Pauperes Christi. Studien zu sozial-religiösen Bewegungen im Zeitalter des Reformpopsttums.* Leipzig.

Wertheim, W. F. 1965. *East-West Parallels: Sociological Approaches to Modern Asia.* Chicago: Quadrangel Books.

Williams, George H. 1962. *The Radical Reformation.* Philadelphia; Westminster Press.

6

Critical Theory and Psychohistory

Freud held that domination and compliance were reflections of that repressiveness without which civilization would dissolve and which was, indeed, the price of such progress as we could claim. He hoped for an ultimate alliance of Eros and reason, an extension of the psychoanalytic project to society at large. In the indeterminate historical interim, however, he resigned himself to a rational acceptance of Eros' defeat.

A Promethean Marx saw in humanity's temporary regressions injuries which would hasten its self-fulfillment. The Promethean aspects of humanity were, for the time being, objectified in the development of its productive powers, in the mastery of nature. That triumph, however, was highly equivocal. It was won precisely by developing a structure of domination and exploitation. This, however, was infused with a particular psychic content, in which human substance was distorted and fragmented. That very distortion and fragmentation, the self-alienation originating in the labor process, was a potential source of a gigantic future reversal of the historical process. The replacement of self-alienation by a conscious and free praxis, in which humanity would realize itself, was the ultimate meaning of socialist revolution. Marx's view of human fulfillment no doubt goes back to the Greek idea of *telos*. The revolution, alas, appears to have been delayed until the Greek kalends.

The failure of Marxist prophecy, the verification of the Freudian one, are the elements of a dreadful secular eschatology. We are parts of a humanity caught in an unending cycle of exploitation, domination, repression and pain. Therewith my despair—and the beginning point of the talk.

This presentation draws upon my own recent work,* but is relatively self-contained. It does rest, as I indicated, on an effort to extricate myself from a certain metaphysical or metahistorical despair. Despite the recent reappearance of an American left, this country still has a long way to go before we even attain an institutionalized opposition like the working-class parties of Western Europe. These countries, of course, have their own problems. Domination and exploitation seem to recur eternally, whatever new forms they may take. All attempts to concretize utopia have been defeated, and much reform is derisory. I wonder whether certain kinds of existential despair are not more appropriate responses to the problem of psychohistory—understood as the inner history of humanity—than our efforts to develop a critical theory of society which claims to be an instrument of liberation. Nevertheless, I would like to explore the problems of a critical theory. I do so, obviously, from the disciplinary bias—if it can be called that— of a social scientist, and not as a practicing clinician.

In the first place, we have to take up the idea of critical theory and its relationship to practice, or praxis as it sometimes is called in a more technical sense (as a human project conceived and executed in a dialectical relationship to theory). Then I want to look at the origins of critical theory in the Marxist theory of alienation (and its counterpart, a less developed theory of disalienation, the overcoming of alienation). I'll continue by considering the complications introduced into (or for) critical theory by the present development of society. Finally, I'll turn to the present tasks of critical theory, particularly in its relationship to psychohistory.

This is a program which may claim a substantial publisher's advance, and, to be realistic, I wonder how much of it I'll get through. With all respect to the conference, I do not think it matters. These ideas are cumulative, but also to some degree repetitive, and when I've gone on for an hour, I'll simply stop so that we can have ample time for discussion.

The idea of a critical theory does go back a long way, but I think

---

* I give further references to work of mine in which some of these themes are developed: "The Crisis of Marxist Sociology," in Norman Birnbaum, *Toward a Critical Sociology*, Oxford University Press, New York, 1971; "Sociology: Discontents Present and Perennial," *Social Research*, Vol. 38, No. 4, Winter 1971; "Beyond Marx in the Sociology of Religion?," Chas. Glock and Philip Hammond (Editors), *Beyond the Classics*, Harper and Row, New York, 1973.

that the best (or most typical) early modern expression of it was *The Encyclopedia*, the eighteenth-century *Encyclopedia* which intellectually preceded (and anticipated) the French Revolution. *The Encyclopedia* treated knowledge as liberating—knowledge, of course, including science. (It is interesting in this connection that the Institute for Policy Studies in Washington has been thinking of a new *Encyclopedia*, which it tentatively terms *Encyclopedia of Social Reconstruction, Plans and Practices for a New Society*.) The notion of science as a liberating force underwent or was subjected to what I call a positivistic degradation. That is to say, first, as a reflection and continuation of the division of labor in the larger process of social production, science itself became a specialized activity. Secondly, no longer within the capacity of the informed citizen (to whom the eighteenth-century *Encyclopedia* was addressed) to understand, it was the domain of an esoteric specialist. More importantly, science was detached from moral and political purposes. This detachment in turn served to attach it again to other moral and political purposes than those of the citizenry as a whole, namely, those which for want of a better term I designate as the technocratic utilization of science. This I understand as the utilization of science by those with power in society for the purposes of administration and domination.

In this context, critical theory is a project. It is not a scientific theory as described in commonplace textbooks on scientific method (which themselves may be now be out of date) or methodological discourse in the prevalent schools of behavioral science in the United States. It is not a theory which claims, or pretends, to be a value-free reproduction of a segment of external reality. As I look for the correct formulation, I'd say that critical theory is not simply an expression of the human capacity for making maps, images, or models of the world. It has something to do with the truth *of* and the truth *for* a higher notion of humanity, an unrealized or utopian notion of humanity. That is, critical theory contains (or entails) a metahistorical notion of the transcendence of the conditions it describes. Naturally, there is an extremely complicated relationship (which has to be specified for each use of critical theory) between this notion or component of transcendence and the empirical or theoretic description of the immanent developmental tendencies in each segment of social process. I think you understand, however, that critical theory as a project has philosophical ambitions which go well beyond the description of reality: these ambitions intend the alteration of reality.

It is important to exemplify this by showing what critical theory is not. It is not, let us say, advocacy social science. Advocacy social science has been much discussed of late in this country. Think of the journal *Social Policy* and of a certain idea of the uses of knowledge developed by the American New Left. Knowledge is to be put at the disposal of hitherto underprivileged groups, disenfranchised by the technocratic oligopolies. There is certainly something noble, and politically justifiable, about the idea of knowledge serving new groups, new publics. But I do not think that this is necessarily connected with the conception of a critical theory. Critical theory goes beyond the expression of the partial interests of segments of the community, to the vision of a truer or more authentic and profound community. That community would be constituted by a transformed, a fulfilled humanity.

Now, I think that the Marxist origins of critical theory are clear, and I'll sketch these briefly in a moment. But I also insist on the curious fact that it was some of the idealistic opponents of Marxism at the turn of the century, working in neo-Kantian or neo-Hegelian idiom, who contributed (unintendedly) to the development of a contemporary critical theory. They insisted on the existence of a plurality of value universes, on the role of human choice in shaping these universes, and on the absolutely irreconcilable nature of value conflict. The view that values are not simply naturalistic derivations of historical process, mechanical derivations, but that they can be imposed upon history by human beings in itself can also contribute to a critical theory. It seems to me that the roots of critical theory in two of the very great Western traditions strengthen rather than weaken it.

Obviously, these ideas of critical theory swim in air, or float in classrooms, unless some kind of connection with social practice or praxis can be found. I'm one of the editors (there are twenty or so) of the Yugoslav international journal *Praxis*. This journal, like other journals which bear names like *Telos, Konkret* and so on, have one central characteristic, namely, an absurd degree of abstraction and remoteness from any concrete human activity. That is to say, praxis as a theoretic idea has become the ideology of a group of Marxist thinkers discontented with every known regime. However, the idea of a higher human practice infused by theory, or praxis, still retains a certain dignity, because I think it can be shown that it can be used to control or to criticize actual efforts at social reform, change and even (as the Yugoslav case indeed shows) revolution. If we look at some of the roots of this notion of praxis, we come closer not only to its philosophical sources but to some of its potential for guiding our own activity. These roots are found, I think, in a chain of thought that goes back from Marx and Hegel to Aristotle. Praxis is the expression of specifically human properties, so that the correct praxis consists of determining the highest human capacities and developing these. On these grounds, the kind of praxis connected with or advocated by a truly critical theory is not simply a step-by-step, pragmatic, empirical practice. Praxis entails an element of realization or liberation of human potential. On this account of the matter, the one thing indispensable to successful social practice would be a correct theory, or at least a theory with a large measure of truth about humanity and its potential. Inasmuch as pragmatic, empirical experiment is necessary, experiment with new social forms (or new styles of life, as they are sometimes called) can never generate a permanent community—unless it filters back, is referred to assimilated, to a continuously evolving, self-critical body of theory which can shed light on the empirical paths to follow.

I do not need to carry on at length before this group on the divergences between philosophical assumptions of this kind and the kinds of ideas received favorably in doctoral oral examinations in the social sciences in most universities—particularly in the English-speaking world, and, above all, the United States. I learned these things myself, after graduate school in sociology in the Department of Social Relations at Harvard, by a process of negation—and in the course of living in Europe. These assumptions require, of course, not only a rejection of what is called the behavioral approach to the social sciences, but, much more profoundly, a rejection of the idea of a value-free social science. There is no absolute demarcation or split between the social sciences, on the one hand, and let us say the moral sciences, or philosophy, on the other. At the same time, it seems to me, there is nothing in these methodological (really, metahistorical) canons which precludes and much that encourages the rigorous examination of evidence. The construction of partial theories, the day-by-day, hard and binding work of social and psychological analysis, is imperative—as long as theories of this sort are recognized as limited.

The roots of critical theory, if we look more closely at them, do lie to a considerable degree in the Marxist theory of alienation and in the tentative Marxist sketches about what I term disalienation (termed by Marx and the Marxists the dissolution or overcoming or transforming [*Aufhebung*] of alienation). Apart from the conceptual structure derived from Hegel's *Phenomenology of the Spirit,* in which the self-alienation of the spirit is expressly dealt with, the sources of the Marxist theory are three. A Romantic aesthetics, in which human beings function as creators of values, was generalized to include the highest creative capacities of humanity. The second source is clearly the Enlightenment criticism of philosophical obscurantism and of the institutional tyranny brought about by an alliance of priests and kings. Third, we find the idea of the realization of heaven on earth, this time put in the language of a humanity transformed and in the rhetoric of the elimination or, more precisely, supersession of religion.

Now, the Marxist conception of alienation, composed from these sources, is curiously obsolescent. That is, whatever efforts we may make to connect it with modern psychoanalytic theory, we have to recognize that the psychology on which it rests is not in its content plausible to us. Its intention, its moral intention, its concept of a holistic humanity or of a mankind healed or restored, may please us; its concrete content can help us very little—a fact which is sometimes overlooked by large numbers of contemporary Marxists and sympathizers with Marxism, who suppose that the concept can be translated immediately into the language of social science. I find this deficiency the reason for the enormous disparity between the theoretic and philosophical promise of contemporary Marxism and its relatively low degree of, let us say, critical performance with respect to contemporary institutions (with certain conspicuous exceptions).

The concept of alienation in Marxism involved a unitary or integral human substance, fragmented and violated by the division of labor. The structures of domination and exchange deprived humanity of direct, primary or expressive relations between human beings. Under these conditions, human activity in the form of work and production itself contributed—paradoxically—to the inhumanity of the human world. Only the fundamental alteration, therefore, of these relationships would free humanity to become itself. In this sense, the view that an economic-interest theory (or an interest theory of any kind) is basic to Marxism strikes me as false. It is under the conditions of alienation that humanity follows, or is obliged to follow, its interests. This occurs in a labor-divided and class-divided society. In the post-alienated, or disalienated, state human beings would be free to do what is most human: express themselves. At times, then, the notion of alienation rest not on Promethean conceptions of humanity as creative but also on Dionysian modes: the expression of human impulse as the substance of humanity. I suppose that in this sense Wilhelm Reich is in the Marxist tradition.

We can think of Norman Mailer's famous essay on the white Negro as to some extent the ideological manifesto of the counterculture many years in advance of the counterculture. Mailer wrote this essay (if I'm correctly informed) at a time when he was directly under the influence of Reichian psychoanalysis. I do not know whether he was in therapy or not, but it is not relevant. Reich's theory of orgasm seems to me, to put it minimally, not incompatible with certain ideas found in the *Economic-Philosophical Manuscripts of 1844*.

But what about the roles of disalienation in the Marxist canon: what do they entail? In the first place,the canon argues that humanity comes to consciousness of itself through blockage, deprivation and frustration. Awareness of its potential is not simply a notion that certain needs are to be satisfied, but a view that its stature has to be altered. That is to say, under the conditions of a labor-divided society, humanity is diminished. From this point of view, revolutionary activity is in itself a form of activity therapy, or praxis. Praxis is a form of the reclamation of humanity by itself. The relationship of this process to knowledge recapitulates some of the themes of critical theory: knowledge and correct practice, or praxis, meet. Because there is a unity of human truth, it is not alone the truth about mankind, or humankind, not alone the truth about humanity, but the truth *for* humanity, the truth lived by humanity in the process of self-development. It is not an abstract theory or a positivistic conception of the truth.

In this view of disalienation, the proletariat functions as a surrogate for all of humanity. It is the most human class because the most suffering, and therefore precisely the class with the greatest capacity to develop the realization of a new human potential. In the disalienated state or postalienated society, as sketched in the *German Ideology*, we do find a utopian vision of human development: a world without the constraint of scarcity, a world in which personalities are free to develop, to exchange roles, as we should say today—an interesting connection with some of the discussion by Ken Keniston and others on the potentiality of a so-called postindustrial society. In this utopian vision of development, then, humanity is free to develop its aesthetic and intellectual, indeed its technical, capacities without the constraints of scarcity and without the division of labor. I should add that Marx asserts that it is not private property which causes the division of labor, but the division of labor which causes private property. This, of course, implies that a certain level of the development of the productive forces is necessary as a precondition of a communist or utopian society.

Now, of course, in the later Marx some of these themes were—so to speak—sublimated. This is an enormous discussion, which I do not think it really pays to recapitulate. The young Marx versus the old Marx, or was the old Marx truer, who was the real Marx, and so on. There is no doubt that what everyone says is true: as Marx grew older, he did turn to political economy and left philosophy, explicit philosophy and metahistory behind. On the other hand, the categories for the description of the working of capitalism are directly derived from the early work. Here I bow to Steven Marcus, who has taken upon himself the task of reading everything Engels wrote. Surely, the old Engels did in fact convert Marxism from a form of Hegelian metacritique of human historical existence to something resembling evolutionist and positivist doctrine. This, however, was not necessarily true to many of the components of authentic Marxism. Our problem is, I think, not one in the textual analysis of the Marxist tradition. It is, instead, a serious historical problem, a conceptual problem. By default, Marxism remains the one critical, social theory (along with Freudianism, which deals with other domains of human existence). Marxism in its entirety clearly does not work any longer, despite all kinds of efforts to save it. I myself protect a series of works under the general rubric the Marxist legacy. We have had a legacy, and like many heirs we are faced with the embarrassing task of spending or liquidating the legacy and yet remaining true to the intentions of the persons who willed it to us. But if we look at the historical problems facing a contemporary critical theory, we are overwhelmed. We are simply incapable of subsuming them under one theory; the division of labor has itself been altered (as we shall see, not least due to the role of what Marx called the "scientific power" in the production process), and a key concept like alienation no longer can function as a key to the riddle of history. Let's look at these problems in a rather concrete way, and then go on to consider some of our present analytical dilemmas.

I want to discuss four problems which a contemporary critical theory has to confront. The first is the failure of the proletariat.

The failure of the proletariat may well be connected with the fact that in the Western European societies and the United States, the proletariat, as depicted by Marx in the middle of the nineteenth century, became less proletarian. That in itself was a possibility that Marx as well as Engels envisaged. They themselves tended to what might be termed reformist politics toward the end of Marx's life. This process (deproletarianization) had the effect of socially integrating the proletariat as part of a national community. Marx and Engels, I think, despite their own fierce German nationalism, curiously underestimated the appeal or the cohesiveness of national ideologies as opposed to the force of class interests. At the same time, the proletariat underwent a number of transformations. It became, not a proletariat, but a working class. It was subjected to the winds or tides of nationalism, even chauvinism; it became an accomplice in the imperial domination of other peoples. And as it was integrated socially into the national community, paradoxically it developed its own counterculture. I use the term advisedly. The parties and movements which originally intended to prepare the revolutionary transformation of capitalist society became vehicles for the adaptation of the working class to it. They formed enclaves within the national communities. This was certainly true of pre-1914 German Social Democracy; it is true today of the French and Italian Communist Parties. Both are powers in their societies incapable of assuming the leadership of those societies even if it would be very difficult to dislodge them from an important share in, let's say, the distributive process (not the administrative process) in their countries. What is at issue is more than the political integration of the working-class movements in Europe: it is, equally, a form of parallel society or culture possessed by that class and organized by its parties. That seems to me to be the first, and certainly a very critical, problem for a Marxist theory which—after all—did predict that working-class organization and culture would lead to the opposite of integration, revolution.

The second problem is what I would term the problem of the wrong revolution in the wrong place. The revolution occurred not in the industrially advanced but in the industrially backward countries, first in Russia, later in agrarian China, more recently in certain Third World countries. These are countries which had the peculiarity, as well, of being outside the Western cultural and philosophical tradition. And since they are outside that tradition I wonder whether the conceptual argument, the conceptual apparatus, involved in the doctrines of alienation and disalienation can be directly applied to these revolutions. When I speak of the wrong revolution, I also mean wrong from the viewpoint of having educative or model functions for the advanced societies. I think that they do not have those functions. I also note that with the possible exception of Yugoslavia and certain experiments connected with the Cultural Revolution in China none of these revolutions has followed what we may call explicit and purposeful disalienating policies. The notion of a policy aimed at overcoming certain forms of human alienation has more or less tacitly (at times more or less explicitly) been dropped in these revolutions.

Of more importance for us, I think, have been the structural changes in capitalism. This I would cite as the third major issue which contemporary critical theory has to confront. And here I would point to three kinds of structural changes in capitalism which I think it is important for us to consider.

The first of these is the pervasive process of bureaucratization which stems from the massive interpenetration of state and society. It is impossible to separate state and economy even in so-called free-enterprise societies. The economic role which the state adopts as a means of distribution and economic control is simply enormous. Modern capitalism is unthinkable as a free-enterprise system. Modern capitalistic interests need, above all, to control the modern capitalist state. At the same time, the scale of capitalist enterprise—national and multinational—is such that bureaucratic forms of hierarchical organization, administration and production in the private sector parallel those in the public sector.

Bureaucratization is a mode of organization of the social forms of late capitalism. That is to say, it is impossible to have a high degree of monopoly capitalism without using a bureaucratic apparatus. This was not foreseen by Marx. It was discussed already by the turn of the century among World War I Marxists of the generation of Hilferding and Rosa Luxemburg, and others. They were attempting to bridge the unbridgeable or reconcile the irreconcilable, namely, to interpret changes in capitalism with a certain fidelity to the original model. But it seems to me that the dynamics of this structural change in capitalism are to be found in what has been called social imperialism.

Here I come to the second point I want to adduce about structural change in capitalism, the development of an entire nation as an imperial community. The phenomenon is old in a county like Britain, perhaps even in this country. It has recently been subjected to an acute or heightened degree of critical consciousness. Social imperialism entails a considerable degree of integration of the working class in the imperialist enterprise or project, making it an accomplice in the exploitation of other nations, the emergence of a global proletariat. And, of course, the organization of the competing capitalist nations for imperialist purposes almost guarantees a perennial situation of international conflict, providing an economic and political dynamism for the system.

The third structural change in capitalism, and one of equal importance to our understanding of the mechanisms of integration of the working class in modern society, is the industrialization of culture. The prime source of our insight into this development can be found in the famous chapter on the cultural industry in Horkheimer's and Adorno's *Dialectics of Enlightenment,* recently available in English but first published in 1947. Cultural industry is the industrial production of a culture for mass consumption. It reproduces, uncritically, the surface of daily life. The cultural sphere, the general sphere of symbolic reflection and image-making, becomes not a protected area in which society and its institutions can be criticized, but a means of ideological consolidation of the status quo.

I'm in agreement with Marcuse, the more so as the ideas found in *One Dimensional Man* and (less so, perhaps) in *Eros and Civilization* directly follow from the *Dialectics of Enlightenment.* Marcuse is, in a sense, the American representative of the Frankfurt School.

Curiously, the fourth point about capitalism is the political effect of what I would term tyrannical socialism, which seems incapable (in our societies, at least) of engendering world historical enthusiasm as a model for transformation. The Soviet Union is, perhaps, the chief example of a terroristic industrialization, with horrors that rivaled and at times exceeded those of primitive accumulation in nineteenth-century Europe. It also has a bureaucratized and centralized administration with absolutely no libertarian or pluralistic component. It manifests a degree of cultural standardization, not to mention philistinism, which makes the American TV networks seem to be functioning in some postrevolutionary utopia. Under these conditions, the absence of a really compelling counterforce, the cultural and political consolidation of capitalism was easier to accomplish.

I have been attempting to give an account, perhaps a litany, of our woes. And we may ask at this point whether, faced with the historical situation as it is, critical theory is able to offer any solutions. Must it not simply lapse, may not its components have to be separated? On the one hand, we have a moral and political critique of existing institutions, with morally motivated political action to overcome these. On the other hand, we have a more or less empirical and historical description of these institutions, descriptions compiled in the hope that in some unsystematic way the information and insight accumulated by the operations of intelligence will be used for moral and political purposes. An alternative or different system would be constructed on the basis of knowledge. If this were the case, this would indeed force us back to a situation not unlike the situation imagined to be true by most of our colleagues in the moral and social sciences. That is a situation in which there is an absolute distinction of spheres, a distinction of discourse between a social science, or a social theory, and a politics— a politics taken in the generic sense of an attempt to shape a human community. Before reconciling ourselves so easily to this situation of fragmentation and ordinary despair, we ought to see whether something can be made in fact of the legacy of critical theory. In particular, I'd ask whether an infusion (and I use the term with real hesitation, since it is so imprecise) of the Freudian legacy cannot save the Marxist one by revivifying it.

First, we must deal with a difficulty in the Freudian legacy itself. There are two somewhat contradictory, or at least very different, moral philosophies explicit in the work of Freud. Freud once praised his small group of early collaborators (those to whom he gave that set of rings) by saying of them that they had learned to bear a piece of reality.

Now, here is what has been called, I think earlier by Ken Keniston the stoical dimension in Freud. Psychoanalysis has an Old Testament-like, awful, moral lesson: that all humans suffer, that life is hard and unremitting, and that health consists in the ability to comprehend and understand that these blows are inevitable. There is a harsh moral quality to this, some of which was expressed in that remarkable letter of what only can be termed no consolation Freud sent to the widow of Karl Abraham after the latter's death. He said that he'd had difficulty in writing the letter, had delayed doing so, but that when he sat down to write, it was not any easier. There was nothing he could tell her. This was an absolute confrontation of pain and the abyss, an almost metaphysical renunciation of hope. Yet we can find at the same time in Freud's hopes for psychoanalysis, for its cultural consequences, an idea of liberating therapy—not just for individual patients, but for a reeducated humanity. Freud situated psychoanalysis, in other words, not only in the tradition of Copernicus and Darwin, who confronted a narcissistic humanity with hard truths, but in the tradition of the Enlightenment. That is a tradition which certainly included or includes Marx. I say this despite the anecdote reported by Sachs. At the beginning of the Soviet Revolution, the Bolsheviks were not unfriendly to psychoanalysis, and Freud had patients from the Soviet Union—including a high official. This person told Freud that Lenin had declared that the first fifty years of the Revolution would be unremitting toil, suffering, deprivation, disappointment. The next fifty, however, would be splendid. Freud, with his characteristic irony, said something like, "Well, I'll give you the first half."

Freud was skeptical and wrote skeptically of Marxism, and yet in the notion of a liberating, an experienced and lived knowledge, there are obviously not alone spiritual resemblances between Freudianism and Marxism but also structural connections. Finding these structural connections is enormously difficult. This is not the place, and we lack the time to review the large, very large, Marx-Freud literature—the best of which doesn't appear in English. There were very interesting discussions in the late 1920s in Weimar Germany (now again in the German Federal Republic), discussions participated in by persons like Bernfeld and Fenichel, some of whom came here and did rather different things, in different *personae*.

I do think that we can say that it is extremely difficult to recognize any direct relationship of a one-to-one kind between the pervasive kinds of character disorders now favored in psychoanalytical treatment (now favored in the sense that they seem to make up many of the clinical reports in the clinical literature), the disorders which introspection and observation combine to suggest also dominate our culture, and the symptomatology of alienation as depicted in the Marxist tradition. The concentration of some kinds of explicit suffering amongst patients from the middle class indeed would make the connection even more remarkable, could it be established. It is frequently middle-class persons who have the most autonomy at work, the most expressiveness in their work and their lives, who in their work enjoy considerable amounts of freedom. Yet this group is most pervaded by psychic malaise and misery, in many of its forms. I am aware that Marx did not locate alienation exclusively in work or in market and exchange relationships; it was, for him, also the consequence of the absence of an authentic human community. Nevertheless, at first glance at least, it is impossible to crystallize, or concretize, or localize, the sources of the psychic malaise we know in any one sector of the society. Familial and sexual relations; work and economic relations; politics and the organization of the larger society; culture and aesthetic expression: the malaise appears equally intense, equally pervasive. We are obviously able to establish (or diagnose) interconnections between these spheres. At the same time it is extremely difficult, even for a skilled Marxist or a dialectically supple neo-Marxist, to insist upon the priority of one or the other sphere. It is this failure of diagnostic success, a failure of causal analysis, which appears, despite promising beginnings, to have prevented the development of a theoretically enriched or articulated relationship between Marxism and the classical Freudian tradition.

This theoretical failure has led, at least in this country and perhaps elsewhere as well, to a new form of disalienating politics—the politics of the counterculture. A theoretical account of the interconnection between character disorder and alienation in the political community is absent. Present, however, are the lessons of both the Freudian and

Marxist traditions—lessons read as schematized directives to go out and liberate yourselves. The counterculture has emerged as what might be described as an artificial, a willed utopia. It has obviously encountered serious institutional resistance, some of it taking the form of encapsulation and exploitation. It is interesting that the original notions of the counterculture as devised by Mailer, and later to some degree popularized or vulgarized by minor prophets like Hoffman and Rubin, has made use of extremely blunt, extremely superficial, notions of impulse expression as the *via regis* of attack on authority. There is even in Jerry Rubin's *Do It!* a parody of the Communist Manifesto, as if instinctual rebellion were all that mattered. Instinctual rebellion or impulse rebellion would in fact serve as a new Joshua's trumpet and blow down the walls of an institutional Jericho. The evidence is not all in, but it does appear that despite the counterculture and whatever long-term undermining effect it may yet have, the institutions of late-capitalist society are still able to function; they work rather well.

Brigette and Peter Berger, our colleagues in sociology, have argued that there are always replacements, that for every middle-class counterculture dropout there is a blue-collar person ready to rise in the hierarchy. This seems to me not to be true. The counterculture is intrinsically a consumer item, and can be consumed to some degree by the working class as well.

The counterculture rests on the notion that administration and production are gratuitous, that distribution is the problem, and that the problem of distribution can be solved by a parody of liberalism, by an absolutely random distribution. People will then seize upon what they need from this distributive cornucopia and use it for their own free and high purposes. That seems to make the counterculture a system heavily involved in consumption and which has nothing, or very little, to say about the institutions of administration and production. Secondly, it is a consumer item in a very specific market sense, that is to say it is sold or vended. Its heroes, meanwhile, sometimes fairly ephemeral ones, are available for the cultural industry. And the society seems to have integrated, or capitalism seems to have integrated, this challenge which was supposed to have undermined it, by undermining amongst other things the will to work, deference to any kind of authority and the like.

I'm reminded that an old friend has said recently in *Partisan Review* that the great thing about the contemporary counterculture is that people insist on having fun. This was Clement Greenberg, a profound critic of mass culture. There is something to it, and I may well be underestimating it. It seems to me that the theory of the counterculture is a curious parody of a fused and undigested Freudo-Marxism. It is almost as if all the hard work, the hard thought, the conceptual apparatus, the slow labor against the real external and intrinsic intellectual difficulties involved in the rapprochement of these two theories had been set aside in favor of a few simplified injunctions, to go out and do it or to live it up. The very frenzy of the injunction suggests the uncertainty of the directive.

Postscript. It may be that for the moment the truest answer is the simplest one. There is an autonomy of spheres, and we have been unable to make (with some significant exceptions) important connections and interconnections between economic-political processes, on the one hand, and the intrapsychic processes, on the other. Freud's long-term educative hopes for psychoanalysis remain unrealized. If we look for new possibilities of a revolution or human transcendence, we may have to revert for the time being to the sphere of political work in social institutions. If we look, however, at the possibilities of what we might term political mobilization, as we seek new modes of organizing new agents of social transformation, new social groupings, new sectors of the labor force, of reactivating consciousness in the working class, of devising real counterinstitutions, of devising forms of institutional and participatory democracy for wider sectors of our public life, including the economy—if we look at all of these matters and seriously pose the question of historical agency, two very great difficulties appear, the first philosophic and the second psychohistorical.

The philosophical one is more easily described than dealt with. Quite apart from our difficulty in putting together the elements of modern society for purposes of analysis, we lack a vision of our ends. We have no conception of the dimensions and structures of a fulfilled or even a viable political community. It may be that only such a conception of our ends can in turn generate the elements of an analysis of our present situation. In other words, a metahistorical idea of community may be the most effective guarantor of an empirically adequate and concrete historical analysis.

The second, or psychohistorical, difficulty is best rephrased as a difficulty in or with psychohistory. Clearly, no idea of a community can dispense with an idea of a fulfilled humanity—of a psychologically matured or developed humanity, its potential realized (or, at least, a good deal of it unblocked), relatively at one with itself. Psychohistory, as practiced up to now, does not quite escape what I would term an empiricist temptation. It offers us a series of discrete images of human development, in several historical situations, some of them very disparate. The elements are always combined and recombined in different ways, historically. Not one humanity emerges; several do.

That is one side of the difficulty. The other is no less problematical.

The concept of identity and renewed attention to symbolization as a defense against the idea of death and recurrent problems of the life cycle point to the psychohistorical search for universals in the human situation. Psychohistory is, then, not alone a record of the working of these universals in specific historical epochs and structures. It is a record of human fate, of a struggle within and against history. Let us put it another way: psychohistory uses the psychoanalytic tradition and our awareness of human historicity in a new search for a human essence.

In its present phase of development, psychohistory's boundaries are difficult to circumscribe. Indeed, there seems to be no particular need to do so. Psychohistory is not only a mode for the understanding of history, but possibly a modern version or interpretation of the task of a critical theory. In that sense the pursuit of psychohistorical explanation and analysis may very well be an authentic derivative of what I depicted as the Marxist legacy.

Increasingly, we can see a conception of, or a project for, a critical sociological theory which would be more viable than nineteenth-century Marxism. Marriage between this and psychoanalysis is not quite the right term. Eventually, perhaps, a synthesis might be possible. For the moment, nothing so definite obtains. I think that the liberating intent of what's been done in psychohistory does coincide with the intentions of a critical social theory. There is too much connection for this not to be so.

Perhaps I gave too totalistic an idea of critical theory, too finished an idea. What I thought of was the infusion of particular activities, clinical and theoretical psychoanalysis, empirical and theoretical sociology, political economy, and aesthetic inquiry, but not so much a finished critical theory as the search for one. The dominant assumption is that we can never completely establish a critical theory as an articulated, finished, much less dogmatic system. But it functions as a set of moral intentions, a set of moral intentions about the world and a set of methodological assumptions about the way certain things, certain institutions, certain attitudes, certain characterological developments are put together. It involves the possibilities of reeducation.

What we may expect of critical theory is to absorb energies from contemporary experiments, but also to assimilate the lessons of the past, not alone our American but other pasts. I conceive of the task of critical theory, therefore, as also being able to situate these experiments. This isn't the first time in America that communes have been developed.

I recall that when I spoke to Berlin students at the Free University in 1965 about some of these themes, I was criticized for having advanced a program for research rather than for action—a fate suffered by Marcuse himself some years later. The maintenance of a critical social theory in hard times, times of encapsulation and integration, let alone oppression, is in fact an act of political defiance—or an act of political hope or faith. The active pursuit of a critical theory in a so-called knowledge-based society is in itself a political act because a knowledge-based society depends on the production and strict demarcation of technically utilizable knowledge, not critical knowledge. It gets critical knowledge without intending it. It depends for functioning upon an educated labor force, a strictly technical education. The mastery of technique presupposes a general education, and that in turn brings students (and the public, addressed by those who work in universities and the contiguous sectors of the knowledge industry) in contact with critical ideas.

I think that there are two points to be made. One is that there seems to be a kind of telescoping or fusing of possibility and achievement. It is true that the productive capacity of advanced industrial societies is such that administration and production are not matters of life or death. But they are matters of political life or death. That is to say, the conquest of power depends upon controlling the mechanisms of administration and production, and turning them to more humane, more just, newer ends, what you call a new social contract. It seems to me that from this point of view, and this is without doubt an old Marxist or old political position, if we look at the emergence and consolidation of the counterculture, the guarantee of the new human existence would have to be the control of these posts. That would call for a different kind of political strategy.

What has critical theory produced? If we understand critical theory to be the Western Marxist tradition, I think it has produced, very roughly, two things. It has produced institutionalized opposition in Western society, in the form of working-class-based political movements, unions and the like. These have become increasingly detached from the remote aim of revolution and increasingly adapted to the modes of class division in Western society, even constitutive of it. Spiritually, it has produced an oppositional set of intellectuals like some of the people Freud went to school with for whom critical theory was an expression of a longing for a better life, an aesthetically and morally gratifying life, hopes which for a time they placed in the working-class movement. At other times, they withdrew those hopes from it. It is interesting that the discussion of the counterculture today was picked up, rather than other things. It seemed to me almost as if we were collectively searching for a newer historical agency for this transformation or liberation, with youth in the place of the proletariat.

It is interesting that the failure as well as the success of the 1968 uprising in France has had a lot of derivatives. Among the most interesting is the turn of the French Socialist Party to the left, the emergence of a strong new body of French trade-union doctrine (particularly in the ex-Catholic or left union, the CFDT, to the left of the Communist-led CGT). That is, it has led to some revivification of French socialism, with the Cohn-Bendits completely out.

I spoke, as other people certainly have spoken, of the difficulty of disengaging casual chains. Family, work, the state, communities—the difficulty is real enough, but certain causal chains probably do exist. There are probably certain nodal points and connections. The point that seems important is that, to a degree not dreamt of by Marx, populations have become instruments of their own subjugation, or have internalized,to use a familiar phrase, domination and exercise domination over themselves.

That is why I spoke of psychohistory as a legitimate derivative of critical theory, why I confer legitimacy as a critical theory upon psychohistory.

Remember Dr. Mitscherlich's remark about the persistence of the superego and the need for a three-generational concept to give it some kind of coherence or shape. Things fall apart, the center does not hold. But in fact we live in a period in which there are historical legacies or historical processes working themselves out in which the generations are not simply the mute bearers of history but are very actively reenacting past histories which may be in part obsolete, in part viable. The psychohistorical contribution would certainly be the way to clarify this psychic inheritance and disinheritance.

If we make an examination of, let's say, the hidden or not so hidden depths of public opinion and political symbolization, of popular political thought, we find phenomena like the self-hatred and internalized self-contempt of the working class, the sense people have that they face chaos if certain things change.

We have to take account of a methodological peculiarity of both Marxism and Freudianism. Remember Erik Erikson's citation from Freud, that education can only develop or work with what is given. Marx held that socialism was inevitable because the inner contradictions of bourgeois or capitalist society tended in this direction, and that socialism was the seizure of the inner movement of reality. It seems to me that what we need is the completion of the liberating, humanly therapeutic dimensions of Freudian theory, an abandonment of its stoic renunciation to some degree. We need to know from the psychohistorians, the critical psychologists and psychoanalysts, what is given in human nature, what are its capacities for growth, development, liberation, its capacity to free itself from its multiple, internalized, secreted tyrannies. Unless we know that, no project in the sense of a model of the future, a social utopia, will be viable. It becomes a gratuitous exercise in speculation. Now, that is a long initial detour but, I think, an important one, and that seems to me to be the task of psychohistory, of the critical theorists in a very general sense, because no other competence will respond to these questions.

We suffer on the one hand from a surfeit of information, stimuli which are available, visible in the number of things unread, communications not responded to, notes, papers, books—especially books— as they pile up. We have a sense, all of us, of missing whole areas of intellectual experience. It is a conceptual deprivation, personal in the sense of impoverishing our abilities to do serious work. It isn't, however, quite a quantitative one; it has other dimensions.

We are all asking whether there are new unifying concepts which we could discover or invent which would play a role analogous to or equivalent to the concept of alienation in Marxist thought, possibly of repression in Freud's thought. Is our deficiency in this sense a conceptual deficiency which, once resolved, would somehow enable us to put together this surfeit of information, to interpret it selectively according to new criteria of significance? Of is this difficulty not part of a much more complex historical difficulty, which in the political sphere expresses itself through the inchoate shape of the agencies of positive historical transformation? That lack of historical certainty about our capacity to transform the world may well express itself in the absence of any clear notion of the inner developmental tendencies of our society. Did not the British anthropologist Edmund Leach write of a world gone wild, a world running out of control, a world which in its inner mechanisms escapes our vision? We do not grasp those mechanisms, we do not understand our world. And that, in some measure, reflects the way in which humanity has been dwarfed, humilitated, by its own history.

• The paper is an edited transcription of a talk given to the Wellfleet Psychohistory Group, chaired by Robert Lifton, in 1972—and the postscript is a response to questions posed, variously, by Margaret Brenman-Gibson, Peter Brooks, Erik Erikson, Kai Erikson, Robert Holt, Robert Lifton, William Phillips, and Richard Sennett. I am grateful to them for their creative, and demanding, counsel.

7

Are We Entering a Post-Marxist Age? Marx After Marxism

Is it accurate to term our epoch post-Marxist? Two decades ago, the critical Left everywhere would have answered "no." It was recognized that while class conflict in capitalist societies had not culminated in revolution, and while the global system of capitalist exploitation seemed more pervasive, the development of the welfare state in the West owed much to Marxism. Social, political, and even religious movements claiming direct descent from Marxism were widely distributed. And today, while state socialist societies hardly represent utopia (socialist appropriation of the means of production by party and state has entailed new forms of exploitation), the multiple forms of alienation and an intensified consciousness of homelessness in capitalist societies suggest that the deformation of the human spirit may be as acute now as it was at the beginning of the capitalist epoch. Marxism, of course, needs to be modernized, adapted to any number of phenomena not envisioned by its founders. But two decades ago, this task was felt to be well under way. It would have been impossible then to declare that Marxism could neither apprehend nor reshape our world. The situation has now changed.

Visiting the East German peace movement a few months ago, I

was struck by how very different is its consciousness. A generation ago, its predecessors in opposition were linked to humanist Marxists, the anti-Stalinists of Hungary and Poland in 1956. Much of the present-day East European opposition is distant even from the Czech reformers of 1968. It seeks to destroy bureaucratic power, develop pluralistic culture, and preserve the earth and its species. Its affinities are with movements like the German Greens. Elsewhere, Friar Leonardo Boff refuses to consider himself a Marxist, saying Marxism is but one among many methods of analysis. He seeks a church prepared to revise its Euro-centrism. In any number of new social movements, the theme of cultural autonomy is as pronounced as the theory of class conflict defined in strictly economic terms. The pathologies of both state socialism and international capitalism have enlarged and fragmented the structure of social conflict.

In short, while the world economy has assumed dimensions anticipated by Marx, the new ideology and sensibility—and even contemporary culture as a whole—escape his categories. Modern social conflicts result from differences in gender groups, generations, nations and regions, as well as from economic classes. Aesthetic and moral values fuse with, and not infrequently define, class interests. It is my sense, then, that we have entered a post-Marxist epoch. If we are to discern its outlines, it is important to understand what has occurred.

Marx began as a poet, proceeding through philosophy to political economy. He adumbrated "the laws of motion of capitalism," and was drawn to the work of Darwin. His own life exemplified the trajectory of the nineteenth century—from post-Christian millennialism to post-religious scientism. His work includes both scientific description and moral prophecy, combining elements that are analytical and eschatological, empirical and religious. The lines dividing these categories were never rigid; Marx's original labors of scientific description were charged with spiritual energy. The existing world was scrutinized for the sake of a higher (and better) world to come.

But Marxism has now been academicized, has thoroughly penetrated much of what was once called "bourgeois social science," and is taught by bourgeois professors who are not Marxists. It has been assimilated into the Western intellectual tradition—a tradition of which Marx was more a part than most of his philistine detractors. Its spiritual impulses have found other outlets: movements of psychological and religious renewal, newly conceived systems of spiritual transformation. Even within Marxism itself, it is proclaimed that the future is now, that indefinite postponement of revolutionary delight denies one of Marx's central tenets. Such claims revert to a more primitive, more poetic Marxism in which the complex structure erected by Marx himself dissolves like the insubstantial world of Prospero's farewell to art in *The Tempest.*

To be sure, a world economic system has emerged (comprising both capitalist and the self-designated socialist states) which fulfills some of Marx's major predictions. Capital knows no national loyalty; its relentless pursuit of profit across frontiers is the only effective internationalism in sight. Our politics has not kept pace with this transformation; its language is unable either to describe how impersonal concentrations of economic power dictate the fate of nations, or to effectively interpret the enormous development of science and technology. New proletariats multiply as more workers perform utterly routine jobs or become superfluous. Welfare capitalism, dependent upon production for a mass consumer market, has engendered needs which it cannot satisfy. None of these developments would surprise Marx.

At the same time, however, revolutionary—even mass reformist— movements in the West are conspicuously absent. A global proletariat may be more combative, but organized international capital has succeeded (often unintentionally) in dividing and exploiting it, just as it has divided Western populations. Put differently, the internal divisions of Western capitalism, as well as the visible incompetence of capitalist elites, are balanced by the incoherence and disunity of the global opposition. The gradual socialization of the means of production has occurred, but its triumphant historical subject is capital itself.

Nor has state socialism processed that differently. Ironically, it is even more vulnerable to a Marxist critique than capitalist regimes. Production is politically centralized, coercion economically organized, consciousness and culture instrumentalized. Even the ostensible masters of the apparatus are servants to it. (This is also true of bureaucratic capitalism.) For Marx, it was precisely the crassness and visibility of this domination and exploitation which would contribute to the collapse of capitalism. Capitalism hardly thrives. But compare it with "police socialism" where parties who call themselves Marxist administer a spiritual vacuum, furtively penetrated by an opposition which is in principle judged to be impossible by the system's apologists. The new society is the old society writ large.

While the record of state socialism is a factor in today's retreat from Marxism, I suspect it contributes less to the genesis of a post-Marxist epoch than to a revival of pre-Marxist consciousness—a resignation to the eternal return of oppression. The crimes and tyrannies of our century have liquidated the belief in progress. As a result, the secular version of transcendence embodied in original Marxism has ceded, especially among the opponents of capitalism, to miniaturized notions of felicity. Alternative movements like the Greens explicitly demand reconsideration or redefinition of the idea of progress. Burckhardt and Nietzsche have triumphed over their contemporaries.

More important to the emergence of a post-Marxist consciousness has been the intractability of capitalist culture: Marxists' political predictions break upon the rock of its immutable autonomy. In capitalist society,the consciousness is fabricated industrially in ways which are strikingly similar to its manipulation by state socialism. I am not referring here to a modern version of "bread and circuses." Rather, the centralization of capitalist societies generates multiple and often mutually antagonistic nodes of differentiation and resistance. But the welfare state neutralizes explosive economic antagonism by proliferating a wide variety of aesthetic, ethnic, and religious values. Economic centralization and cultural fragmentation thus supplement one another. We dare not overlook the possibility that mass unemployment and brutal, rapid declines in living standards may yet engender large-scale class conflict in some capitalist societies. But for the moment, these societies use adversity very differently. New corporativisms and older identities (rooted in family, region, religion, ethnicity, language), alternate. Multiple allegiances and split social roles (e.g., those fostered by the separation of work and residence) preclude the kind of class consciousness Marx expected. No matter how inauthentic or instrumentalized, the culture of capitalism perpetuates itself. Analogous developments are evident across the world: movements like the Islamic revival, the Catholic renaissance in Latin America, political Buddhism in Asia, doctrines like Negritude—all are the new foci of social consciousness.

None of this should astonish us. The history of nineteenth- and early twentieth-century Europe will surely sustain a reading quite different from the standard Marxist interpretation. Even the concept of "totality," advanced by modern Marxists as essential to understanding Marx's thought, may lead, as Lukacs felt, to a critical revision of Marxism. And consider the challenge of psychoanalysis to the Marxist theory of human nature. Despite Marx's complex depiction of human interests, the depth of Freud's vision is missing. Marx ignored the relative autonomy of the development of character in a given historical milieu; the thinker who thought in epochs came to believe that humanity could leap over its own historical shadow. One day, perhaps, humanity will actualize its communal or higher self in a revolutionary furor. In the meantime, authoritarianism and aggression threaten to prolong our wait.

The most recent challenge to Marxism comes from the school of historians closest to it: the *Annales* group in France. Insisting on the primacy of "the long term," they depict structures like the family, community, and habitat as inextricably linked to class configurations. And newer historical examinations of the relationship between politics and the state reveal how much of what we earlier identified as economic factors are indeed political—leaving us quite unclear about which is primary. These ideas, along with psychoanalysis and other psychologies, give us fresh insight into the notion of historical totality. They destroy the linear clarity of Marx's theory of an economic base with a cultural and social superstructure.

In his vision of a unified science of man and nature, Marx was a typical nineteenth-century figure. But recent transformations in the history and philosophy of science have led us to question the Marxist and positivist reliance on a single canonical scientific method. Marx himself never doubted that humanity's highest task was the mastery of nature, but his own critique of technocratic rationality has prompted us to question our previous trust in instrumental reason. When this distrust is joined to a renewed interest in ending giganticism in social structures and to the ecologists' demand for a less arrogant approach to nature, we come to see Marx as a prisoner of the assumptions of early capitalist industrialization. We return, in a sense, to the roots of Marxism itself. Marx sought the transcendence of capitalism so that humanity could be restored to wholeness.

Marx expected to find a key to this wholeness in art, especially in the epic and tragic poetry of the Greeks. He was enormously impressed by the fact that, despite their dependence on "immature social conditions," the works of Homer and the tragedians "still constitute for us a source of aesthetic enjoyment and in certain respects prevail as the standard and model beyond attainment."

A return to human wholeness, a search for irreducible virtue in human nature, a willingness to be instructed by the past (even our own past as children) will certainly give us a view of transcendence very different from the progressive hopes of the age. By renouncing Marx, we may return to his spiritual intentions. The post-Marxist epoch, then, will be marked indelibly by Marx himself.

III

THOUGHT IN ITS SETTING

"Students, Professors and Philosopher Kings" was written for one of the volumes produced as part of the Carnegie Commission on Higher Education's large assessment of American universities. The essay criticizes some of the illusions of the hyperactive left of the 1960s, illusions about the feasibility of converting the American university into a vanguard of revolution. Our society was far from ready for revolution, and our universities were (and are) extremely improbable *foyers* of revolution. The essay is anything but a conventional defense of the liberal university and is, rather, an examination of the failure of liberalism to sustain a publicly engaged academic culture, a criticism of the technocratic servitude of the American university. I connected the discussion to themes found in the essays in the previous sections, concerned with the nature of citizenship. An authentic democracy requires educated citizens, and the hermetic closure of much academic culture has contributed to the deformation and decay of what was once an American public. To be sure, it is also a resigned response to the absence of a public by those who would address one if they would locate it. I leave it to my readers to judge whether, in the light of recent debates on "political correctness," the essay retains some timeliness. Its method is, interestingly, rather like the one I employed to discuss both the condition of sociology and the argument about Marxism. I sought to go beyond immediate antinomies to situate the argument on terrain shared by supposedly antagonistic camps. In sociology, empiricists and theorists agreed that there was a self-contained science of society. Marxists and anti-Marxists shared a linear conception of history. Liberal and technocratic interpretations of the university referred to sustaining social contexts which are, now, rapidly eroding.

Ten years after the publication of the essay, I found myself at the Sorbonne as one of several hundred guests of the President of France, who had convened something like an *assisses des intellectuels*. What struck me first in Paris in 1983 were the common elements, across the frontiers of the industrial democracies, in our situations. Critical thought was limited, the opportunity for critical practice even more so. This was the case not only for Reagan's United States but for France, governed by socialist intellectuals. The event was instructive in that some of the participants were French technocrats—the very sorts of figures I had criticized in the Carnegie Commission essay. *Autres pays, autres moeurs?* The technocrats in France (who were, of course, public officials and managers of state enterprises) at any rate seemed

avid for new ideas, but that is what the intellectuals at the conference most definitely lacked. Still, France in 1983 seemed to
be a society in which there was an educated public. I returned
to Paris for two months in the Spring of 1991 and had the dis-
concerting impression that this was no longer so. Fragmentation
and privatization marked French society as much as any other.

The general conclusion of both efforts, bound as they were
to specific times and places, still weighs upon me. Thought is
free when not tightly bound to one interpretation of the world,
but then it is also likely to float weightlessly in historical space.
Can social thought be both free and rooted? Can we live and
think at sufficient distance from the powers in society to maintain our independence, and still draw upon the moral energies
of engagement?

8

Students, Professors and Philosopher Kings

Introduction

The invitation to prepare a chapter giving "a critical view of the university: academia as a defender of the existing social order and its potentialities as a critic" was both an honor and an embarrassment. Honors are easily dealt with; embarrassments tend to prolong themselves. Have not much ink, typewriter ribbon, photocopy, and print been expended to treat precisely this theme? Universities in the United States, in Western and Eastern Europe, in Latin America, in Asia, and in Africa have been discussed *in extenso* (if not *ad absurdum*). Heads of state, ministers of education, rectors, presidents, and deans have delivered opinions of varying degrees of ponderosity and ponderability. The working professoriat has been heard from. Indeed, a new academic specialty has arisen from the ashes of academic conflagration: the study of universities themselves. The image of the phoenix comes to mind, but it is not entirely appropriate, as the fires which burned in some universities were never all-consuming. The owl of Minerva, that metaphysical bird, has flown off at too many dusks to be cited now. Some critics might turn to the Bible, but here the possibilities are too many: Lazarus, King Solomon's mines, and the Tower of Babel are but three. Perhaps we ought to impose a certain ascetic rigor upon ourselves and seek to discuss the university's problems in terms relatively free of imagery. Straightforward discourse, however, may be difficult. Imagery is useful when customary conventions of thought and fixed patterns of experience are dissolving. That is our present situation, and it is possible that straightforward discourse will make sense only when we can count upon a degree of institutional stability unattainable for the moment. Yet the idea of asceticism is attractive. A determined limitation of discussion to the essential issues (rather than the effort to resolve, in and through the universities, every problem of our society) may at least mark out the ground on which discourse can take place.

Certainly, asceticism has not been a prominent attribute of the student movement's contribution to the discussion. The student literature on universities is enormous. The energies invested in it, used for academic work, would have constituted prodigious dutifulness.[1] Indeed, the dutiful aspects of the recent deluge of literature on the university—whether written by students, teachers, or administrators—are striking. Analysis, criticism, and protest continue unabated. Have not all positions been taken, all objections mounted? Nothing has been left unsaid, or unwritten, in any number of languages. I have written on higher education recently, and I am exceedingly uncertain that I can say anything new.[2]

Embarrassment may be the beginning of wisdom. The student revolt may have resembled a ritual of rebellion and made all of us participants in a charade.[3] However, rituals do generally express real social and psychic conflicts in human societies, particularly those which defy easy resolution. The university has lacked clear self-definition, is confused as to its social role and political obligations, is divided internally, and is the object of public political dispute. These difficulties are not consequences of the student revolt. That revolt has refracted problems originating long before the conversion of academic self-reflection from a cottage industry to its present, multinational form. Every argument on the universities by now has a familiar ring. Suppose that we pose our dilemmas in terms which entrap us. We may have attained the limits of our capacities to think anew. Reality itself paralyzes our imaginations and blocks our efforts to create new ideas.

Two contrasting courses are open to us. We may take a principle on which many of us are agreed and implement it pragmatically. That the university ought to be an intellectual free market is, perhaps, the most widely professed principle of this kind. Of course, the term *intellectual* is just as important as the term *free market*. Not ideas of any sort, but ideas promulgated according to disciplined and publicly accepted

---

[1] Cockburn & Blackburn (1969), Leibfried (1967), Nagel (1969), Schnapp & Vidal-Naquet (1969), Wallerstein & Starr (1971).

[2] Birnbaum (1969*a*, 1970*a–d*, 1971*c*).

[3] Aron (1968), Brustein (1971), Habermas (1968), Meyerhoff (1971), Scheuch (1969).

procedures, have rights in the university. Empirically, we can conclude that university thought encompasses radical social criticism and a higher social apologetics, as well as all the positions between these poles. We may depict the university as a protected space for the most divergent and contradictory ideas, seek to minimize the costs of reconciling their often opposed social consequences, and attempt to enjoy the very different rewards brought by the different sorts of ideas. A pragmatic option of this kind is attractive. It enables us to situate debate on common ground. It allows us to work within limits which are conventional, but certainly not ignoble. Above all, it appears to respond to the stringent demands of reality. Beginning with the university as it is, we can weight the competing claims of tradition, immediate social pressure, and higher public interest. Perhaps, in the end, we shall arrive at a conception of the university's political role that is far more compelling than one derived from new principles as yet uninvented—perhaps, but there is no point to burdening the public with yet another gloss on our present alternatives just to declare them immutable.

I shall take another course. The university contributes immensely to society's thought, but usually does so in a fragmented fashion. It divides reality into separate sectors, advances mutually incompatible ideas, and promulgates contradictory values. To complicate matters further, it sometimes embarks upon social and political action itself. Even when it does not, other forces in the society use university-generated ideas for their own purposes. Is there an underlying unity in all this diversity, a philosophical meaning implicit in the current confusion? I am not sure that either unity or meaning can be established easily—particularly since I conceive of these end products of reflection as beginning points for academic policy. I am certain that it may be rewarding to examine the possibility that new conceptions of the university may be found, or developed.

In doing so, I shall necessarily tread on philosophical grounds. This chapter is not a treatise on the theory of knowledge, but it must touch on questions which cannot be left to philosophers alone. Much academic thought, particularly in the social sciences, is interpretative. We do not describe social processes with mathematical exactitude and observational rigor. Instead, we construct images of the social order which transcend particular data. Frequently, we make a rather hard distinction between the cognitive components in our thought and its evaluative dimensions. The two are not as separate as is sometimes supposed. We require a new understanding of cognition—and, beyond that, of science generally—if we are to think critically of the future of the academy.[4] I do not pretend to offer that view, but the assumption that one can be found is indispensable to this chapter.

---

[4] An interesting progression has taken place. Discussing the debate on academic freedom earlier in this century, Metzger shows how much of the argument for academic

A moment's reflection about the theme of the chapter may illustrate the direction we shall have to take. The university can criticize the social order, or it may defend it. We would do well, however, to avoid thinking of the academic mind as passing judgment on a world entirely outside it. Much of the recent discussion of the university has reversed this notation and has considered the academy as an agent of social action, if at times an unwitting one.[5] Total engagement, in other words, has been opposed to pure contemplation. That some parts of the university are engaged and others are contemplative is obvious enough. Engagement, however, presupposes previous contemplative activity. Contemplation, further, may provide points of reference and directions for engagement. The two are not as separate, then, as simplicity would demand. I propose, now, to sketch some of the dimensions of the problem.

Implicit Partisanship

It would be difficult enough to consider the university as politically partisan. We might distinguish between partisanship by the university in its corporate identity and the political activities of some of its members or segments. I do attempt, later on, to examine these questions. Difficulty is compounded, however, when we examine the implicit partisanship of the university. Activities ostensibly devoid of political intent (and frequently actually devoid of it) may have indirect but important political consequences. The university may align itself with the ruling elites of a divided society, and it may serve these most effectively just when rendering services to their subjects. Finally, higher education is of itself a valuable economic good. In distributing it, the university participates in the play of market forces in the society. Put another

---

freedom rested on an unquestioned belief in liberal values (Hofstadter & Metzger, 1955, pp. 407ff.). When Harvard published its report *General Education in a Free Society* (1945), the inculcation and defense of liberal values had become an explicit task of higher education. These values, in other words, were no longer regarded as immutable components of the setting of higher education. The problem brings us into realms properly philosophical. The writings of Juergen Habermas constitute an attempt—in the midst of the turbulence of the German university—to state the problems in terms adequate to modern social science and contemporary philosophy. See Habermas (1969) and his most recently translated *Knowledge and Human Interests* (1971b).

    [5] The Cox Commission, investigating the Columbia University disturbances of 1968, has stated the problem in fairly clear terms: "Choices have to be made: there are not enough hours and resources to go around and often the alternatives conflict with one another. Moreover, the more the application of knowledge brings the university into involvement with society, the more apparent it becomes that the choices depend on judgments of social and political policy. . . . Making decisions on the application of knowledge to society must, to some degree, politicize the university" (*Crisis at Columbia*, 1968, p. 21).

way, we may say that even if the university eschewed practical activity and professional instruction, it would still be an element in the relations between social classes.

The university's partisanship may take several forms. It may endorse the goals and policies of parties to social conflict in the larger society. The university may issue judgments on social and political conditions, their causes, and their putative consequences. These judgments may incite groups outside the university to act, or they may reinforce them in courses of action already begun. The university may appeal from the concrete public—fragmented or inert or ignorant—to a public supposedly more real, if in fact ideal.[6] These partisan interventions may be highly focused, direct forays into the political sphere. They may be indirect, seeking to influence politics by working upon the spirits of the intellectual elite, and of the elites responsive to the latter.

Examples are plentiful enough. During the May rising of 1968 in France, ad hoc bodies of teachers, students, and staff declared themselves for a larger social revolution. (The representativeness of these bodies was later challenged. Their institutionalized successors, established by the Faure reforms of 1968, have generally confined themselves to the less exalted and far more familiar task of attacking the government for not giving the universities enough money.[7]) In May of 1969, the teachers and students of Amherst College addressed a letter to President Nixon on national policy.[8] In the aftermath of the 1970 protest on the Cambodian incursion, President Nixon appointed Vanderbilt's Chancellor Alexander Heard as a spokesman for the universities at the White House. Heard was clear about his mission: It was to represent the universities to the White House, and not the other way around (*The New York Times*, May 11, 1970, p. 15; July 9, 1970, p. 21; July 24, 1970, p. 1). The universities were not authorized to take these steps. The institutional and legal issues involved are still obscure. The fact is that university institutions as such took positions on matters of public policy.

The American university's teaching in the social and administrative sciences has frequently been criticized on political grounds. The past decade of criticism has made us extremely self-conscious, but the

---

[6] Arrowsmith (1970). See also the classical statement of the Regents of the University of Wisconsin (1894) in defense of academic freedom. The celebrated 1915 Declaration of Principles of the American Association of University professors is even more explicit: "The public interest is served when the vagaries of public opinion are disregarded" ("Report of the Committee. . . ." 1915).

[7] See Birnbaum (1970c) and Alliot (1971). Rector Alliot was a leader in the professorial movement of May 1968 and subsequently an advisor to the (ex-)Minister of Education, Edgar Faure.

[8] April 24, 1969, letter to President Nixon from Dr. Plimpton.

tradition of criticism (from every position on the spectrum of political opinion) is not a decade but nearly a century old. The most profound political criticism we can make is a philosophical one. The university develops categories for the analysis of the social order.[9] These may legitimate that order by accepting its forms and boundaries as given or by discouraging thought in terms of other social possibilities. The technical discussion of *reification* in social thought is not invariably light or lucid. However, a good deal of social and administrative science does employ concepts which reify the social order by taking its own notions and limits as definitive. The study of public opinion, for instance, has often enough taken the liberal ideal of free and morally sovereign citizens as if it were a reality. The recent varieties of political behaviorism have made the opposite mistake, by supposing that the ideal is impossibly vague—and, in any case, almost certainly unattainable. Social science has flattered the citizens by assuming that they are intellectually and morally autonomous, or it has insulted them by supposing that they respond blindly to mechanical pressures. It has far less often assumed a pedagogic task, that of helping nominally free citizens to become actually free. To do that, social scientists would have to criticize their own work in terms both political and philosophical.

It is necessary, however, to venture into these depths to discuss the political implications of social science. Its emphasis on some themes and its exclusion of certain problems may give a pronounced political cast to analyses of society supposedly objective. I shall give two examples. Until the Poznan riots in Poland and the revolution in the German Democratic Republic in 1953, American studies of the Communist states insisted on their monolithic character. Our specialists on communism might have served us better had they not mirrored our prejudices so faithfully. The prevalent assumptions of the makers of American foreign policy need not have served as working hypotheses for scholarship. Poverty became the object of much public interest in the early 1960s as a result of the civil rights movement, the reception of Michael Harrington's book, and a policy decision by the Kennedy government to tackle this problem. Most American economists and sociologists, however, had previously chosen to work on other problems. The rediscovery of conflict in Communist society and of poverty in our own were not consequences of the immanent movement of social thought. The cases are different, of course. Events in Eastern Europe were such that previous stereotypes could not be maintained. Domestically, a political decision to reduce poverty resulted in the mobilization of academic resources through the reallocation of research funds. The radical groupings in the various academic and professional

---

[9] I have dealt with this theme before in "The Arbitrary Disciplines" (1969*a*).

organizations have often criticized the scholarly disciplines for this sort of unconscious or semiconscious partisanship.[10]

Thus far, I have written of the "university" in an extremely general way. The question of the corporate self-definition of the university is difficult. Meanwhile, a considerable segment of public opinion persists in its own notions of the university's corporate nature, attributing to it a mechanical and uniform character it does not possess. Were the matter one of governance, it would be relatively straightforward. Trustees govern American universities, even if they have allocated specific areas of competence and power to faculties (Rauh, 1969). Were it a matter of scholarly competence, the problem would be more complicated, but not impossible of solution, although the criteria of competence in some fields are equivocal. Faculties have scholarly competence, but they are not the only university group to have interests or opinions. The precise limits of scholarly competence ar hard to establish, and however imprecise these may be, some scholars exceed them with remorseless consistency. Finally, we must consider the public authority of the university, the respectful hearing given to university pronouncements in the society at large. (A good deal of public hostility to the universities is also a tribute, exaggerating their power and influence beyond measure.) Possibly, the university's public authority is a residue of its theological past. Possibly, it rests on a naïve belief in the power of knowledge, a vulgarized Saint-Simonianism. Possibly, it is a remnant of the liberal belief in enlightened moral inquiry. I shall examine in later discussions the ways in which contemporary universities have departed from their liberal antecedents, but clearly they still profit from them. Finally, some of the university's contemporary authority rests on the public's perception of the relationship between academic knowledge and power. Political pronouncements issuing from the university are often obscure about the bases of their claims. Do they rest on the scholarly competence of the institution, or do they appeal to other legitimations? When we consider the prevailing uncertainty and dispute as to authority and power within the university, we understand why the debate on the university's political role continues.[11]

Most expressions of explicit political opinions by the university have been the work of particular members of it: individual teachers or groups of teachers, individual students or groups of students. They have not

[10] See the publications of the New University Conference, and in particular *The Student Rebellion* (1969b). The several causes in the disciplinary and professional associations have also initiated publication programs. See, for instance, *Science for the People*, a journal published by the Scientists and Engineers for Social and Political Action. See also Ohmann (1968).

[11] See Carnegie Commission on Higher Education (1971) and American Association of University Professors (1971).

claimed to speak for the university as a whole, but they have used the public authority given them by their university membership to claim attention for their pronouncements. The individualized or segmented nature of political pronouncement in the university (the term *political* designates pronouncements which refer to the distribution of power in society) has resulted in one rather common political theory of the university. On this account of the problem, the university is a protected space in which political views may be developed, expressed, and criticized. Indeed, it is the university's duty to society to maximize political debate within its walls—as a guarantee of its moral seriousness and to provide society with ideas it might otherwise never consider.[12] The university as such cannot endorse any of the ideas expressed by its members, but on the same ground it cannot censor these. We may recall the celebrated dictum by Harvard's A. Lawrence Lowell that the university could not censor its teachers' ideas because it might appear to be endorsing the ideas of those whom it did not censor.[13] What the university could do was to offer public guarantees of the competence and neutrality of those in its service. These very terms, *competence* and *neutrality*, have been used by the scholarly authorities on the history of academic freedom in the United States to describe the justification for allowing teachers liberty of political expression (Hofstadter & Metzger, 1955, pp. 400ff.). It is clear that the justification rests, *inter alia*, on a theory of ultimate consensus: Views of social truth are initially partial, but in the end are reconcilable. They are reconcilable because the search for truth presupposes disinterestedness and common standards of judgment on the part of all who are engaged in it. The notion of a free competition of ideas in political society is similar. (These justifications touch student political activity only insofar as we can depict it as part of the learning process.)

There is no such widely agreed-upon justification for a corporate pronouncement by the university as a whole on political questions. Indeed, given the divergence of viewpoint among students, teachers, administrators, and trustees, the elaboration of a justification for a corporate university politics would stretch the abilities of a generation of casuists. The Carnegie Commission, in its recent recommendations, summarized the prevailing academic opinion when it said that the institution has the "right and obligation not to take a position, as an institution, in electoral politics or on public issues, except on those issues which directly affect its autonomy, the freedom of its members, its financial support, and its academic functions" (Carnegie Commission on Higher Education, 1971, p. 40). A substantial segment of uni-

---

[12] Regents of the University of Wisconsin (1894), "Report of the Committee . . ." (1915).

[13] A. Lawrence Lowell, quoted in Hofstadter and Metzger (1955, p. 503).

versity opinion, however, would disagree. That disagreement has a number of components, but an essential one is the theory of the administrative partiality of the university.

The theory has two components. The first concerns the university's endorsement, in effect, of the work of its teachers. Since that work inevitably entails an evaluative or political component—explicit or implicit in content, direct or indirect in consequence—the university in appointing and rewarding teachers cannot claim adherence to standards of neutrality and objectivity. As an institution, it assumes responsibility for the development of thought in one rather than another political direction. The same argument extends, of course, to grants to university scholars by external agencies. Indeed, a political scientist, Marshall Windmiller, has called for a form of ideological pluralism in the allocation of research moneys.[14] It may be noted that this pronounced negation of A. Lawrence Lowell's thesis does not rest on the impossibility of objectivity in scholarship. It suffices, for its proponents, to assert that at any given moment, scholarship is insufficiently objective. Their appeal, then, is from partiality to a larger or higher standard of truth.

A rather different set of arguments (although the two are often confounded) concerns the university's role as a social agency. In rendering a multiplicity of services to institutions outside itself, the university assists in the pursuit of their political goals. The university enters the arena of interests—and often does so in an unreflective and unacknowledged fashion. The demand that the university contribute to the solution of urgent social problems (the decay of the inner city, race relations, the quality and quantity of health services) is sometimes a demand that the university reverse its alliances—or, at least, contract rather different ones (Birnbaum, 1969; Lynd, 1970). That these choices are frequently political has been increasingly acknowledged, and the recent suggestion by the President's Commission on Campus Unrest that the university reconsider its activities in these areas was, not least, an effort to pacify the campus. Interestingly, the Commission did not suggest a withdrawal from service activities but, rather, a redirection

---

[14] See "International Relations . . . ," (in Roszak, 1968, p. 130). Professor Windmiller is also quoted, interestingly, in Wallerstein and Starr (1971, vol. 2) in defense of the dismissal of a radical colleague for violating academic propriety by leading students in disruptive activity. See the exchange between Windmiller and Gerassi, the colleague in question (Wallerstein and Starr, 1971, pp. 341–370). Windmiller's comments make it clear that his conception of university legitimacy rests on a pluralistic philosophy. Insofar as the university is genuinely pluralistic, with respect to the availability of intellectual options, it is legitimate. The dispute with Gerassi concerned not the latter's opinions but his conviction that the pluralistic university could not exist under current conditions: the fraudulently pluralistic one, therefore, was a proper target for unlimited attack.

of these—in directions more congenial to protesting white and black students and to radical faculty (*Report of the President's Commission on Campus Unrest*, 1970, pp. 191–195). A rather differently composed body—the Cox Commission, which investigated the Columbia University disturbances of 1968—had reached similar conclusions previously. The Cox Commission, however, was rather more explicit about the political and economic dimensions of the choices at issue (*Crisis at Columbia*, 1968).

The university is a social agency in another, more primary sense. Access to the university and the acquisition of a degree are modes of occupational and social selection.[15] Admitting some applicants and refusing others, setting conditions of entrance which automatically preclude university education for a substantial percentage of the relevant age group, the university in effect controls entry to entire strata of occupational opportunity—and, therewith, the life chances of an entire generation. The recent extension of higher education, accompanied by explicit emphases on the internal differentiation of the higher educational system, is also a response to the demands of the economy for a different sort of labor force.[16] The relationship between the economic and cultural functions of the university is complex, but it cannot be said that this relationship has received the attention it requires from the university itself.

A hitherto irreducible false consciousness has marked the university's approach to the confused and contradictory relations between its cultural and economic roles. The student movement's attack on that false consciousness has been heavy-handed. In a parody of the Marxist theory of the extraction of surplus value from the working class by capitalism, some student movement theorists (often faculty members) have depicted grading as the extraction of surplus intellectual value from students. The analogy presupposes that students do add directly to society's stock of intellectual capital, but here it is inexact. Heavy-handed it may have been, but the student movement has had the merit of forcing discussion of the problem. It is far from absurd to suggest that universities do educate important segments of the labor force. The university educates, but it also engages in occupational socialization.[17]

The most profound political influence of the university is its impact on the minds and spirits of the citizens who pass through it (Withey et al. 1971). It would be reassuring to record unequivocally enlightening

---

[15] Blau and Duncan (1967) suggest that education in turn probably reflects the continuing influence of class structure. A somewhat different view is found in Bell (1971*a*).

[16] See the valuable work of Samuel Bowles, exemplified in his paper entitled "Contradictions in U.S. Higher Education." [Published in *The University and Revolution*, Gary Weaver and James Weaver, eds. (Englewood Cliffs: Prentice Hall, 1969).]

[17] Klawitter (1969). The works of Paul Goodman touch on this theme, as does Ivan Illich's proposal for "deschooling."

results of higher education, everywhere. We may recall, however, the disturbing observation that national socialism conquered the German universities before it won the streets. The educated were early and important recruits to Italian and central European fascism between the wars. In the United States, university education does make a difference. University graduates are often broader in outlook than others. As the number of university graduates grows, differences within the group may also grow larger. These may reflect the differences between the universities its members will have experienced (Spaeth & Greeley, 1970). Further, the initially broadening effect of education is generally narrowed by the graduates' subsequent immersion in community, family, and occupation. These qualifications are important. Nevertheless, it is essential to see that the chief political activity of the university is education.

The conclusion is traditional, but it prevents us from losing sight of the university's primary function. The institution's active role in society is important, but we would do well to think strenuously about what universities teach. Curricular problems are of course related to the university's multiple entanglements in society. The university's specific vocation, however, obliges us to think of higher education not simply as a derivative of other social processes. The current notion that the university is an especially efficacious agency of direct political change is dubious. This chapter is intended as a modest contribution to a new sobriety. My point in analyzing the university's bondage to society is not to arrive at the excessively banal conclusion that everything is related to everything else. Neither do I suppose that university reform is the *via regis* of general social change, much less a beginning of social revolution. Rather, I hope to suggest that some freedom from bondage may be attained, if the price for it is paid. The first task is to examine the nature of our present bondage. Perhaps, within it, we may find unexpected, if small, possibilities of liberation.

The Liberal University

Earlier, I remarked that imagery has its uses. I plan to employ two images to describe the university of yesterday and the university of today: the liberal university and, as its dramatic antagonist (or bastard offspring), the technocratic one. The colleagues who commented, upon reading an earlier version of this chapter, that the liberal university may be my own invention have understood my metaphorical intent. I note that none denied the existence of the technocratic university, even if some insisted, quite rightly, that it contains important liberal elements. I have used the metaphor for reasons of economy, which are not entirely different from aesthetic ones. Designating types of universities in terms of the larger political society in which they are embedded may sharpen our perception. We have to examine, after all, the ways in which the educational process were and are related to the political one. I think it possible to show that the relationship has been most pervasive when it has been one of consonance and correspondence rather than one of domination and direction. The university has formed minds which proved themselves subsequently attuned to the rhythms of the society, organized for the mastery of its tasks, and inwardly adapted to the nuances of its culture.

We have recognized the quantitative transformation of the university, but we have as yet to understand its changes, conceptually. The demise of the liberal university (whatever historical vocabulary has been employed by different scholars) has been treated as a fact—deplored by some, welcomed by others, and thought inevitable by nearly all.[18] Analysis and description have not always been free of a nostalgic pathos. I am skeptical about assertions of the linear continuity of our own university with the medieval one, and that for historical reasons (Chenu, 1957; LeGoff, 1957). Medieval culture had a relatively coherent vision of things eternal and temporal. Medieval thought embodied the effective sovereignty of philosophy in an epoch in which the physical sciences were still empirical. Medieval society was conflict-ridden enough, but its conflicts were fought out within defined boundaries. (In that social order, the bourgeoisie were quite literally those who lived in cities.) The use of medieval academic structures as models for modern reform strikes me as hopelessly anachronistic. We should be wrong, moreover, to think of medieval universities as inexorably dedicated to the pursuit of the beatitude of truth. Kings, popes, bishops, and princes were continually intervening in their affairs. Theological inquiry was politically charged. The late medieval universities condemned Luther's heresies, but also harbored many crypto-Protestants (Schwiebert, 1950).

It is not nostalgia but historical analysis which has led me to designate the early modern university in terms derived from the political society of which it was a part. European and American society in the nineteenth and twentieth centuries experienced the emergence, the (temporary) consolidation, and the increasingly precipitous decline of a liberal social order. Liberal ideals were developed in France and Britain, were transplanted to the United States with considerable success, and were influential if never fully assimilated in Germany. Moreover,

---

[18] Aron (1968, fn 1). See also Nisbet (1971) and the protests of the German defenders of the liberal university, Maier and Zöller (1971). Critical views of the liberal university in its German version will be found in Habermas (1971*a*) and Sontheimer (1971). See also the special issue of *the Public Interest*, "The Universities," Fall 1968, and the critical essay by Lasch and Genovese (1969), as well as Lasch's essay in Voss and Ward (1970). Bouwsma's essay in the same volume may also be read with profit. Finally, see Wolin and Schaar (1970).

the continental societies differed fundamentally from the Anglo-Saxon ones. Roman law and the state bureaucracy marked the former, and common law and considerable local self-government characterized the latter. The varieties of capitalist development were also different, and the resultant market structures engendered very different class systems. Compare the Evangelical business and professional elites of late-nineteenth-century England with their bureaucratized counterparts in Bismarck's Germany. Contrast the Boston Brahmins at Harvard to the elites who made their way into the Grandes Écoles of Paris. Surely, if the conception of a liberal university is not a fiction, that of liberal society is. Why not employ a more concrete term which does not round off the jagged edges of history? Would it not be more appropriate to write of bourgeois society, and therefore of the bourgeois university?

I still prefer the term *liberal university*. Liberalism describes the ideals of bourgeois society, ideals it was in the end unable to maintain, much less transmit. For a time, at least, the bourgeois university was the bearer of those ideals—in the explicit values it communicated, in the modes of spiritual and intellectual discipline it embodied, and in the methods of work it objectified. The very contradiction between liberal ideals and the society which professed these was to give rise to the successor to the liberal university, the technocratic one (Veysey, 1965). That anticipates the subsequent argument, but will do to explain the choice of the term. The purpose of the analysis, after all, is not to describe a static past but to inquire into the origins of a turbulent and conflicted present.

What were the cultural ideals of liberalism? In the first instance, the liberal university treated intellectual work as an individual performance. The cultural tradition, in other words, was real only insofar as it became part of the conduct of life by autonomous persons. Their road to autonomy was the use of reason. The liberal understanding of reason, however, did not make of it an independent or metaphysical entity. To be reasonable meant to respect science, to arrive at orderly (reasoned) moral judgments, to bring rationality to the working of social institutions. The development of the natural sciences, the enlargement of our knowledge of society, and the improvement of our capacity for moral reasoning were the aims of the liberal university. The assumption of a progressive direction to history was an essential element in liberal culture. Not the pursuit of knowledge alone, but its moral organization and direction, made learning liberal.

The notion that knowledge and morality were connected had another, political assumption. The persons who possessed liberal culture were supposed to be able to apply it in the institutions of the society. Indeed, those institutions were defined as liberal precisely because they were supposedly open to redirection and alteration by a rational citizenry. Liberalism held that the learning transmitted by the university,

both substantive and moral, exercised a continuous influence upon society. Educated individuals supplied a continuous self-correction to institutional development.

Did the larger society really function in this fashion? The graduates
of the liberal university entered a social order no less fixed than any
other. The working of the market, the class system, and the state set
limits upon the citizenry. It is certainly important to recall that only a
very small proportion of the latter had a university education and,
therewith, full access to liberal culture. Liberalism understood itself as
a political philosophy appropriate to autonomous individuals, making
choices about the framework of their society. Viewed from the vantage
point of a fixed social order, liberalism was something quite different.
It was a scheme of explanation and justification which enabled the
elites of bourgeois society to go about their business effectively, and in
good conscience. That society offered far less scope for moral choice
than the liberal ideals of the university supposed. It did demand effective performance from individuals with responsibilities and power: the
university prepared them for that performance (see Faber, 1957). We
may define the liberal university as one in which the transmission of
knowledge and moral education were joined to shape individuals. On
this view, the intellectual openness of the liberal university was less
important than its character as a community of culture. It is interesting
that some academic spokesmen for liberalism inserted reserve clauses
in their doctrines. In situations of political conflict, liberalism often embraced restraint and even constraint.[19]

Sometimes, the migration of ideas illuminates their inner tensions.
Max Weber, the great German sociologist of the early twentieth century, was in many respects a German liberal. He favored rationality in
the university and even denounced its politicization, not an altogether
popular view in imperial Germany. However, in politics he sympa-
thized with doctrines not alone of *raison d'état* but of *Machtpolitik*. In
the end, he opted for sheer irrationalism in the choice of moral and
political values, denying in despair that these could be arrived at by
moral discourse.[20] The German social and political setting was strikingly different from the Anglo-American one. A coherent liberalism
could work only in the absence of institutions like those of Germany:
highly centralized capitalism, the bureaucratic state, and the adoption
by the educated of the ethos of state service. Liberalism really required

[19] Nicholas Murray Butler's highly elastic interpretation of liberal principles is indicative of this tendency. See Veysey (1965, pp. 381ff.). The general background in the
movement of American thought will be found in White (1949) and Lasch (1965).

[20] See the classical essays "Science as a Vocation" and "Politics as a Vocation" in
Gerth and Mills (1946) and the intense disputes at the German Sociological Association's
1964 centenary celebration of Weber's birth (Stammer, 1965).

free-market capitalism, a state zealously watched by its citizens, and pluralistic institutions as a sphere for the activity of the educated. Precisely these things, however, have changed in the societies (like our own) which were originally liberal in politics.

The strength of the liberal university was drawn from institutional continuity in the world it served. As long as it educated new bourgeois generations who could count on entering an intact bourgeois society— whether in its British, French, or American variants—it could promulgate a relatively coherent intellectual and moral vision. Education consisted of the academic and moral formation of a spiritual elite. The phrase seems strange, perhaps, when applied to those who were unwillingly analyzed (at a distance) by Freud, derided by the Bohemians, and anathematized by the modernists in art. There is a lesson to be learned, however, from the fact that those still raised in the bourgeois tradition could undertake psychoanalysis, comprehend Bohemianism, and patronize the modernists. Their sensibility and the attacks on it were compounded of the same language, the same conception of character. The spirituality of the liberal university assumed that the world could be mastered by the conscious effort of a generation: reason, science, and morality were modes of cultural creation.

The transformation of bourgeois society into something very different precipitated a decomposition of these notions. Reason was fragmented, so much so that its precise identity and location became matters of argument. Wherever it was to be found, it could be located neither in cultural tradition nor in the individual judgment. Science became, at once, instrumentalized and isolated. Indisputably a power in the affairs of men, its connection to a general notion of culture dissolved. As for morality, social and individual, the universities offered large debates and small convictions. The system of cultural exchange between the university and the large society broke down. Its graduates could take with them into that society a certain conversational facility; some valuable notions about the past, and possibly a set of techniques for acquiring and assimilating information. They did not acquire a coherent conception of culture which could infuse their lives. That conception had disintegrated.

We can use yet another metaphor, that of cultural reproduction (see Bourdieu & Passeron, 1971). (Just as the economy in its productive cycle reproduces society's means of existence, the institutions of culture reproduce its means of interpreting itself and the world.) The liberal university claimed that it could reproduce the world. It supposed that the education it provided enabled its graduates to give cultural continuity to society while mastering its tasks. The world of the contemporary university defies reproduction in this way. Continuity and mastery have not disappeared entirely, but they have been seriously attenuated. The inner coherence of the liberal university has dissolved, as liberal culture has broken against the resistance of a world it never made—and cannot remake.

The Technocratic University

Some time ago, an experienced and distinguished university administrator, himself a working social scientist and a student of universities in their new social functions, told me that there is nothing wrong with universities, except for the problem of the undergraduate curriculum in liberal arts. (am paraphrasing perhaps, but not—I trust—in a tendentious way.) It is not necessary to indulge in nostalgia, however, to insist that the liberal arts curriculum informed the rest of the university with coherence and a sense of vocation. The professional schools applied the principles communicated in basic instruction in the learned disciplines, the graduate schools enlarged knowledge on the disciplines' frontiers, and the educated citizenry carried into the world a set of reflective principles which could guide it.

I use the term *technocratic university* to describe the present one. Like all concepts, it has its difficulties. An unmistakably pejorative cast attaches to it. The notion of a technocracy is itself not entirely clear—even among the experts.[21] Let us define a technocratic society, not entirely arbitrarily, as one in which science and technology have become important instruments of administration, production, and power. Technocratic culture instrumentalizes reason and fragments hitherto intact cultural and symbolic totalities. The liberal university reproduced a world, even if its sense of freedom was illusory. The technocratic university has no such pretensions. It supplies (indispensable) means to a world which can reproduce itself. The unit of reproduction has changed—from the person and spirit of the individual shaped by the educational process to the agencies and institutions using knowledge. In the circumstances, it is not surprising that the technocratic university has no center, nor even a doctrine. It has as much or as little coherence as society imparts to it, directly and indirectly, in imposing tasks upon it.

From this point of view, the position taken by a notable segment of the left is a distorted mirror image of the position it attributes to the right—or to a vaguely circumscribed technocratic middle. The view that the university should serve new publics, different clients, is not a view that the university should reclaim the autonomy enjoyed—at least formally—by the liberal university. It is a view which enjoins upon the university a self-definition in terms of the tasks imposed upon it. Other

---

[21] Bell (1971*a*), Birnbaum (1971*b*, pp. 367ff.), Lefebvre (1967), Lichtheim (1963), Touraine (1971).

varieties of this position, in the form of demands for "deschooling" or "universities without walls," entail no less of a renunciation of the autonomy of the university. The crumbling and gradual disappearance of liberalism seems to have effaced the very claim made by its university—that thought is autonomous and potentially sovereign and that the university in its liberal form is a privileged site of thought.

The Tension Between Concepts of Universities

In face, the antithesis of liberal and technocratic university conceptions is too schematic. The conceptions coexist, with a maximum of tension—and the dialogue between them resembles nothing so much as a dialogue of the deaf. It is for this reason that so much confusion exists about the university's political function. In the positions taken in accord with the liberal tradition, standards of principle and of utility both claim coherence in terms of an image of a liberal society. On this account of the polity, it functions according to choice and, after deliberation, to maintain—and create—values. The technocratic vocabulary is a very different one. That it is also a discourse with a strong evaluative component no one would deny—especially the intelligent technocrats.[22] Technocratic objectives, however, concern the optimization of resource allocation (including, of course, human resources) and the supply of knowledge (as if it were a commodity—which, for many contemporary purposes, it must certainly is). If any model of the polity infuses the technocratic one, it is a model of a political servomechanism. The university serves as a brain, with limited functions—keeping society on a course determined by inputs into the university. The metaphor is strained—but the operating conception is no less so. What is essential, for present purposes, is that in the technocratic conception, value choice—and value creation—have migrated from the university: they have somehow become immanent in social processes themselves. (Again, there is a significant left parody of this conception. The view that educational content is nothing, but that process is all—education as a very long trip—reflects a total loss of faith in the autonomy of reason. The alliance between the advocates of a totally antinomian education and those who favor new, community-service universities may not be accidental. Both factions unite in despair over the capacities of thought.) Small wonder, then, that some of the new university's analysts have proposed that it would be logical to carry the conception of hierarchy in university systems to its logical conclusion—an elite sector

---

[22] Organization for Economic Cooperation and Development (1971). The document in question, a report by a panel of advisers to the OECD in science policy, is remarkably illuminating. In it, the advisers call for a redirection of scientific work in the hope of developing a drastically improved system of social measurement and control.

for thought, a separate sector for the application of thought, and a lower sector still for training.[23] Plato's *Republic*—in rather American guise? What is left out, of course, is precisely the notion of an educated citizenry—a legacy of the liberal university, and not a contemptible one.

The Public's Concern

These historical tendencies have altered the university. They are inextricably fused, of course, with the enormous quantitative expansion of universities. The change in scale, the extraordinary differentiation of the modern university, has inevitably resulted in a change of function. Neither expansion nor differentiation, however, can relieve us of the moral necessity of finding humane purposes to reshape these functions. History has not left unaltered, of course, the polity and the public, and new demands upon the university reflect these changes. A sector of the public, let it be said, is frightened. Did not the *New York Times,* awhile ago, quote a citizen of Middletown (Muncie, Indiana) as saying that he feared nothing so much as a college professor (Whitman, 1970)? He was a father preparing to send a child through higher education: the putative economic gains must have been matched by the supposed spiritual threat. But what threat? Loss of cultural continuity, abandonment of familial and local values, new modes of thought and being—or the painful infliction (along with the other things) of a sense of cultural inferiority upon persons with a dim sense of having been cheated in their lives? It is difficult to give a definite answer. The recent rediscovery of the American working and lower middle classes has hardly gone far enough to permit us to reconstruct the inner structure of their thought. That many Americans view the university as already a center of counterculture is clear—but what, precisely, they object to is not. Social and sexual experimentation, critical ideas, the predominance of the young: these are the usual answers. They clearly object to students who accept public subsidies and work very little, if at all. But suppose that they object, as well, to intellectual discipline, abstract thought, a cosmopolitan ethos? In other words, they may reject both the oppositional university of the new student culture and the old liberal and the new technocratic one.

The public demand upon the university, that it should contribute to individual and collective economic welfare, is clear (Eulau & Quin-

---

[23] James Coleman, in his chapter in Carnegie Commission on Higher Education, *Content and Context,* ed. Carl Kaysen (1973), does not entirely escape this. The tendency is very general: Mass or democratic systems of higher education usually eventuate in internally stratified ones. Bell (1970) summarizes much of the current argument.

ley, 1970). What else is expected of the university by the public is difficult to say. A contribution to the general spiritual welfare, perhaps—but not in terms that would be recognized as such by many of those, in and outside the universities, who debate these matters (Wicker, 1971). Not the least of the problems before us, then, is that we work in a context of public opinion, with pronounced points of negation. The positive ones are hard to fix.

Public opinion, of course, does not make politics in our society. It follows directives, advice, and persuasion from our elites. The recent debate on universities in this country has been held, generally, among the educated—or, at least, among those with college degrees. The inchoate hopes and fears of the rest of the population have been taken account of, used, or even exploited. They have not dictated policy, and if they have set limits upon it, it is hard to establish these with any precision. David Riesman has reminded me that in some states, power struggles among local elites and counterelites have taken place at the expense of the universities. Even though educated, these elites have not hesitated to exploit popular anxieties and prejudices against universities. All the more reason, therefore, for those within the universities to attain some clarity on their own position with respect to their political role.

Continuities and Discontinuities

The reading, or rereading, of the history of academic freedom offers no unequivocal lesson to us. When the famed seven teachers at Goettingen were dismissed in 1837 for having criticized a royal decree, the motto imposed upon the day was "Mannesmut vor Koenigsthronen" ("Manly courage even before the thrones of kings"). Many celebrated cases of academic defiance, upon examination, turn out to be somewhat less clear-cut (Veysey, 1965). Not kings, but the far less imposing although more pervasive influence of public opinion—however ill defined—have constituted a limit to academic freedom. Matters are made more complex by the fact the university authorities (in the United States, trustees and administrators) have at times anticipated public opinion by imposing sanctions on those thought likely to offend it grievously. Finally, the academics themselves have usually wrought codes of conduct which expressed limits set by the academic community on its members—limits, no doubt, cast somewhat wider than those congenial to some publics or some university authorities, but limits nevertheless.

The social organization of all intellectual activity renders rather imaginary the notion of solitary spirits defying convention and consensus.[24] Even Freud, at odds with academic medicine, worked to gather about him a group of collaborators (Jones, 1953–1957). Indeed, one of the more interesting (and, as yet, substantially unwritten) chapters in the history of thought may be entitled "the socialization of dissent." Critical ideas require development, and development in turn requires response and resonance—even critical or antagonistic response. The so-called bourgeois critics of Marxist economics and sociology, from Boehm-Bawerk to Aron, have contributed much to the emergence of a modernized Marxism—precisely by recognizing Marxism's claims as legitimate matter for academic scrutiny and by (in effect) admitting serious Marxists to the company of scholars. Academicization may rub the polemical or cutting edge off some doctrines, but it is often a pre-condition of their survival beyond those rare moments of inspiration (and even rarer ones of genius) in which they are created. I shall ex-amine, below, in more detail the modes of academic organization for the processing—I use an industrial term advisedly—of ideas. For the moment, it suffices to recall that universities are concerned not only with knowledge in a quantitative and tangible sense but also with the ideas (sometimes radical and new) which organize and generate knowledge. The frequently adduced nineteenth-century examples (Marx, Mill, and Spencer—among others—outside the university, Renan ejected from it) are upon examination not entirely convincing for the argu-ment that original and critical ideas flourish only outside universities. The thinkers in question were dependent upon a high culture with a substantial academic basis. Our contemporary problem is one of find-ing the optimal conditions for a university culture that can generate ideas: this, too, will be considered a bit further on.

External Alliances

The immediate social relationships of intellectual production, then, are important. Of equal importance, however, are markets for ideas—and, to continue the analogy, investments in their production. The history of academic freedom, I have said, gives us few unequivocal lessons. It does suggest, however, that academics are most undisturbed (I do not use the term *free*) when allied to protective groups outside the univer-sity. Those alliances have their servitudes: consider the vast and at times profound output of the German imperial universities in the social sci-ences—and the inability of the vast majority of the German academi-cally educated (in politics, the professions, and the state) to compre-hend the dimensions of their national and social problem (Ringer, 1969). Consider the mid-nineteenth-century American college teacher, in bondage to a clerical board of trustees and under the vigilant eye of a

---

[24] Coser (1965). See also T. Kuhn (1970).

clergyman president. Little wonder that this group of men did not develop deep anticipations of the process of secularization which was about to break over American culture (Rudolph, 1962). Their own intellectual perspectives were defined by a theological frame of reference, just as the Germans—in spiritual harmony with the class and the culture which so esteemed the professoriat—accepted the imperial regime's ideology. The lay republican morality promulgated by the philosophers and historians of the Third Republic was quite consonant with the views of the educated French bourgeoisie. The proponents of these themes, however, so convinced themselves of their truth that they overlooked the fact that these had been developed in a conflict with the integralists. The latter's interpretation of French tradition took very different forms: the enlightened French professoriat was surprised by the texture and temper of the Vichy regime (Aron, 1971; Thibaudet, 1927). Chomsky's portrait of a segment of the new American professoriat—living in a world defined by federal agencies, the opinion of our ruling elites, and concrete rewards in the form of posts, commissions, and grants—is all the more regrettable for its accuracy (Chomsky, 1967). Ostensibly, the university addresses the entire nation. In fact, it works with (not necessarily for) a highly limited part of it. It is not surprising that the university's immediate public appreciates what we may term *ideological reassurance.* It may, indeed, even appreciate a form of creativity—providing that it is consonant with its experience and requirements. Those American academics who in the 1950s and early 1960s labored on problems of education, welfare, health policy, and the cities may fairly complain that they were ignored when the nation's elites were preoccupied with rather narrow conceptions of national security. By the middle of the decade 1960–1970, academic specialists on these problems of American social structure could complain about neither want of attention nor what of resources.[25] In the words of a recurrent mode of critical discourse, they had been "co-opted."[26] Does a notion of political purity as entirely oppositional, of the spirit as working most independently when solitary or indeed beleaguered, infuse the conception of co-optation? In the current literature of university criticism, at any rate, it is linked to a very different one—the notion of finding new publics for universities, in effect, new alliances.

[25] See my essay (Birnbaum, 1971*a*) on recent changes in the domestic policies of some of the foundations. A very good analysis is given by Harold Orlans (1971).

[26] The conversion of the term *coöptation* from a technical neologism in sociology to a word guaranteed to make every right-thinking person on the left aware of dangers to his or her immortal soul is an interesting chapter in contemporary rhetoric. A philological-historical investigation would repay the effort. My own first acquaintance with the term came from Selznick (1949). The current usage of it is a contemporary derivative, apparently, of a somewhat less recent version of moral decline: the history of the bureaucratization of the socialist movement.

The critical aspect of our present situation may lie, indeed, in the very high degree of sociological self-consciousness possessed by most parties to our debates. Laurence Veysey argues that the consolidation of the modern American university was made possible by the protective functions of ignorance. Professors, students, and administrators (along with trustees) were careful not to probe too deeply into one another's conception of the university. The opposite situation prevails now: a certain amount of protective ignorance (or, at least, insulation) might give us pause to think. At the moment, the academy suffers from a surfeit of analyses of the (supposedly) spurious logic, (alleged) psychopathological foundations, and (imputed) ideological tendentiousness of every single position taken on the university's social role. Another point made by Veysey seems more important. The enlargement of academic freedom attendant upon the rise of the university at the turn of the century, he argues, owes much more to general changes in the social and political climate than to the intrinsic effects of doctrines of academic freedom. In the progressive area, academics who were critical of the dominant American institutions found political allies (Veysey, 1965). A minimum of pluralism in the larger society seems to be a necessary (if not a sufficient) condition of pluralism within the university. Veysey's point, if I understand him correctly, is entirely consonant with the earlier findings of Hofstadter and Metzger (1955, pp. 420ff.). The point also suggests some future and unintended consequences of the demand that the university reverse its present alliances.

The demand is unlikely to be met in its entirely. Short of an abrupt social revolution, American universities will continue to work closely with the larger corporations, with the federal bureaucracy, with the agencies of power in American society. A dispersal of alliances, however, is entirely possible. Critical and reformist groups in the professions, the newly developed "public interest" advocacy—however uncertain its present legal and philosophical assumptions—and the organized politics of groups and strata hitherto excluded from politico-economic decision will singly and severally find academic defense, justification, and assistance.

We have come a long way from the late 1940s and the 1950s, when government, the foundations, and the universities collaborated in making of social science an administrative technology for the nascent American empire. The 1960s, with increasing amounts of technical and political debate in the universities on public policy, may have been a return to normalcy. Certainly, the universities during the cold war period, by contrast with their comportment in the 1930s and 1960s, may be compared with the universities during World War I, as contrasted with the periods 1900–1916 and 1920–1940. The contrast, in each case, is between ideological mobilization for a single political task and a more pluralistic and much broader set of concerns and alignments. There are similar phenomena in the natural sciences. In the 1940s and 1950s, debate on the integration of science in the national defense effort was not absent, but muted. The recent concern with the social and political uses of science, with questions of the environment, and the hierarchical structure of big science is a counterpart to the diversification of opinion in the social sciences.

The historians of academic freedom argue that thought has been most free where it did not conflict with concrete interests (Hofstadter & Metzger, 1955, p. 434). We seem to be on the verge of adopting another solution, quite unintendedly: the adumbration of opposing schools of thought, backed by opposing interests. The disadvantages of the solution are obvious. It is not a principled one and therefore leaves the university intellectually defenseless should the situation change. It is not a positive solution, in that it may leave other possibilities for university thought unexplored, tying it to a foreshortened conception of contemporaneity.

I have discussed, in effect, two rather different sorts of alliance contracted by the academy The first entails a general relationship to the perspectives of a public, or to a stratum or class which can claim to impose its interests and conceptions upon the nation. The second involves a specific relationship to a group with a focused political program. I have also suggested that much of the autonomy of the liberal university may have been due to the consonance of its thought with the views of a public. Finally, I have argued that pluralism, if not without its advantages, may take the rather constricting form of multiple and contradictory alliances between different groups within the university and groups outside it. The analysis thus far seems to suggest that historical view offers little or no hope that thought may rise to authentic critical autonomy. Perhaps the difficulty resides in our conception of thought itself.

The Influence of University Thought

Thus far in this chapter, I have used an excessively general notion of thought. It has encompassed everything, from the governing assumptions of philosophical systems to the methodological assumptions of the empirical social sciences. It has—by implication, at least—included aesthetic conceptions, insofar as these entail views of social order. It also includes the physical and biological sciences, with methods, findings, and consequences which influence—indeed, at times form—conceptions of social power and order (Himmelfarb, 1968). Is there some utility to distinguishing the social sciences, with their actual impingement upon the conduct of affairs, from the other aspects of university thought? Would it be wise to distinguish between abstract, or theoretical, disciplines and empirical, or concrete, ones?

Clearly, any number of possibilities are open. It is striking that the intensity and extent of university thought's influence upon prevailing political and social conceptions have not been connected in any recurrent way with thought's formal properties. Paleography, biblical archaeology, comparative ethnology, vertebrate biology, clinical neuro-psychiatry, economic theory, political philosophy, and empirical sociology have shown equal capacities for disturbing the ideological equilibrium of society—from the late medieval period onward. Perhaps, in the absence of any compelling pattern in the evidence, we can make the following distinctions: University thought may affect either public thought or public interests. In the first case, it may touch upon general interpretative notions, or it may refer to specific objects. In the second case, it may propound new conceptions of interests, or it may endorse (or attack) prevailing ones. We might expect discussion of interests to have more immediate effects, but we should not be surprised to find that alterations in prevailing schemata of thought have more enduring ones. We may put the matter in another way: History does not allow us to make a priori judgments as to the socially disturbing possibilities of types of university thought. Certain kinds of psychological theory, and the clinical derivatives these generated, were for years treated as benign in this country. Recently, however, we have been told that the student revolt is in fact a consequence of a mistaken psychology, or of incorrect deductions from a valid one (Bettelheim, 1971). The social utilization of knowledge (more precisely, the social interpretation of knowledge) is a process which often escapes the control of the university once knowledge is published in the sense of being made public.

The immediate public use of knowledge, in any case, is not always an indication of its ultimate use. Impeccable in his liberalism, implacably ironic in his celebrated remarks on the economics of pyramid construction, the late Lord Keynes did not quite anticipate the utilization of his work by the modern technobureaucratic state—to keep in motion a vast military-political complex which has increasingly become autonomous of the purposes for which it was developed. The proposition on the distinction between the immediate and ultimate uses of knowledge is even more true of abstract forms of thought. Not all the young Hegelians who deplored in their master his ultimate accommodation with the Prussian state saw the potential explosive force of applying a dialectical view of society to historically transient social institutions. In our own American history, the late Richard Hofstadter has shown with force and delicacy how the same general social ideas have at times reversed their political directions. Big government and minimal government, strong federal power and states' rights, trust in popular wisdom and extreme skepticism about it, a belief in the intrinsic value of the market and a disdainful rejection of it—each antithesis has had not merely different but contradictory political meanings (Hofstadter, 1955).

A glance backward in time, then, produces no very clear answers to our questions. Continuity and discontinuity seem of equal weight in the history of the university's involvement with the social order. Purposeful involvement of a partisan kind has often been less important than the unintended consequences of university thought. Knowledge has been socially used, even if not supposed to be useful. Architectonic structures of conservative ideology have sometimes had radical consequences. Radical proposals, meanwhile have not infrequently turned out to be parodies of (and, therewith, contributions to) conservative realities.

The Demise of the Liberal University

The end of liberalism has been a recurrent theme of so much recent social thought that its introduction in this setting will not surprise my readers. Liberalism, with its conception of an enlightened citizenry, did have certain cultural assumptions. These, in turn, shaped a particular conception of the university. The Jacobin French university and the imperial German one, as well as the ancient and modern British foundations and the American universities, bore the imprint of this conception. Despite all specialization, higher culture in the liberal epoch was sufficiently uniform to possess content as well as form. The liberal university had a purposeful and conscious relationship to the high culture of its epoch. (By *high culture*, I mean a system of sensibilities, values, knowledge, and techniques transmitted by formal means across generations. High culture entails self-conscious effort and reflection—in its acquisition and its alteration. It can be distinguished from popular culture, which is not self-consciously or reflectively acquired, and from mass culture, which is produced for a market and passively consumed by those who buy it.)

Knowledge of the classical tradition in letters and philosophy, some appreciation of universal as well as national history, and the rudiments of a grasp of the developing cosmos of the natural sciences were the standard elements in this culture. They were integrated—or, more accurately, held together—by the mind's supposed capacity to reason critically about the cultural inheritance. The idea of progress was given concrete form. Progress was the capacity of the culture to utilize the past respectfully, but selectively: the very idea implied confidence in reason's ability to shape the future. No doubt, these were legacies of the Enlightenment. No doubt, as well, the Enlightenment was insufficiently assimilated by the educated Germans and rigidly codified (in a curious mixture of positivism and Jacobinism) by the French bourgeoisie. In the Anglo-Saxon countries, it was fused with strong components of Protestant moralizing and utilitarian calculation. Yet even the early philosophical justifications for the modern German university attribute holistic and personal spiritual values to scholarly and scientific specialization. The liberal university formed persons whose cultural acquisitions became part of their personalities (Anrich, 1964). The late Theodor Adorno, if I recollect correctly, once said that it was only recently that his contemporaries had begun to write of cultural "values" *(Werten)*. He pointed to the verbal similarity in German between this phrase and the term for describing holdings in corporations (the French term *valeurs* shares this dual function too). Adorno (1951) supposed that this was evidence for the alienation of culture, its new status as a commodity. The analysis if familiar enough. In the period of the liberal university, not exteriorized goods but persons were thought of as cultured. Moreover, the person could not become cultured by a process of accumulation: he was formed and formed himself in a process of interrelationship with his milieu, but his contribution to the process was singularly important.

Two processes altered this conception. In the larger society, the fundaments of a liberal society were eroded. Groups and organizations everywhere replaced individuals as agencies of social organization. It would be fatuous to suppose that liberal society, at those rare moments when it most conformed to its philosophical image of itself, was an aggregate of sovereign individuals. There were periods in which the organization of the larger society, however, imposed tasks on individuated social roles: in the liberal professions, in the conduct of the economy, in the sphere of cultural creation itself. The enormous increase in the scale and complexity of industrial society—in part, a consequence of the release of energy facilitated by the organization of bourgeois society—required other forms of social organization.

In the sphere of culture, specialization became the precondition for the mastery of anything but a dilettantish fragment of the whole. I have previously written of Max Weber and the internal difficulties of liberalism. Weber was also the prophet, if that is the word, of the inevitable triumph of specialization in the learned disciplines—including the social sciences. He did not entirely like the process, but he felt it to be inevitable. What had been a unified world, accessible to reason, became a fragmented one—explicable only by very different types of intellectual activity. The familiar and continuing debate on the "two cultures" comes to mind. Suppose, however, that there are not two cultures but several? With no particular effort at systematization, I can list (1) a historical culture, which would include the study not only of history as past politics but also of institutional and cultural history; (2)

an aesthetic culture, in which the inner structure of the work of art is essential; (3) a social-scientific culture, with its search for underlying regularities in social life; (4) a natural-scientific culture; (5) a culture concerned with the structure and content of moral discourse; (6) a culture concerned with the nature of discourse in general, the study of language and linguistic philosophy; and (7) a philosophical culture, in the sense of institutionalized reflection on knowledge. It is clear that many of these concerns are interrelated, but even in these few lines, we have an indication of the multiplicity of intellectual interests institutionalized in the academic disciplines. Who can forget the episode in Thomas Mann's *Dr. Faustus* in which the musician-hero of the novel has a psychotic episode in the presence of his friends and acquaintances? One of them rose: he was only a specialist in numismatics, he declared, and the problem exceeded his competence.

At the apogee of the liberal university, it was torn by conflicts over the general implications of ideas. The Darwinian controversy, with its ramifications in philosophy, psychology, ethics, and politics, comes instantly to mind. In fact, so does the dispute between the historical and classical economists, with its explicit political components (Eisermann, 1956; Schumpeter, 1954). Mach's reflections on knowledge played some role in the genesis of Einstein's work on relativity, which in turn gave rise to philosophical dispute (Clark, 1971). Is it entirely an artifact of distance that makes us think that other days knew giants? The balance between the exposition of general ideas and the development of specialized techniques within circumscribed disciplines then seems to have been different. The liberal university assumed that general culture formed persons, and it also assumed that general culture was constituted by ideas. The liberal university was not by any means a focal point of social criticism or social experimentation. (The case of the Russian university at the end of the nineteenth and the beginning of the twentieth centuries is obviously different.) Moreover, the liberal university knew very little of what we should today think of as a counterculture: Bohemian styles of life were sought out by some students in special, urban enclaves (Michels, 1931, pp. 181–199; Venturi, 1960). Its interest in general ideas, however, meant that social and political criticism could in principle enter the universities. The methodological disputes in the social sciences at the turn of the century were often disputes about general ideas, not matters of technique. Even Max Weber's rigorous insistence on the distinction between fact and value in the social sciences was meant to facilitate debate over values (Weber, 1949).

This is a useful place at which to recall that John Dewey's educational ideas were also impregnated with liberalism (Dewey, 1922). It is quite true that the traces of his early interest in Hegel are to be found in his belief that the ultimate worth of ideas was to be measured by their contribution to a social process. Individuals, however, were bearers of that process—and shaped themselves by their reflections on their encounters with it. Changes in the individual's relationship to culture, as much as changes in the large organization of society, marked the eventual implausibility of this version of liberalism.

The increasing domination of canons of specialization in the university, then, meant that it was impossible to form individuals by imparting a limited set of cultural principles. The intrinsically dynamic force of the specialized science did not compel those exposed to these sciences to think anew about their fundaments—continuously. The dynamic force of the specialized disciplines was turned outward. It was codified in disciplinary procedures for registering and integrating new knowledge (insofar as the disciplines were scientific, and in ways frequently illusory insofar as they were not). Society was influenced, even changed, by the application of new knowledge—persons were not. (We shall see, below, that the technocratic university seems to lack a view of the person it forms.)

Decline of the Idea of an Educated Public

The liberal university, as it was transformed, gradually abandoned—we might even say stealthily abandoned—the organization of teaching and scholarship for educating a public. The decline of the liberal university, indeed, was a historical correlate of the decline of the idea and substance of an educated public. The Nazi regime in Germany did not politicize a university dedicated to the universal values of enlightenment. Rather, it imposed a uniform ideological cast on a university whose teachers had already (some of them with indignation) rejected the view that they had public responsibilities of a general kind. Their responsibilities, they argued, were to the impersonal canons of their own science. Others, to be sure, had interpreted their public responsibilities in rigidly national terms—not in terms of general ideas but in terms of their specific historical location. The failure of the German Enlightenment had had this dreadful historical sequel. The Nazi university was a curious union of forces professing absolute scientific neutrality and others insisting on fanatical partisanship.[27]

Elsewhere, of course, developments were less dramatic. General ideas, themselves, became the property of academic specialists. Alternatively, they migrated from the university to circulate among groups of urban intellectuals (Gilbert, 1968). High culture became the property of a group of mandarins—numerous, to be sure, but far from serving as the avant-grade of a generally educated public. Indeed, the mandarins were cut from that public. They did have a vocabulary in common with some socioeconomic elites in some countries (most notably, Brit-

---

[27] H. Kuhn et al. (1966), Lilge (1948), Mann (1958, pp. 820ff.).

ain and France), but their conceptual world was different (de Beauvior, 1959, 1966).

In the United States, collegiate culture in the form familiar to readers of F. Scott Fitzgerald meant, among other things, that the liberal university had either failed or (worse yet) declined its charge. That universities should have impressed philistinism upon a new generation is not the least of the singularities of the history of higher education in America (Veysey, 1965). The development of a mass culture outside the universities was, in some measure, the work of half-educated university graduates.

These developments were not without political consequences. Insofar as the university provided highly specialized instruction, it ignored the social context in which its graduates were to apply scientific and professional knowledge. Insofar as the university provided a stereotyped general education, transmitted without rigor (and often in the despairing conviction of the teachers that the impartation of this education was more important to them than to its recipients), it did little to provide the American elite with critical distance from, or new approaches to, its tasks. As for a more diffuse kind of public influence emanating from the universities in America in the first four decades of the twentieth century, the following can be said.

Did not the universities contribute to civilizing a country whose head of state could still declare, in the third decade of the century, that the business of the nation was business? Did not new social policies and administrative techniques develop under the first Roosevelt, the New Freedom and, during the second Roosevelt's administration, first in Albany and then in Washington, because of the collaboration of university teachers with men of politics? Indeed, did not the period witness the reemergence in America—for the first time since the days of the educated gentry who wrote the Constitution and gave us our first few cabinets—of scholar-politicians? To be sure, these often served as counselors to presidents, governors, secretaries of federal departments, and the Congress—but their influence was enormous. Finally, was not the period 1930–1940 one of intensive political activity on the American campuses, some of it hardly of a conformist, much less technocratic, kind (Altbach & Peterson, 1971)?

The points can hardly be denied, but note their implicit limitations. The permeation of government (and, indeed, subsequently of business) by academic specialists in the social and administrative sciences did not generally entail the promulgation of new ideas. Rather, the techniques brought to public life by these specialists were related to ideas already in the public domain very early in the century (White, 1949). The triumph of these specialists was in fact a triumph for the technocratic university, living off liberal intellectual capital.

Erosion of Religious Foundations

There are moments in social history when forms seem to retain their structure, but when content changes—imperceptibly at first, with consequences visible only later. There may have been a moment of indeterminacy, as Veysey suggests, between the period in which American higher education was dominated by official Protestantism and the emergence of the modern university proper. Veysey (1965) holds that in this moment, professorial governance of the university might have been established, and the subsequent pattern of trustee authority and presidential governance might never have come to pass. Perhaps the failure of the professoriat to assume command of the American universities expressed a failure of spiritual nerve. The universities were already divided in the type of educational aim they pursued and the type of culture they mediated. Criteria of practical utility coexisted (in the same national system, if not always in the same institution) uneasily with moral and aesthetic views of American life which represented a poorly disguised snobbery. The erosion of the religious foundations of American liberalism deprived secularized liberalism of that kind of self-confidence, or élan, without which no doctrine triumphs. It became a codex for the operations of mind, an open mind, and not a source of spiritual judgment.

In the circumstances, three kinds of activity could and did fill the vacuum. The first was a form of cultural indoctrination, or socialization, administered by peer groups on the campuses. On the elite campuses, this was accompanied by an infusion of high culture by its votaries, the cultivated professoriat. The second activity was the pursuit of progress in the several learned disciplines—learning, often enough, being conceived of as its own end. The third was a utilitarian technology—applying knowledge in a variety of contexts for the solution of concrete social and technical tasks. The university became an instrumentality for the pursuit of these ends, singly or in combination. The multiversity had its origins not at Berkeley in 1945, but a half-century earlier, in the predispositions of a university system at cross-purposes within itself.

Is this a repetition of what we may term the "new theology of academic decline"—an eschatology handmade not for the world but for the campus? I am struck by the tonal similarities with the views of Hutchins. (1936). Even Robert Nisbet's lament for the disintegration of the medieval scholarly cosmos does not seem entirely remote, despite my own belief that it rests on altogether too schematic a reading of academic history (Birnbaum, 1971c). Perhaps the reference to Hutchins is not out of place. His critique of the American university, it is sometimes forgotten, has two components. One is that the university fails to concentrate on the adumbration of a new metaphysics. At times,

Hutchins's views have had a faint resemblance to the late Dwight Eisenhower's curious stand on religion: He felt that every American ought to have one, but he did not care which one anybody chose, Is it so with metaphysics for Hutchins? There has to be one—if not Aristotelian, then some other kind. The second element in Hutchins's position is related to the first one, but is distinct from it. The university has to educate a citizenry which is spiritually mature and sovereign in its judgment—above all, in its judgment of cultural and political issues which cannot be left to (often self-proclaimed) experts. Metaphysics, on this view, is a tool of judgment. Hutchins, again, was an exponent of an evaluative social science—one which would go beyond empiricism to make critical judgments on the polity.

Lack of Consensus on Ends of Education

Was the university, however, ever really liberal? I have used the term to designate both a mode for intellectual activity and a sense of moral purpose. The liberal proceeded empirically, in obedience to the dictates of reason, but did not doubt that reason would help him realize (or actualize) the sovereignty and moral autonomy of the person.[28] I have also asserted that this view of the ends of education presupposed a certain kind of social order, and I have employed the historical shorthand term *bourgeois society* to identify it. It is obvious that the internal differentiation of Western history in the nineteenth century renders this shorthand difficult of transcription. History is far more complex than these codes would allow (Trilling, 1950, 1968). I would argue, however, that the argument does allow us to depict a certain kind of university culture. Despite all the differences between national societies, this culture dominated the universities of the nineteenth century. Indeed, the figure of the academic virtuoso would be inconceivable without it.

What, concretely, can be said about the nineteenth- and twentieth-century universities which will show the utility of the argument? I have advanced it as a heuristic principle, to organize this chapter—but I do not on that account suppose that historical reality may have an entirely different structure, and that this approach to it is entirely arbitrary.

The first thing that can be said is that without some such assumption in the minds of those who taught in the nineteenth- and early-twentieth-century universities, their activity makes no sense. Specialization did develop, but the specialists during this period insisted on the organic intellectual links between their work and the elements of a

[28] See chap. 3, "Culture," of my book entitled *Crisis of Industrial Society* (Birnbaum, 1969*b*).

total world view. That view may have been transmitted on the Continent in classical secondary schools, but teachers in the latter were educated in the university and often were promoted to its teaching ranks. In the United States, the colleges transmitted this view to those who were later to go directly into employment or to the professional schools. Even the elective system in American higher education had as a major justification a faith in the possibility of rational choice by students among alternatives. The reaction against the elective system at the time of Eliot's succession by Lowell was, after all, based on the view that the university as such had responsibility for the content of education—that it could not be left to chance arrangements among and between specialists.

The second thing to be said is that *liberal* in this sense did not preclude an acute sense of the limits of permitted political discussion— and an awareness of the specific public to which the university was attached. The universal pretensions of liberalism were limitless. It did tend to identify the public welfare with conceptions of it peculiar to the educated and prosperous groups which supplied its political cadres. Veysey (1965, p. 97) has observed that Eliot had the habit of putting controversial figures into temporary or ancillary posts: many liberal academics (in countries besides the United States too) reported for intellectual mobilization when the First World War broke out (Bourne, 1964).

The most cursory of glances at four separate cases of the modification of classical liberal ideas of the efficacy and primacy of the free market in the economy will show how closely university liberalism was attached to influencing its publics. The *Kathedersozialisten* in Germany, the social liberalism of T. H. Green and his school in Britain, the socialism of the Durkheimians in France, and the academic advocacy of new social policies in the United States (particularly in institutions like Wisconsin) represent what may be termed departures from formal liberalism on liberal principles (Durkheim, 1970; Richter, 1964). Those who, after an examination of state, society, and economy, reached these conclusions did so in the explicit interest of serving liberal values. New forms of economic regulation could alone contribute to that public rationality and private autonomy which were espoused by liberalism. The present point is not to discuss the validity of these ideas. It is important to see that the liberal university facilitated critical and general political discourse of a principled kind. In abstract terms, indeed, it went as far as criticizing some of the practical assumptions of a liberal polity. It did so, however, precisely when sections of its public were turning from a total affirmation of the value of unregulated market capitalism. The university, at that historical moment, served its public by allowing principled debate of very general political alternatives. It did so in the conviction that an educated public could in fact give effect to these alternatives. At the end, in other words, of the epoch of the liberal university, that institution could justly claim one of its most singular triumphs.

Ideological Limitations of Its Public

It never pays to exaggerate. The liberal university, in general, had a rather poor record with respect to academic freedom for Socialists and socialist doctrine. Again, we may attribute this to the ideological limitations of its public. As debate over changes in the economy was in full cry, one theorist of educational liberalism, Alexander Meiklejohn (1920, pp. 55ff.), intimated that perhaps liberal education had been overly concerned with distributive justice and questions of production. What was wanted was a code for the decent and dignified enjoyment of life, for intelligent use of resources. Did Meiklejohn—a formidable pedagogic theorist and practitioner—assume in 1912 that economic problems had been solved sufficiently for decent consumption to be a focus of liberal education? I suspect that his position entailed an unconscious defensive reflex, a fear that the explosive stuff of social debate would shatter liberal education. Meiklejohn, it should be noted, was a resolute opponent of the fusion of the liberal arts college with the technocratic university. His interest in the purity of philosophical purpose of liberal education may have induced in him a reluctance to risk the supposed corruptions of closer and continuous contact with issues of wealth and power.

The customary defense of the liberal university against these corruptions, and against the many excitements, vexations, and dangers of political involvement, was the standard of neutrality. The liberal university, on this reading, was dispassionate. What are we to make, however, of the influential 1945 Harvard College report *(General Education in a Free Society)?* In it, the defense and inculcation of liberal values were made the chief aims of the proposed curricular changes at Harvard College. (In fact, as those who have studied or taught in that program know, Harvard's general education courses quickly enough developed into forums in which these values were examined.) Compare this by way of a doctrinal commitment with the views of Woodrow Wilson, who in 1896 in an address declared in effect that it was not Princeton's office to give society values (Wilson, 1961). The passage of a half-century had, apparently, two effects. First, the threat to liberal values was so great that spiritual mobilization on their behalf seemed necessary. Second, the connection between a form of education and a definite set of values had become clear—or clearer. That it did so just as these values were submerged in new academic currents is, possibly, a lesson for us. Perhaps this time we can enlarge our choices by attaining clarity on the relationship between university values and social context.

The Rise of the Technocratic University

The technocratic university developed on liberal foundations. A response not to the immanent growth of knowledge but to the social organization of knowledge in industrial society, the technocratic university has reinforced some of that society's more recent tendencies. (I at first wrote "capitalist societies," but the thought that universities are even more technocratic in the Soviet Union demanded a change in the phrase. Nevertheless, American universities certainly do respond to the technocratic imperatives of American capitalism.) The free market has diminished in importance; the bureaucratic control of ever-larger segments of the economy has replaced it. The technocratic university does not vend knowledge; neither does it administer it. Rather, it organizes (or administers) knowledge-producing units. The criteria for the production of knowledge in the technocratic university have two sources. The first is the prevalent intellectual structure of the separate fields of learning. The second is the demand of social agencies outside the university for knowledge—a demand which may be communicated in the intangible (but effective) form of cultural and intellectual opinion, or political preoccupation, and in the tangible form of resources and rewards for certain kinds of work. Upon examination, one sees that the two sources are not isolated from each other (Birnbaum, 1969*a*). The notion of self-governing academic units, working according to criteria of reason, is of course an element of continuity with the liberal university. What has changed is the relationship to a public. The technocratic university produces knowledge for specific social agencies and no longer confronts a public with whom it shares a common discourse.

Is any other organization of the contemporary university possible, particularly in view of the enormous expansion of knowledge and its increasing inner differentiation? Put in another way, is talk of a common discourse simply utopian? Perhaps, but in that case, all the more reason to examine the roots of our present situation. If common intellectual discourse is impossible, we still have to live together. But how? Possibly, we may develop discourse about discourse, or at least enough to enable an educated citizenry to control, from time to time, the decisions of their technocratic governors. In any case, a plethora of proferred solutions to these problems is not available.

The Morrill Act of 1862, as amended in 1890 by the second Morrill Act, is sometimes thought of as the charter of the technocratic university in the United States. The text is interesting, in that it calls for "the endowment, support, and maintenance of at least one college where the leading object shall be, without excluding other scientific and classical studies, and including military tactics, to teach such branches of learning as are related to agriculture and the mechanic arts, in such manner as the legislatures of the states may respectively prescribe, in order to promote the liberal and practical education of the industrial classes in the several pursuits and professions in life" (Hofstadter & Smith, 1961, p. 568).[29] The consequences were, ultimately, rather different—but if the text is to be believed, the land-grant universities were to be agencies of social betterment by virtue of the fact that they would educate social groups hitherto without access to higher education. These were to be educated both liberally and practically. The choice of both terms suggests that the framers of the act, like many of their contemporaries, had a clear notion of the distinction between liberal education and practical activity.

Giving Knowledge Private Status

It is the erosion of that notion which gives the technocratic university its peculiar temper—a vertiginous ascent which knows no limits, encompassing increasingly large areas of activity. The relationship be-

---

[29] Verne Stadtman was good enough to offer the following comment, which I cite in full:

"My first reaction to this paragraph was that the sentence 'These were to be educated both liberally and practically' was not a valid interpretation of the intent of the law. But after thinking about it, I am not so sure. I have often suspected that the phrase 'without excluding other scientific and social studies' was included for two reasons less exalted than the one you offer: (1) to enable existing institutions, like Dartmouth, to make use of the act without sacrificing their mainline studies, and (2) to provide access to college on the frontier not only by engineering and aggie students but also by the sons and daughters of college-bred parents who regarded Eastern models as the only legitimate ones. There was also, of course, interest in raising the farmer's and mechanic's status to that of a 'professional.' Much of the rhetoric of the Grangers expressed this notion at the time. But almost a concomitant of 'professional' status was the liberal training that undergirded the education of theologians, doctors, and lawyers. In practice, as I'm sure you know, few of the early attenders at land-grant colleges pursued agricultural or mechanics courses right away. The quality of available instruction in such fields wasn't very good, and besides, many of them had come to college to escape the farmer-laborer caste, not to rise within it. Allan Nevins wrote about all of this very succinctly in his essay on the land-grant colleges prepared for the land-grant centennial.

"There is an interesting sidelight on the whole thing offered by the description of agriculture as taught by the University of California's first professor of agriculture: it began with 'a thorough course in fruit growing in the Garden of Eden, passing spiritedly to grain growing in Egypt and the conditions surrounding the corner in sorghum which Joseph contrived for Ramses II, pausing to look carefully into the dairy practices of the Scythians, and was rapidly approaching the relatively modern cabbage growing of Cincinnatus when, as tradition declares, both instructor and pupils fell asleep. . . .' This is obviously a burlesque, but suggests the efforts that probably were taken by early agriculture teachers to make their subjects respectably academic."

tween the university and the society no longer passes exclusively through a public, no longer takes the central form of the education of a future public. It consists, rather, in a complicated—even subtle and at times opaque—cycle of relationships between parts of the university and social agencies outside it. This is not the place for demonological fantasies. Sponsored "defense" (or "war") research in the universities of a secret kind was estimated for 1970 at about 1½ percent of the total research budget of the American universities. The estimate was made by Kenneth Keniston and Michael Lerner (1971), who are unlikely to be thought of as apologists for the Pentagon. Moreover, it can be argued that directly sponsored research is less important, quantitatively and qualitatively, than research suggested and then planned and executed by the development of a "pure" or nonapplied learning (Organization for Economic Cooperation and Development, 1968).

The critical point about the technocratic university is the detachment or disengagement of inquiry in many fields (including the social sciences and the humanities) from a sense of its public context. The assertion may be paraphrased, with little change of sense. An altered public context governs inquiry (and influences, of course, teaching). The specialization of the several disciplines has, as we shall see, varying degrees of authenticity. The specialization of the pure natural sciences has *no* demonstrable relationship to the utilization of the sciences in a technological way. The general dictum that an increase in pure scientific activity must have technological benefits need not be true (Kaysen, 1970). It may not even have to be believed to be true by the society's elites. A technological society without a basis of scientific activity is nevertheless difficult to conceive of.

The influence of the larger society on the intellectual production of the technocratic university, then, is not easy to describe. Part of that university, given to the pursuit of pure knowledge in fields in which specialization seems to be technically and intellectually justified (theoretical physics, let us say, rather than urban sociology), spends most of its effort on reproducing itself. That is, it produces new scholars to replace old scholars, new knowledge to replace obsolete knowledge, new ideas to replace old ideas. The ways in which the development of canons, of criteria, for the choice of objectives in the fields of pure knowledge is influenced by the social context of the university are not clear to us. The sociology of science and of knowledge, curiously, is more advanced with respect to the internal organization of scientific work than with respect to its social context (Ben-David, 1971).

With respect to applied knowledge, less of a problem confronts us. The university may and does accept commissions from outside agencies which ask for reliable (and, of course, valid) knowledge on the problems which interest them. Here, too, distinctions are important. The knowledge requested of the university may be assimilated in various ways, rejected in various ways. In an enlightening and even entertaining piece, the German sociologist Helmut Schelsky (1969, pp. 232ff.) has enumerated the many ways in which expertise may or may not be used by those who seemingly seek it. In the social sciences, one considerable difficulty is that knowledge may not lend itself readily or easily to practical use.[30] Moynihan (1969) has shown the uncertainty surrounding, and the obstacles in the way of, the utilization of the social sciences for decisions affecting social policy. He might have gone further and drawn the conclusion that the delineation between objective knowledge and social and political judgments in the social sciences is impossible to maintain. A further question concerns the extent to which the university, so often accused of selling its soul, in fact has anything to vend. The Coleman report made clear that the factors adduced by the social scientists, or at least by a consensus among them, as accounting for school performance did not seem to play the role ascribed to them (U.S. Office of Education, 1966). And Robert Nisbet, in his commentary on the lamentable Project Camelot, has declared that the worst thing about it was not its perversion of social science to the political purposes of the Pentagon, but rather the fact that the social science on which it rested was devoid of content, significance, and cognitive efficacy—was, in effect, not worthy of the designation *science* (in Horowitz, 1967).

In what way, then, may the technocratic university be described as technocratic? Our criteria, upon reflection, seem negative—characterizations of what the technocratic university is not. It does not communicate very much to the public—or does so in a haphazard and fragmentary way. Its activities, whether pure or applied, lack the internal coherence which could be supplied by an underlying doctrine. Their dynamic, insofar as they have one, is connected to the notion of the immanent development of knowledge. But the contemporary peculiarity of this idea of knowledge is its detachment, in turn, from a conception of the public status of knowledge. The world has become one dominated by science, but we lack a political philosophy for public control of knowledge. It is the merit of Wilhelm Hennis (1970, pp. 47–62), the German political scientist, to have insisted on our want of conceptual resources to deal with the problem. A recent report by a panel of advisers to the Organization for Economic Cooperation and Development (1971) insists on the necessity of public control of the technical uses of knowledge. The panel, however, had no recommendations to make on the development of public criteria for the evaluation of the uses of knowledge—though it offered some on the concrete institutional mechanisms which could assure a public control of this sort. It is in this general setting that the technocratic university func-

---

[30] Orlans (1971). See also Birnbaum (1971*b*, pp. 214–231).

tions. Its lack of what we may term a *political theory* is a reflection of a general deficiency.

Points of Consideration

The cycle of intellectual exchange with the larger society, then, proceeds unreflectively. A cycle of this sort does not rest on a large and explicit conception. It is most certainly not planned in any general way. Nevertheless, it has nodal points of concentration, which reveal the implicit social and political patterning of the cycle. It is to these that I now turn. But it seems most useful to begin with some organizational data on the cycle. I have made the distinction between a university which (through its teachers) addresses a public and one which serves special social agencies. We may call these latter *clients*, but the terms of the usual professional relationship do not quite apply. The agencies (governmental or private) may seek knowledge and reserve the utilization and application of the knowledge for themselves. They may seek advice on the application of existing knowledge. They may make long-term estimates of their interest in supporting pure inquiry of one or another kind (as the Office of Naval Research did for a long period). The aims of the agencies may be open to scrutiny and control by the public, but in many cases they are not. Even governmental agencies may mount large-scale research operations which for a longer or shorter period escape close congressional scrutiny.[31]

These agencies utilize the university's resources for their purposes. In a complex set of transactions, the university (and those within it) may derive considerable benefits from the relationship: the funding of activities which could not otherwise be supported, more ample funding for activities which in any case would have been pursued, additional funds to pursue other activities outside the scope of the immediate transaction. In addition to these material benefits, intellectual ones accrue—not least, contact with a sector of reality outside the academy. Finally, there is the possibility of exerting influence on the conduct of society's business in a very direct way. In all these relationships, parts of the university (teachers in their individual capacity or as members of knowledge units, departments, research groups, or laboratories) make choices. If they do not endorse one specific set of policies rather than another, they lend their knowledge to agencies which do have policies.

It is very difficult to apply the notions of criticism or defense of the social order in a context of this sort. Limiting cases are clear: a professor at Harvard may serve as an adviser on Southeast Asia to the United States government and may be excoriated by a colleague at MIT for doing so (Chomsky, 1967, p. 13). The issue of criticism or defense

---

[31] Orlans (1971) has a valuable bibliography.

seems to have been resolved, for those who take positions in this way. But not all cases are so clear. Research for the Department of Health, Education, and Welfare may have the effect of increasing that agency's effectiveness and may favor a bureaucratic conception of welfare administration (Pliven & Cloward, 1970). This last is a large concept, and research may also have the long-term effect of preparing administrators and the public for rather different institutional approaches to the problem. It may do so even if conducted in a technocratic context, that is, without systematic and explicit public attention to the issues of policy and choice involved in the problem.

We have arrived, then, at another distinction between the liberal and the technocratic university. The first, it will be recalled, concerned the social group to which knowledge is communicated. The liberal university communicated knowledge to a public; the technocratic one communicates it to a specialized agency or group. The second distinction concerns the philosophical structure of the communication. The liberal university communicated knowledge in a consistent and generally explicit philosophical framework, on clear political assumptions. Communication by the technocratic university is segmental, detached from a statement of assumption. The knowledge units making these communications serve as groups of technicians, relay stations, experts—but not as thinkers. It is not necessary to assert that their work has implicitly conservative consequences. It may, indeed, have implicitly radical ones. The point is that it is explicitly devoid of political position.

The technocratic university, indeed, cannot take an explicit political position. Its operating principle is one of ostensible decentralization. Decisions as to the pursuit of lines of inquiry, the conduct of the inquiry, and the solicitation or acceptance of contracts and grants from outside agencies are the province of the knowledge units of the technocratic university. We encounter, here, an interesting distinction. The technocratic university is formally liberal: Having assured itself of the competence of its teachers and scholars, it leaves these free to teach, conduct research, and write as they like. Most such universities, however, do exercise a formal control over the solicitation and acceptance of funds from outside (matters like individual fellowships for leaves may well be excepted, but larger research grants are not). Generally, these are left to the free play of market forces: the control is usually purely formal. Universities have at times made academic decisions to exercise that control—on the grounds that a particular grant or project would constitute a source of academic imbalance and compromise the future utilization of the university's resources, for instance. Sometimes, the decisions have been political, as in the decision of some universities to terminate secret research. It is interesting that decisions of this sort (the same may be said of the debate on ROTC on many campuses) frequently use academic justifications—in the one case, the necessity of preserving the openness of academic communication; in the other, the necessity of maintaining academic standards. I have termed these decisions *political,* nevertheless, because it is clear that they rested on a considerable repugnance in the American academy toward the specific policies of the American military-political apparatus. The debate at MIT in connection with the "research strike" of March 4, 1969, suggested that some faculty members objected to the principle of universitywide decisions of a political kind on the acceptance and utilization of research funds (Allen, 1970). The familiar argument of those who favored such decisions was that the abstention from decision also amounted to one. Leaving the research effort of the university to the chance play of market forces, or the availability of funding, must inevitably weigh the results in favor of the highest—and therefore the most established—bidder.[32]

With this argument, we leave technocratic rationality behind us. What we face is an effort to restore a conscious or self-conscious political dimension to the technocratic university—in an epoch in which the liberal political assumptions have been shattered. To whom, however, shall the altered university appeal? On what shall it base its choices? I shall deal with these questions under the section entitled The University and Politics. Before moving on, however, we must consider other aspects of the technocratic university. As we shall see, the matter is more complicated than many of its critics allow.

Retreat from the Content of Liberal Education

The familiar argument concerning the university as an agency of cultural socialization and standardization hardly requires recapitulation.[33] On this account, the technocratic university's retreat from the content of a liberal education is inevitable. The new university trains and does not educate. It processes manpower and does not assist persons to develop—nor could it, even if it wished to do so, since the larger economy and society require not persons but trained capacities. Even this last term is suspect, since it is a form of trained incapacity which is wanted, a specialized and fragmented set of skills—combined with only so much general perspective as will enable the alumnus or alumna to take his or her place in a changing technobureaucratic system. The

---

[32] Wallerstein and Starr (1971) give ample (and repeated) statements of this position. See also Wolff (1969, pp. 37ff.).

[33] It is interesting that this argument has also been used not alone against the technocratic university, but against the liberal one. The standard liberal arts curriculum, it is claimed, does not meet student needs—but, rather, forces students into an alien mold. See the summary of recent discussions in Mayhew and Ford (1971).

operative term, here, is *place:* the university is designed to prepare a new sort of worker for a new type of assembly line.[34] Its lack of a unifying conception, as an institution, expresses the lack of moral and political coherence in the culture it transmits. It is precisely this jagged, almost deranged image of the world which it communicates. In the void left by the decomposition of liberalism, thought can easily rigidify into ideology. A reasoned examination of the humane possibilities in the polity becomes a foreshortened and compulsive defense of the social order with all its irrationalities and cruelties, and a reasonable insistence that the social order be examined critically becomes an unyielding antinomianism. In the world of the technocratic university, ignorant armies may indeed clash by night—there is no day.

Yet the clash is in some considerable measure a consequence of the technocratic university's continuity with its liberal past. In the nineteenth- and early-twentieth-century market societies of Britain and the United States and in the bureaucratic societies of France and Germany, the university could form (or contribute to the formation of) persons who had reasonable expectations of the work awaiting them in adulthood. In a relatively fixed social framework, socialization by means of a single set of intellectual or spiritual assumptions was possible. The recourse of the technocratic university to socialization by induction into a limited form of intellectual technique, or, in the most vapid case, by exposure to a form of peer-group culture, followed the historical erosion of these assumptions. That erosion, in turn, was not the fault of the liberal university—but was caused by the movement of the larger society.

I have said that we lack a political theory for the utilization of knowledge in modern society. The technocratic university lacks a theory for the organization of knowledge and instruction—and has had, perforce, to utilize liberal traditions and structures. The notion of the university as apolitical, in the sense of refusing to interpose itself between its units and the society at large, is a legacy of the liberal tradition. But what price a liberalism designed for a society in which individuals were supposedly sovereign, in a society in which very different forms of social organization constrain and limit individual choice?

The conceptual difficulties of the technocratic university would, by themselves, account for its political confusions. Political action and political attitude usually derive from a more complete view of an institution's social location and task. When to these confusions are added the multiple demands upon the university, we can see why recent dis-

---

[34] The most coherent analysis of this sort on the left has been developed by the French socialist André Gorz. A philosophical associate of Sartre's, he is also an economics editor of *Nouvel Observateur*. See his contributions in *Les Temps Modernes* (1970, 1971).

cussion has been so tangled, so at cross-purposes.[35] It is as if different participants in the debate were considering very different definitions of the university—and arguing, with syllogistic rigor, from beginning points not only different but often antithetical.

The many demands upon the university are well known enough. It is to perform a public service, however we conceive of both these words. It is to provide mobility opportunities for those who could otherwise not advance in the social structure—and to maintain the advantages of those to whom that structure has given, in effect, their own head start. It is to conduct advanced inquiry and to form future savants. It is also to bring to fruition the intellectual education begun (badly, in our own country) in the earlier years of the educational experience. Finally, with very different forms, contents, and ends assigned to the project by the parties to the debate, it is to socialize the young. Rather different ranges of political or critical possibility attach to each of these functions. When the functions are combined, the political possibilities multiply. No image will do. The Tower of Babel comes to mind, but there, a common project was impeded by the absence of a common language. Here, there is no common project. We are reduced to a Hobbesian ideological condition, a war of each idea against every other.

Multiple Targets of Criticism

Some of my readers will be impatient by this point. Is this not overdoing a method useful if confined to a modest compass, the historicization of sociological argument? Have I not constructed notions of the university, liberal and technocratic, only to show their interpenetration? Does not the argument refer to the general conditions of university existence rather more than to its political role? It is difficult to deny these contentions. It is difficult to deny, too, that if the functions of the university are in fact multiple, different arguments may have to be employed when dealing with these. The kinds of criticism that a university may focus on the social order in its teaching office may differ from the criticism it can effect in other ways. Finally, why have I refrained from mentioning the university campaign against the war in Vietnam; the apparition of figures as diverse as Chomsky and Kissinger, Leslie Fiedler and Kingman Brewster; the counterculture; and—inevitably—the backlash? It is quite true that I have said almost nothing about the ways in which universities today still contribute—if not quite in old liberal tones—to the making of a public opinion. Who writes for—indeed, who else but professors read—*The New York Review*

---

[35] I claim for my review in *The New York Times Book Review* at least the merit of depicting the tangle (Birnbaum, 1971c).

of Books, or *The Public Interest* (Kadushin et al., 1971)? The culture of the university does extend significantly outside it, to the center of media production in New York, to Washington, to the increasingly technocratic reaches of corporate enterprise, and of course to the professions. If the universities do not influence what these important social groups think, it is difficult to see who or what else does. Quite true, but perhaps these matters may now be dealt with more effectively, a setting, for better or for worse, having been supplied.

The University and Politics

I have given the term *politics* a larger (or Aristotelian) meaning. Politics occurs when larger issues of the common life are discussed, not only when concrete and specific questions on the political agenda are at stake. That even work in the physical sciences has political implications is by now a commonplace. Since no university worthy of the name can avoid discussing the common life, since none indeed would wish to do so, university inquiry and teaching must inevitably entail either defense or criticism of the social order. And since the university performs—for better or for worse—a certain number of additional functions bearing on the common life, these too are political.

The often decried politicization of the university, then, has already taken place. It is so pervasive, however, that very little seems to follow logically for our thinking about new modes of university organization and function. We cannot retreat from the present situation to some other one—and very little in the situation itself gives indications of a possible way forward to more fruitful arrangements. Our judgment of what is and what is not fruitful must depend, moreover, upon what we like, in politics and academic function.

As useful a beginning point as any, and better than most, is the liberal remnant in the technocratic university. The view of the university as a field for the pluralistic competition of ideas has been given a pragmatic sanction. It is to society's interest that ideas should contend in the university, which may serve as a laboratory for intellectual experiment. If I understand it correctly, that was the sense of the celebrated defense of academic freedom by the regents of the University of Wisconsin (1894) in the case of the economist Richard Ely. The university, with respect to its teachers, guarantees the seriousness of their ideas by guaranteeing their competence. For the rest, it allows history (or the larger society) to decide—and asks society only to leave it in peace. This notion is part of the liberal remnant in the technocratic university, but I note that some contemporary university radicalism claims shelter on these grounds. Indeed, Robert Paul Wolff (1969) has argued that radicals would do well to espouse this particular derivative of liberalism, lest they be swept out of the university.

At least two very large assumptions attach to this position. The first is that the university is in fact intellectually pluralistic. Unfortunately, it is less so than it ought to be. Perhaps this is a historical fatality, of the sort a sociologist cannot protest: ideas develop in universities when the larger society is ready to receive, or at least consider, them—and not before. Perhaps so, but the university could do more to enlarge the range of debate within its own walls. The processes by which prevalent social opinion influences the university may be rather subtle. In the experience of many of us, a narrowing of social criticism in the social sciences has been accomplished in good, indeed exalted, conscience by influential colleagues professing methodological purity. On occasion, the principle of competence has been abused, to impose sanctions upon those with unconventional views. That, however, is rarer than the more placid process by which intellectual conventions develop, forestalling or foreclosing debate.

The solution to this problem may well be one entailing an ethos— and therefore peculiarly unsusceptible to immediate institutional innovation. Other solutions are possible. If ideas develop in universities in response to social demand, however inchoately transmitted, will an alteration in social demand increase pluralism in the universities? Those who have proposed new alliances for the university have often conceived of these in terms of alternative patterns of service, to different groups and publics.[36] Suppose, however, that a relationship to sponsors rather different from private trustees or state educational authorities or federal funding agencies were developed. One of the rationales for the autonomy of black studies programs is that only close contact with the black community can guarantee the authenticity of such programs (Wallerstein & Starr, 1971, vol. 1, pp. 335ff.). Would universities, or institutes, sponsored by the trade unions enlarge the margins of debate in political economy and sociology? We may recall that in those European societies in which social science, at least, has a rather strong (academic) Marxist component, there are Marxist political movements. In France and Italy, a quarter of the electorate is Communist, and another sizable fraction is socialist. At first sight, the argument appears convincing—but we do well to remind ourselves that the intellectual and historical traditions of these countries (particularly, but not exclusively, their Jacobin components) lend themselves to Marxism. Traditions have to begin sometime, of course, and perhaps a radical tradition in the American university may take root in response to the consolidation of radical political opinion outside it.

There is another possibility. In a recent paper, Martin Trow (1970)

---

[36] Birenbaum (1969) is a good statement of this position.

has evoked the possibility of the permanent pedagogic and ideological fragmentation of the university. He writes of "consent units"—in which groups of professors and students with ideological affinities would develop their own programs of education. These might be academic programs or combined action-study programs of some kind. Presumably, in forms of this sort, the current wave of student and faculty radicalism could institutionalize and perpetuate itself. We may note that this would be an initiative from within the university—not a response to a specific social demand from outside it, although of course it would be a response to the demands some new students bring to contemporary universities. Trow's image of the future has already found confirmation in parts of Germany, where new university laws in some provinces have allowed students and younger teachers in some faculties and institutes to reshape academic programs, to the horror of a good many senior professors. In at least one case, the new programs have already brought a ministerial, or governmental, intervention: the city government of West Berlin has forbidden certain Marxist courses—on grounds of their supposed academic deficiencies ("An die Macht," 1971). It may be asked, however, why it took a total recasting of the structures of university governance to win ground for Marxist approaches in a university which prided itself on its name: Free University.

I have discussed the assumption of intellectual pluralism as a component of the liberal university ideal. Another of its assumptions merits examination, that of the intellectual laboratory. How may general social ideas be tested, rather than examined, in a university? We may adopt the view that the university is a small polis and suppose that social and political experiment within it can generate models of reform (or revolution) for the larger society. I would not deny the validity of the thesis that a considerable amount of socialization, even political socialization, takes place within the university. It is absurd, however, to suppose that it is a mirror image of the larger society. Ideas may be examined, debated, criticized, and developed in the university. They may persuade students, who will subsequently carry these ideas into the larger society—but to be tested, in any real sense, ideas will have to be converted into action. That is, they will have to be accepted by groups or agencies outside the university and used as general or specific criteria of social choice. The university may propose, but society will continue to dispose.

There are data which bear on this problem, and on the problem of pluralism. The evidence suggests that many American social scientists, in the universities, are more radical than either colleagues in other disciplines or the general public (Lipset & Ladd, 1971b). Radicalism decreases, within the social sciences, in the policy sciences (economics and political science). The closer the university, then, to the central institutions of the society, the less radical its members. As I write these lines, I am aware of a difficulty. Surely, the radical students and younger faculty (the surveys report that the younger faculty in all fields are more radical than their senior colleagues, although they tell us little about the possible permanency of these attitudes) are close to some of the central institutions of our society: family and school, to take but two. Have I unconsciously, or semiconsciously, accepted a notion of reality which is ideological in that it transmutes categories of social location into categories of evaluation? At any rate, the radicalism of the university teachers is not easily or directly transformable into social influence of a long-term sort.

I have, thus far in this section, written of the ideas promulgated in the university. What about the social policies promulgated by the university or, indeed, executed by it? We have seen that a considerable range of policies is in fact carried out by universities—from the adumbration of criteria for admissions to the conduct of social experiments for one or another public or private agency. Insofar as the latter are entrusted to parts of the university (parts I earlier termed *knowledge units*), they have until now fallen under the usual pluralistic conceptions. The university has generally left the choice of these policies to the discretion of its knowledge units. The general reassessment brought about by recent events, particularly the nationwide student strike of 1970 with its component of faculty support, has also encompassed activities of this sort ("Neutrality or Partisanship," 1971). The borderlines between thought, advice, advocacy, and action may in many cases prove difficult to draw. I return to this theme shortly. For the moment, let us say that it will be increasingly difficult to accept any university involvement in social policy exclusively on the libertarian and pluralistic grounds on which university thought is allowed, in the best case, an exuberant amount of freedom. There is a difference between action and thought. The franchise and the arguments which extend to thought are not always applicable to action. One of the reasons is that actions taken by the university may adversely affect its primary mission in the sphere of thought. Another is that the official engagement of the university in social action ought to have a high degree of assent from the different members of the university. These members easily agree to accord one another freedom of thought. The process of obtaining assent to the university's social policies is likely to convert the university into a permanent forum for political debate on issues of concrete politics. The objection to this is, or ought to be, clear: The university has other things to do. There is a minimum of issues on which that debate may have to take place: university admissions and employment policy, university investment policy. It is difficult to believe that these limits, already large enough, can be enlarged indefinitely. I am painfully aware that this position apparently conflicts with one I shall shortly take on the corporate university's obligation to control its members' use of university facilities for activity which is scholarly and partisan at the same time (for instance, applied research for a government agency). The corporate university's obligation to do that rests, I think, on the need for continuous self-clarification about the aim, form, and content of its primary mission.

Freedom of Thought

The problem of freedom of thought is not easily dealt with. My own formulations, in the preceding section, are comfortingly banal: a strengthening of the ethos of pluralism and a hope (in default of an expectation) that unconventional university teachers, particularly in the social sciences, may find influential allies outside the university. I am aware that this path may lead to another sort of fragmentation of the university, in which teachers represent institutionalized political and social interests. Metzger records a case, during the populist era, in which changes in state government brought about repeated turnovers in the academic staff at Kansas State University (Hofstadter & Metzger, 1955, pp. 424–425). We are reminded of the confessional politics of the Wilhelmenian epoch in Germany (as well as of Max Weber's celebrated complaint that no Socialist could expect academic advancement in that society [Weber, 1946]). Did not Meinecke take his first professorial appointment in the full knowledge that a Catholic chair of history was being established parallel to his own? Distinctions are important. The existence of extrauniversity social conflicts which find expression in intellectual conflict with the university need *not* entail institutional representation for the conflicting groups in the academic process itself. A good deal of the advocacy of black studies or Afro-American studies in the university has taken the line that special measures are needed to right a pattern of neglect become intolerable because unjustifiable. The institutional extension of the argument poses dangers, not the least of which is a *reductio ad absurdum* of the university to a corporation in which intellectual control is exercised according to shareholding in the polity outside it. This argument is not so dangerous when applied to the composition of trustee bodies. Indeed, it has more merit to it than a situation in which trustees appear to be mainly elderly, white, Protestant, wealthy, and Republican (Rauh, 1969, pp. 88ff.). (I am aware that some private trustee bodies of this sort have at times been more protective of academic freedom than trustees of public institutions who have been more responsive to immediate political pressures. Unfortunately, the patrician elites are passing: ways will have to be found to make popular bodies more patrician in spirit.) The notion of optimizing academic freedom by controlling the political identity of the players in some ideological game is not a very satisfactory one.

It is not satisfactory because a university with terms of reference restricted to the present spectrum of social and political alternatives is likely to be denuded of its theoretical capacity to transcend those alternatives. The ground for deploring a consensual social science, of the kind that dominated the American academy in the 1950s, is not alone or primarily its lack of a representative quality (Howe, 1959). The social science represented all too well a nation which was in many ways morally somnolent. The ground for our (retroactive) repugnance is that thought ought not to be closely bound to fluctuations and aberrations in the climate of national opinion. Put another way, it should lead and shape, and not like a servitor follow opinion.

Sociological pessimism here conflicts with philosophical optimism. The relative servitude of the university is a historical fact. Is there any reason to expect that it will change, and is there any mechanism that can facilitate the change? The term *relative* offers some restrained grounds for hope. From time to time, the university (or, rather, some of its teachers) has overcome servitude. We live in a society about which all the clichés are true. The rate of change is considerable, and possibly accelerating; knowledge rapidly becomes obsolete; the importance of general, even visionary, intelligence in the direction of society is obvious; a highly educated citizenry is an imperative if a new technological barbarism is to be avoided. In the circumstances, critical thought in the university is a historical necessity—but it is so only from a higher viewpoint than that customarily taken by those with concrete interests to defend and the means to defend them.

A possible next step in the reasoning is to assign the university, or rather its teachers, a position apart from the battle. Mannheim (1952), in his familiar description of "free-floating" intellectuals, did just that. Unfortunately, intellectuals do not float freely: a hundred ties bind them to routine, to economic constraint, to spiritual limits. Recent surmises as to the emergence of an intellectual estate in the United States are very varied. Some see in this estate primarily an occupational grouping with indispensable functions in a knowledge-based economy, and Galbraith's phrase, "the educational and scientific estate," points to this conception (Galbraith, 1967). Others see in it a partially retrograde element, desperately attached to values which have only antiquarian interest, and distinguish intellectuals in a literary sense from those who perform economic functions of a new kind (Brzezinski, 1970). It may be observed that even this putative attachment to outmoded values, if manifested by enough persons concentrated in institutions like universities and the centers of media production, constitutes a definite interest—if a spiritual one. Suppose we do cast caution aside and define the new estate in terms of its spiritual interests. The multiple pressures of familial obligation, economic dependency, and psychological conformity may work in opposite directions—but spiritually, the intellectual estate will demand recognition for itself and an enlarged space in which to work. One implication is that it will ask for more intellectual freedom.

It is by no means certain that a majority of the newly educated graduates of the American universities will do so. The study of Spaeth and Greeley (1970) suggests that the young are more critical of conventional definitions of American social values and institutions—but there is other evidence to suggest that this criticism has in itself become a convention (Mankoff & Flacks, 1971). Thinking about the future of this generation, Lipset supposes that a growing conservativism is very likely.[37] If the present experience of the enlarged university generation in the academy leaves any residue, however, it may take the form of a considerable sympathy for intellectual experimentation in general rather than for radical ideas in particular. Much depends upon the ways in which the generation is taught—and we see that we have come full circle, to the intellectual life of the university.

Not objective social necessity or concrete group interests or an infusion of the present university radicalism into the larger society can singly or in combination create the conditions for a new intellectual pluralism in the American university. The chief conditions for it are two. The first is a recognition by a significant group of university teachers that their responsibilities are of a general critical kind. (On this criterion, some of the most dramatically critical of present-day teachers will be found wanting: thrown up by a movement of recoil from earlier pieties and stereotypes, they by now have developed their own [Birnbaum, 1970b]). They will have to represent a social totality which as yet is unable to represent itself, a higher public interest than any concrete version of that interest. The second condition is more important and no less difficult—possibly, more so. The university will have to develop a new theory of cognition and of science, particularly in the social sciences and possibly in the humanities.

Philosophy is a desperate recourse. I resort to it here because I must. The element of self-criticism in the intellectual work of the universities, of reflection in an authentic sense, will henceforth have to be built into its epistemological canons. That the categories of thought are influenced and at times constructed by social categories, that intentionality is often a covert component of social thought, and that structures of thought change profoundly in response to fusions of immanent (cognitive) and extrinsic (social) pressures are propositions which find considerable assent. The propositions remain to be utilized as a source of new procedures for evaluating intellectual work (Chomsky, 1971; Habermas, 1971b). Whether these propositions also entail implications for the social order of the academy remains to be seen. The facile use

---

[37] Lipset and Ladd (1971a). See the larger discussion by Lipset in *Rebellion in the University* (1972).

of conceptions of academic democratization does not help very much, since the quantitative accumulation of knowledge and the mastery of rules for its ordering are not distributed equally in the academic community. (Teachers who sit on the floor in a circle with their students may or may not be indulging in a form of psychodrama: the epistemological consequences of their behavior are nil.) There may be, however, more subtle notions of academic democratization which will facilitate the critical examination of received doctrine. Something like a public defense of the bases of academic decisions (examination standards and appointment criteria) may be in order. Much more important is explicit attention to the mechanisms of academic succession, with their customary confusion of criteria of competence and of adherence to conventional categories of thought.

I do not refer to open and outrageous violations of academic freedom. I do refer to the more pervasive and common phenomena of the imposition of criteria of intellectual judgment upon a discipline by influential colleagues within it. This is something other than the frequent domination of scholarship by one or another methodological or conceptual fashion. Describing matters in this way renders them more harmless than they are. In the social and administrative sciences, and in the humanities, conceptual and methodological fashion often precludes the study of some questions and predetermines the range of answers to others. That the same thing occurs in the natural sciences is true, but is not a legitimation for its imitation elsewhere. The natural sciences are much more genuinely cumulative than the other disciplines, and criteria of competence are easier to establish in the natural-scientific fields.

That much said, it is extremely difficult to suggest concrete procedures for making appointments more open. The institution of visiting members, from the same discipline but other institutions, on appointment committees is useful. My own observation in Britain suggests that it does not always work against the domination of received opinion in the field. The inclusion on appointment committees of colleagues from other disciplines is also useful, but it too has been tried. Perhaps there is no institutional corrective available except for a more generous and rigorous ethos on the part of those who make appointments.

Freedom of thought, then, is its own exercise. Freedom of thought, in the university, is the freedom to transcend received and current categories of thought. That transcendence implies, where it does not directly entail, criticism of the social order. The social order generates its own categories. It is not the highest office of the university to reproduce these as if they were its own. Rather, the university's task is not exclusively the pursuit of knowledge. It is, equally, the criticism of the categories which organize knowledge. It will be seen that these ideas bring the discussion onto a plane removed from some of the pressing problems of the past decade—but they may provide a means of reanalyzing our experience and of preparing ourselves for what otherwise would be surprises to come. The fact is that the university, until the present crisis, worked to a unilinear notion of the accumulation of knowledge, to a civics textbook conception of its role in forming citizens, and with consummate complacency about its own social policies and political options. Social criticism engendered by a philosophical enterprise of the sort sketched in this section may be deeper than a conventional academic scrutiny of the day's political problems. It will certainly be more connected to the university's knowledge-seeking and knowledge-imparting functions.

As for defense of the social order, my first impulse is to set down some very simple notions. There are parts of the social order which may very well require defending—particularly the traditions of rationality embodied (however imperfectly and at times lamentably) in the university itself. If the university's intellectual task is primarily critical (in the rather philosophical sense employed above), it has to reserve the right to defend other parts of the social order or not, as it sees fit and with the means it thinks appropriate. For the rest, the university may recognize that historically, most social orders have little trouble defending themselves—or, at least, have shown a considerable ability to pass on to successive orders their own worst features. The sheer facticity of the social order may very constitute its most effective defense: with so much energy in the university expended on the description and analysis of the social order, its antecedents and functioning, it may well impress its own categories upon the thought of the university.

I have always been skeptical of those who argue that the university needs more immersion in the realities outside it. It is certainly true that many university teachers would profit from doing something else during their lifetime: many have so profited. The issue strikes me as one rather different from asking that the university concentrate on the affairs of the society, in terms derived from society's perceptions of its problems. Those perceptions, upon examination, are usually the perceptions of elites and groups with interests to defend. University thought ought to be ruthless with prevailing notions, not submit to them.

Problems of Governance

My discussion, like some others I have read, shows a distressing tendency to reify the notion of the university. What (and who) is the university? It is clear that it has a corporate social identity in terms of its activities. It is far less clear that it has one in terms of its purposes. Indeed, many theorists of the university (from the most traditional to the most modern) have defined it as precisely a body which has activities, but no chosen purposes apart from these activities.[38] The distinction is more than verbal. It points to the curious pattern of growth of universities recently, through the acceptance of (very different) social tasks—and their lack of organization for philosophical self-scrutiny. Can this last be so, given the deluge of publications about the institution's problems? These, like the avalanche of reports by self-scrutiny committees, are invariably *post-festum*. They may even propose changes in priorities and structures, but institutional inertia seems to be very strong. Let us say that the American universities (and not alone they) show a commendable degree of self-criticism, but that this has as yet to produce noteworthy alterations in their structure. In particular, despite the avant-garde role of a number of institutions, the American universities have experienced few changes in type of governance—few, certainly, in comparison with the amount of psychic energy expended on the problem.

This is not a chapter on governance, but problems of governance do arise when we consider the university's participation in the larger polity. Trustees may be depicted as absentee landlords or as distant guardians; administrators, as Machiavellian oligarchs or harassed bureaucrats; professors, as irresponsible egoists or noble corporativists; and students, as troublesome adolescents or younger academic citizens. The possibilities, if not infinite, are very great. Our choice of adjectives expresses our (academic) political preferences. Two very different issues arise, not entirely unconnected but often enough confused.

The first concerns the relationship between governance and academic process. That, by and large, faculty have widened their powers over the past decades is a general observation. This may well have been due as much to their advantageous bargaining position, vis-à-vis administrations, as to the intrinsic appeal of libertarian principles. (It is significant that faculty in state colleges and in municipal and community college systems are increasingly resorting to trade union organization in order to secure—among other things—the academic freedoms enjoyed as a matter of course, or nearly so, by their colleagues in more favorable circumstances.) The power of faculty over curriculum, appointments, and the actual conduct of inquiry is indeed very great. The reserve power of the trustees and the financial power of the administrations have not recently been counterweights to faculty strength on these issues. Recent developments in California (here, as in other matters, a limiting but historically significant case) suggest that this period may be coming to an end. A scarcity of university posts may encourage illiberal administrators and trustees to impose a more strin-

---

[38] Perkins (1966), Kerr (1963). See also the essay by Fritz Machlup in "Neutrality or Partisanship" (1971).

gent and repressive political discipline on academics. There is distressing evidence that this has begun to happen. For the moment, whatever new struggles may lie ahead, we may say that faculty in the leading sectors of American higher education possess sufficient autonomy to teach, inquire, and recruit as they see fit. The issue of criticism or defense of the social order (within the academic process) arises in terms of the prevalent criteria of what is and is not appropriate. It is hardly a question of governance, but is one of philosophical and political assumption.

There is one important exception to this generalization. Some recent conflicts within faculties (frequently opposing senior to junior colleagues) concern the modality and content of teaching. Younger teachers who refuse to engage in grading on one or another principled basis, others who modify syllabi in exceedingly unconventional ways, and still others who consciously attempt to develop antiauthoritarian roles in the classroom (or what they conceive of as such) are now not rare. In some cases, trustees and even state legislatures have intervened to insist upon a return to discipline. But *discipline,* in this sense, is one definition of what a university should be like and what its teachers should do (Carnegie Commission on Higher Education, 1971). Where trustees speak of discipline, administrators and senior faculty members not infrequently speak of standards. The literature of the New University Conference is full of precept and example:[39] the American Association of University Professors' usual conceptual resources do not cover these phenomena (American Association of University Professors, 1971). It may be said that the innovators sometimes can rely on two justifications. When their opponents sanction them for violating academic standards, they retort that these are simply apologies for political views. When their opponents, alternatively, criticize them for converting the classroom into a political theater, they claim the conventional freedom of the individual teacher to conduct his or her class autonomously. In fact, as most of the innovators recognize, their program is both academic and political; they make no conceptual distinction, on principle, between the spheres.

I am at a loss to advance any solutions for these difficulties. One precept is simple enough to follow: Lack of talent is relatively easy to detect. Innovations of this kind sometimes reflect a refusal, due to an incapacity, to work in the terms of high culture. At other times, they represent a reasoned position—with antecedents of a philosophically honorable kind.[40] In the first case, a question of standards does arise; in the second, a genuine philosophical and pedagogic problem is at

[39] See *The Radical Teacher* (1969) and other publications.

[40] See, again, the New University Conference documents—with their echoes of Rousseau (and of *Rameau's Nephew*).

issue. The fact that the second is the rarer case does not affect the principle. Probably, the solution will emerge only after a lengthy period of experimentation. The pluralism of the American system, here, may serve as well—provided that it is made pluralistic in practice as well as in ideology. There seems to me to be little case for allowing lay governing bodies to require specific forms and content for the teaching process. The matter can be left to faculty, however, only if faculty bodies are prepared to be critical about their own preconceptions.

It remains to be said that the attack on political socialization within the university is, often enough, a radical caricature of liberal conventions. A free market of ideas is to be replaced—by a free market in sensations, in default of one in sensibilities. The absence of persuasive liberal ideas is to be met not by radical ideas, but by radical experiences. The problem of reforming an entire culture is to be solved by branding as "elitist" *(horribile dictu)* the notion of high culture—and giving to American philistinism left-wing sanction (see McDermott, 1969). The liberal university did not give an identity to its students. It gave them the cultural means with which to assume identities, if that is the term, in a relatively defined society. The notion (not entirely exclusive to the political left, but certainly the property of what we may term the *pedagogic left*) that the university can undermine the contemporary social order by allowing its students to substitute "authentic" identities for "conformist" ones is a grotesque oversimplification. It is a form of pseudopolitics, using the campus as a foyer of psychodrama. Politics is not the expression of, or search for, identity; it is the effort to create conditions under which certain kinds of choice about identity may be made. There is no reason for faculty attached to the values of rationality and high culture to be complacent about these aberrations. What in our previous promulgation of that culture has led a new generation to such empty and desperate expedients?

One source of the critical attitude of our students and younger colleagues is, surely, the contradictions of our own existence. We bespeak rationality in the classroom and, often enough, in our writings—and, sometimes, in our lives as private persons or citizens. Those who were undergraduates in the 1940s and 1950s will remember their universities, to a considerable extent, as suburbs of culture on the outskirts of the affluent city. In choosing academic careers, we had the satisfaction of helping ourselves and participating (or so we thought) in a civilizing mission. The university we inherited from our teachers has multiple involvements in a society which has proved recalcitrant to that mission. Further, in many respects it participates itself in that society in ways we did not envisage when we took up academic careers. We thought of the university's mission as cultural, and instead it has been programmed as a gigantic mechanism for occupational recruitment and selection. We supposed that we could think about history within its walls, and we found that our own institutions have been making history—not infrequently on sides we think are wrong (or dubious). Worse yet, we find that we are implicated in all these choices without having willed them. I earlier said that the university, particularly in its technocratic version, has activities and not purposes. We cannot relate these activities to our purposes—and yet this is the institution which limits (if it does not entirely define) our own work.

The second question about governance, then, does not concern inquiry and teaching within the university: it concerns the university's activities in the larger society. These can no longer be left to the inclinations of individual teachers or the directors of knowledge units. They cannot be left to administrative decision or to trustee decree. Ways will have to be found to relate these activities to the university's intellectual purposes. Easier said than done—and often said (*Report of the President's Commission . . . ,* 1970, pp. 13ff.). Suppose the constituents of the university are divided, if not on these purposes, then on their practical consequences for politics? Seymour Martin Lipset and Everett Carl Ladd, Jr. (1971*b*), have shown that the professoriat does not think uniformly about politics—nor yet about the recent challenges to the technocratic university developed by the student movement and its faculty allies.

For the moment, let us concentrate on the faculty. On the usual, but not entirely unambiguous, criteria of competence and disinterestedness, the faculty does assume a corporate responsibility for the quality and aims of teaching within the university. In effect, it assures society that faculty autonomy is the best guarantor of a continued presence in the university of competent teachers, beholden to nothing but the good opinion of their intellectual peers. The same principles apply to inquiry of a pure sort. (On this definition, pure inquiry may well concern a politically debated subject; it is not undertaken, however, with an immediate and concrete intervention in the political process in view.) The faculty, at least, assumes no such responsibility for the external activities of the university. These are either left to the judgment of individual teachers or undertaken by the trustees or administrators of the institution.

Let us consider the consequences of a corporate faculty control (to be understood in a large and loose sense) of the external scholarly activities of its members. The normal range of a citizen's activities would be exempt from control, of course. Ordinary civil liberties and the present canons of academic freedom would make it possible for teachers to publish what they wish and to participate in politics like anyone else. They could place university facilities at the disposition of an agency exterior to the university, however, only after seeking agreement from their peers. Something like a "research council" or "research senate" might have to process, initially, proposals for activities in the applied sphere. (To simplify the argument, let us eliminate personal consultancy from consideration. There may be a case for subjecting consultancy to control, but the problem is difficult. For the moment, let us say that a teacher who accepts a telephone call in his academic office or who dictates a letter to a government agency or corporation for typing by his academic secretary is in fact using university facilities. There is a difference, however, between this sort of thing and the mounting of a research project with an annual budget of several hundred thousand dollars.) The singular advantage of the arrangement is that it would facilitate debate within the faculty on a new conception of academic propriety. It might not alter much (my own view is that very little would be changed, at least at first)—but it could initiate a new form of academic self-reflection. The disadvantages are not, of course, to be dismissed lightly. Some colleagues may refuse to submit themselves to controls of this sort and may retain their academic positions while establishing private research corporations outside the university framework. On second thought, reordering of this sort may not be an entire disadvantage: it may also have the result of clarifying our purposes. How, further, are we to differentiate between pure and applied inquiry? The answer is that at the extremes, the cases are clear—and it is in the extreme or limiting cases of applied inquiry that the university does become engaged in politics.

Finally, what would become of academic neutrality if the corporate faculty were to approve and disapprove projects of applied inquiry? Its present restraint is not quite tacit approval of such projects, but has many of the same consequences. Moreover, present restraint is a continuation of the making of university purposes by abstention or drift. It will be recalled that I have asked for a new process of reflection about those purposes. That much said, two very different answers may be given to the question. Control exercised by the faculty may indeed guarantee neutrality by limiting or ending university involvement in partisan ventures of one or another kind. I find the answer curiously unconvincing, myself, and prefer to give another one. The university, in performing research for one or another social agency, would not be neutral. It would, however, have in the first instance related its activities in the larger society to its academic purposes. In the second instance, it would have taken a step toward assuming responsibility—in a society in which knowledge has become an indispensable element of politics—for the use of the knowledge it produces. Put another way, it would be transmitting knowledge to society in a much more self-conscious context than it has hitherto employed. Our situation may not be new, in qualitative terms. In quantitative ones, it most certainly is new—and new procedures may be necessary if we are to meet our critical responsibilities to society.

(The Carnegie Foundation for the Advancement of Teaching has recently published a set of essays entitled "Neutrality or Partisanship:

A Dilemma of Academic Institutions" [1971]. The essays are instructive. Fritz Machlup provides an eloquent plea for the corporate neutrality of the faculty, but applies his argument against the expression of corporate political opinion to the problem of corporate responsibility for scholarship by implication only. Walter Metzger and Richard Sullivan venture into these troubled realms more explicitly.)

I turn now, very briefly, to those social activities which are in the purview of trustees and administrators, as governors and executors of the university's will in its present American form. These are of the most varied kind. They include an ultimate control, however, of the scholarly activities of the faculty—however sparingly exercised in direct form or subtly employed in an indirect manner. They include investment policy and the university's social policies as an employer. They include the responsibility for the university's relationships with its neighbors (and, often enough, tenants). They include, as well, policies on expansion and admissions with direct social implications.

Two questions may be asked about the selection of policies in these spheres. Insofar as these policies concern, even if indirectly, the scholarly activities of the university, it is difficult to see on what arguments faculty may be denied a considerable role in policy determination. Insofar as these policies concern matters of the general welfare (investment decisions, employment patterns, programs of physical expansion), it is difficult to see why trustees and administrators are on principle more effective guardians of that welfare than faculty representatives. I am aware of the argument that policy decisions by universities require a delicate balance of considerations of general welfare and those entailing the (somewhat more narrowly defined) welfare of the university. All the more reason for a very considerable enlargement of faculty participation in these realms.[41] The larger society may not soon become a republic of the spirit; there is no reason why universities cannot begin to approach this ideal. The universities' policies in these realms do entail social and political choices, and will continue to do so no matter how removed the decision from the forms of public debate. It would seem more appropriate, in a university at least, that decisions of this sort be rationally considered—and that the manner and results of their execution be subjected to critical and public scrutiny.

The Role of Students

As I write, I have on the bookshelf above my desk some thirty titles referring directly to students. The plethora of analyses, tracts, and an-

---

[41] Walter Metzger's argument in the Carnegie Foundation document ("Neutrality or Partisanship," 1971) is persuasive. See also the book by Simon, Powers, and Gunnemann (1972).

thologies on the students in the contemporary university system—in several languages—is one of the reasons for my own reticence, in this chapter, on the subject of student politics.[42] Another, however, follows from the political position I have taken. The university is obliged to assume a critical position with respect to society by the nature of the academic process—the organization, extension, and criticism of knowledge. It is also obliged to assume responsibilities for the application of knowledge in the society, particularly when it communicates that knowledge directly in the form of applied inquiry. In both respects students play a distinctive, but secondary, role. With respect to knowledge, they are in the process of acquiring it. They are not on a plane of equality with their teachers with respect to competence (however valuable the differences in experience, insight, and vitality between the two groups in the academic process itself). With respect to the application of knowledge, students have as yet to enter the occupational system (with the reservation, of course, that students as such constitute what has been termed an *estate*). Changes in these relationships may well occur should the age and occupational composition of universities alter significantly, but for the moment we deal with students who are predominantly young.

Yet the age of voting has just been lowered. Students are now, by and large, not future citizens but full citizens. Moreover, they are unbound by occupational routine and obligation, concentrated in campuses in such a way as to develop a maximal awareness of their distinctiveness, and open—if sometimes semiconsciously and, in any case, within limits—to new cultural and social currents. The recent expansion of higher education has made more visible for many of them the connection between their status as students and their future occupational and political roles, however crudely they may conceive of that connection (or those roles). In the circumstances, some kind of oppositional movement among students was to have been expected.

The student movement has three components, related but distinct. The first is the least tangible and the most ambiguous, but probably the most pervasive. It entails those diffuse conceptions known as the *counterculture*.[43] Its elements are many: a comprehensible demand that *joie de vivre* become a general condition of existence, a refusal of more ascetic values, a disinclination to accept bureaucratic and impersonal routines, a generalized familism which at times resembles a new tribalism. The counterculture may be explained as an aberrant derivative

---

[42] Professor Lipset has been ascetic enough to work on this theme for years, and his most recent publication is an extremely valuable summary and analysis of the available findings. See Lipset (1972).

[43] See my essay contra the counterculture in a review of Theodore Roszak's *Making of a Counter Culture* (Birnbaum, 1971*b*, pp. 360ff.).

of the tradition of high culture (Trilling, 1968), but is every contemporary adolescent really a descendant of Emile? (We may take some consolation, at least, from the fact that there is little resemblance to the young Werther.) Some characterize the counterculture as a new religion or religious movement (Bell, 1971a; Goodman, 1970)—but accents and judgments both positive and negative attach to these descriptions. Orpheus come alive or Raskolnikov gone soft? My own view is that the counterculture in its American form is a singular and unstable mixture of American philistinism and its negation, historically regressive and progressive at the same time, and that it does not necessarily have historical staying power. Some forms of a great refusal may turn out to be a revolutionary playlet (as Marcuse intimated in his dismissal of Charles Reich [1970]).

The second component is the critique of the larger society, its institutions, and its politics. In Europe, this critique developed as a variant or derivative of the socialist movement, and the European student left recently has been seeking rapprochement with that movement (Birnbaum, 1972). In the United States, the student movement's critique of liberalism (in the recent American sense of the term, which refers more to Arthur M. Schlesinger, Jr., or John F. Kennedy than to John Stuart Mill or Gladstone) was its beginning point (Teodori, 1970). In each case, the sons (and daughters) scrutinized the ideals of the fathers and found the elder generation wanting in both moral seriousness and political efficacy. I have said that the European student left has recently been reintegrating itself, to some degree, with the socialist movement. It is taking the American student movement longer to reach a conclusion the Europeans have by now accepted: that the university is not a total surrogate for all the institutions of power in society. It follows that an effective student politics has to be conducted away from the campus. This entails the question of the utilization of the campus as a base for political action. Alternatively, it entails measures to break down the boundaries between the campus and the larger society.

The third component of the student movement does deal with the structures and processes of the university. The attack on university "complicity" with the agencies of power in the society does not, of course, rest on a notion of the necessary and benign separation of the university from politics. It generally is connected with a demand for a different politics, what I have termed a *reversal of alliances*. There is another, possibly more important element in the student movement's apprehension of the university itself. Its mode of governance, intellectual authority, and educational techniques have been called into question—on two grounds. The first is a generalization from the argument about complicity. The university, it is held, is so bound to the present distribution of power in society that it engages (purposefully or not) in a form of political socialization of its students. The second ground is

that university authority is illegitimate, since students do not participate fully in its exercise. The two grounds coalesce: If students could
have their share in university governance, it would be impossible to
socialize them (or to try to do so) in ways we may briefly term *conformist*. Further, students with power in universities would in fact alter these
institutions fundamentally. Or so the arguments run.

The terrain is, I think, familiar enough. What follows for the university's role as a critic or defender of the social order? Note that the
phrase *critic or defender* can have some interesting meanings. Suppose
universities were run entirely by students: they might be considered
defenders of the interests of the student estate, grown to the status of
a major power in the society. On this view, "student power" may be
interpreted as a radical slogan with some conservative implications.
Indeed, within the European student movement the defense of student
interests (scholarships, degree requirements, conditions of study) has
been interpreted by the very left of the student movement as implicitly
conservative or even reactionary. Parts of the French student left have
denounced the French Communist party for its willingness to encourage student participation in the governance of the French universities
under the new reforms.[44] A similar critique of the Italian Communist
party has been developed by the group around the journal *Il Manifesto*.[45] This sort of defense of student interests has not been very prominent in recent years in America, where discussion and conflict have
moved on a plane of a more spiritual kind. I am reminded of the remark by Engels that the English dominated the sea, the French the
land, but the Germans the air. By this he meant, of course, that his
fellow countrymen, in their lack of real power, had turned to metaphysical speculation and abstract historical interpretation. Perhaps the
metaphysical exegesis of a few not very complicated propositions about
American society is all that can be accomplished by a student movement which has not yet organized itself about the concrete interests of
the students. Perhaps, too, the (occasionally) concrete tones of the programs of black or other ethnic student movements, and the grievances
of students in the lower levels of the higher educational system (state
and community colleges), will entail a change. American trade union-
ism as a whole, combative and aggressive on specific problems, has
failed to develop a totally oppositional ideology like European social-

---

[44] See my essay in *Change* (Birnbaum, 1970c).

As I revise this chapter, I read in *Le Monde* (June 28, 1972) that in the recent
French university student elections for places on the governing bodies of the universities,
participation was low—so low that in many places the number of student representatives
was lowered, as the Faure reform law provides. The Communist-led student group (UNEF-
Renouveau, Union Nationale des Etudiants-Renouveau), however, turned out as many
voters as it could.

[45] See the work by one of the founders of *Il Manifesto*, Rossana Rossanda (1968).

ism. It is possible that the organized student movement in America will develop along similar lines. For the moment, no such development appears imminent.

The political implications of the counterculture are difficult to specify. That the campuses as sites of this culture are frequently objects of popular anxiety, concern, and antagonism (verging on murderous hatred) is obvious. The proponents of the counterculture have argued that its very existence is a political datum of considerable significance, since it represents a break in the continuity of the dominant culture, a demonstration that alternatives exist, and a refusal by the student generation to accept the roles for which it has been cast. If this represents a criticism of the social order, it is clearly an implied one—although large sections of the American population have gotten the message and do not like it. That the relationship between the counterculture and other university values is troubled is not a point which it is easy to convey. The academy, after all, rests on an ethic of discipline and work. The counterculture, whatever its metaphysical bases, does not. To what extent the counterculture represents an exaggeration and vulgarization of the collegiate culture of the 1930s, I cannot say. My own classmates at Williams College, even if they wore white bucks, clearly realized that they would have to go out to work soon enough. They did drink a lot, but they refrained from justifying themselves as the advance guard of a new and freer human culture. There is no future situation in which universities will cease to provide material opportunities for new psychocultural experiments like the counterculture. A thorough change in the age composition of student bodies, with far more students recruited from older and occupationally engaged groups, may diminish experiments of this sort. Yet the campus as a locale for experiment is precisely in this respect a magnet of attraction for some older students. The elimination of anything that could be remotely construed as a counterculture, or a student culture of any kind, has been pursued most relentlessly in China. There, the integration of university and society has become a central theme of politics (Macciochi, 1971). The Carnegie Commission has invited distinguished observers of the American University from Britain, the Federal German Republic, France, and Israel to comment on our system of higher education. As yet, however, it has to my knowledge not opened discussions with the Ministry of Education of the Chinese People's Republic. Both the proponents and antagonists of our own parochial version of the cultural revolution might be surprised at Chinese reflections on our problems.

The chief implication of the counterculture for the university's social role seems to me to lie within the university. The counterculture may well have provided, and may continue to provide, a powerful impetus for pedagogic and curricular programs which stress personal development, immediate experience, and a (supposedly) presuppositionless search for a coherent vision of the world. It may, also, provide an incentive for a critical social and aesthetic theory: the rejection of old forms may encourage the search for new ones. However, the counterculture's total rejection of the technocratic university is in most cases not simply a demand that it be humanized. It is a withdrawal, which would leave the field entirely to be disputed by powerful technocrats and powerless liberals. It is, in effect, also a repudiation of high culture—the university's distinctive resource in criticizing society. A university system made up of "consent units," most of which were conducting experiments in communal living, reinventing the alphabet, or encouraging the invention by their students of new selves, would be a system which would pose no immediate threat to the present system of power in America. True, the long-term implications of the development of new life-styles (as they are termed) might be different. There is no evidence, however, that the counterculture itself can generate a counterpolitics. Indeed, the emphasis on the counterculture may be due in part to a turn from politics.[46] For the moment, let us say that the criticism of the social order implicit in the university's neutrality (sometimes, benevolent neutrality) toward the counterculture may have long-term political implications. These, however, may be rather different from those envisaged by the counterculture's advocates. A sector of the university system given up to the counterculture may be encapsulated, deflect dissent, and assist the process of turning the counterculture into another range of goods sold on the cultural market—a process which, in any case, is well under way. I am aware that episodes like the Kent State shootings and the disturbances over the People's Park in Berkeley and those which occurred adjacent to the Santa Barbara campus took much of their emotional coloration from popular antagonism to the counterculture (as expressed in the antistudent attitudes of local police and local opinion). True, no doubt—but the episodes did entail direct confrontations between police and students, a challenge not to the cultural conventions of the populace but to the political power of the state.

The relationship of the university to student politics as such may be considered under two headings. The first is the question of student political organization directed to the larger society. The entire range of questions connected with institutional neutrality has been explored in this connection, with the qualification that students—of course—can hardly commit entire institutions to political interventions of one or another sort. There is no reason why students cannot, however, commit themselves to such interventions. The issue of whether general student representative bodies (in contradistinction to explicitly political groups) may take political stands seems to me not impossible of solu-

[46] See footnote 43.

tion. If enough students consider that they should, they will (as they have done). If enough are opposed, they will not, and from time to time they will presumably vote out of office the representatives who in effect have misrepresented them. On pragmatic grounds, there may be reasons for a certain restraint in this kind of intervention. On grounds of principle, it is difficult to find rigorous arguments for rejecting occasional political interventions by corporate student bodies. The argument that such bodies should confine themselves to matters directly affecting student interests is persuasive. However, the most cursory examination of the content of the notion of "student interests" will suggest that in our epoch, these are touched by every facet of the university's relationship to society and by many of its political conflicts. It may well be that we shall approach a condition not unlike the French one. There, contending political groups (some of them allied to political parties and movements outside the university) do present alternative policies and candidates in elections to bodies representing the students as a whole. These bodies are particularly important since, under the new French law, they participate directly in the governance of the university—and, indeed, of the entire system of higher education (Birnbaum, 1970c).

What of the utilization of the university as a base by student political groups whose views and activities are extremely unwelcome to the surrounding populace? Here, familiarity breeds not contempt but strong aversion. No university can censor or restrain students in terms of the indices of their extrauniversity popularity. It is equally clear that if society may be impelled or cajoled, at various times, to allow the university to function as an intellectual sanctuary, it will not extend to the university more privileges of political organization than it extends to other institutions. Students may, then, use the university as a base for extrauniversity activity, but they are on risk when they do so. I am aware of the theory, now less prominent than some two years ago, that the university may serve as a base for the conquest of power by a new American left. The theory rests on a large overestimation of the importance and political potential of the university—called upon, in the theory, to make good all the defects of the American trade union movement and of American reformisms and to compensate for the absence of a socialist—much less a revolutionary—tradition in our country.[47]

What of the view that the institutional integrity of the university demands a strict separation of its activities from politics—particularly its academic activities? Enough has been said to indicate my own skepticism about the empirical appropriateness of this view. There is a sep-

---

[47] No other university system has been so overburdened—however contested it may have been.

aration which is necessary in the interests of thought, but it is unlikely to be strict. The demarcation line between academic thought and politics may prove to be a movable one. Moreover, the university cannot afford to accept from the larger society the imposition of a limitation on the political activities of its students just because they are *in statu pupilari*. As long as it is understood that student political activity does not commit the university as such, discrimination against the students would not only violate their rights as citizens—but probably also pose a threat to the integrity of the university itself. It is significant that those most indignant about student politics do not share, in general, Professor Hook's undoubted concern for academic freedom for professors (Hook, 1970). Those who want docile students generally also will require a quiescent professoriat.

A final component of the question of student politics concerns student power within the universities, the third element in the student movement's somewhat inchoate program. A distinction must be made at the outset. Student participation in the general governance of the university is something else than participation in the control of its academic processes. Questions of curriculum, appointment, and evaluation are different in kind from questions about the university's investment policies, the global allocation of its resources as between different activities (even academic activities), and its relationship to the agencies of power in the larger community. The two types of question are, undoubtedly, related. (One could imagine certain student representatives on a university governing body questioning the allocation of funds to "irrelevant" subjects—but one wonders whether this is a worse possibility than the actual allocation of funds as between fields by technocratic university governors.) They are, for most practical purposes, distinct. It will also be seen that I have employed the term *student participation*—deliberately using one a good deal less strong than the omnibus term *student power*. There seems to me to be no case for total student control or domination of universities. There seems to me to be a considerable case for student participation in their governance, within rather precise limits.

The final question about student politics concerns the relationship between student opinion and the academic process itself. It is not to the credit of the American university that the critique of its technocratic servitude was developed at length by extremely junior members of the teaching profession or by students who were often intellectually more junior, still. The editor of *The Dissenting Academy*, in his introduction, called for a higher form of and purified social mission for, knowledge. (The same scholar, in his *Making of a Counter-Culture*, changed his mind—seeing very little social use in any form of academic or intellectual knowledge.) He explained that he had not included an essay on sociology because C. Wright Mills's critique of that discipline, published in 1958, was still valid (Roszak, 1969).

A reexamination of Mills's *Sociological Imagination* will show us the distance we have come.[48] Mills's critique of sociology was also a general critique of the social sciences, for their ahistoricism, for their mechanical and servile imitation of the natural sciences, for their political conformism in the guise of political neutrality. Sociology is now in conceptual fragments, although there are interesting developments in it—not least, the revival of what Mills termed the "grand tradition" of historical and theoretical work. The other American social sciences, under the influence of a critique of their ideological limitations, have experienced more interesting changes. American historians have embarked upon a major reexamination of our past. Instead of a more or less benign interpretation of our institutional development, we have had treatments of racism, of imperialism, of the corporate tendencies in American liberalism. In political science, in opposition to the dissolution of institutional analysis in a formalistic (and contentless) behaviorism, there has been a serious revival of political philosophy. The new political philosophers have attempted conceptual and evaluative discourse about contemporary problems: authoritarianism, bureaucracy, participation. In economics, there has been a revival of the political dimension in political economy. The categories in which economic data are ordered and the uses of data have been analyzed in political terms. These tendencies, it should be said, are rather distinct from the insistence of many social scientists that their disciplines serve underprivileged groups in particular or new publics in general. The new temper among some of the social scientists is both critical and theoretical. It is, in other words, highly academic.

The recent critique of the humanistic disciplines has been less profound. The mandarinism, real or alleged, of these fields has evoked a curious response. Some of the younger scholars have invented a genuine American popular culture (in contradistinction to an industrially fabricated mass culture), in the face of the evidence that none exists. Others have had recourse to a literary populism of considerable crudity, a denial of the value of high culture.[49] (It is a dismal kind of

---

[48] The historians appear to constitute an exception—for reasons which might well repay investigation.

[49] Some of the recent discussion is a curious recapitulation of older debates. But with some exceptions, the Russian debate in the mid-nineteenth century on the moral functions of literature is not familiar to many contemporaries. See the article on these themes by Frederick Crews entitled "Offing Culture: Literary Study and the Movement" (1972). See also the article by Leo Marx entitled "Susan Sontag's 'New Left' Pastoral: Notes on Revolutionary Pastoralism in America" (1972). Both appear in *Tri-Quarterly*, Winter-Spring 1972, nos. 23, 24. This issue of *Tri-Quarterly* is to be published as *Litera-*

respect for others which would leave them at their present cultural level, but it is not only in literary studies that we find intellectuals paying this dubious tribute to their fellow citizens, while abasing themselves.) At least, some of the discussion in the humanities has concerned the very real problem of the communicability of high art in an era of ostensible general literacy. It has taken up, in other words, the question of a politics of culture in circumstances much more complex and troubling than those which gave rise to the early American discussion.

In the physical sciences, discussion of a critical kind has focused on the uses of scientific and technical knowledge. The participants in the discussion have concluded, quickly enough, that these were not problems which the university alone could solve. In any event, the discussion has greatly enlarged the participation in the debate on science policy—once the preserve of a few specialists, it is now seen as a prime concern of the reflective scientist.

What is significant about these developments is that a critique from the margins of the disciplines has, quickly enough, fused with movements within it to develop new directions in academic thought. The process, however, is a professorial one. Student sensibilities, student insight, may have provided a context for it: the process remains one which can be brought to maturity only by the arms of inquiry and thought.

There is a lesson in this sequence, if a rather old one. Intellectual work, not least work on the frontiers of thought, entails preparation and demands special competence. These can be acquired, but they cannot be acquired overnight. Academic citizenship, then, differs in one dimension from political citizenship: It presupposes certain kinds of experience, certain sorts of competence. Membership in a university, then, cannot be equated directly to membership in a political community. There are respects in which the members of the university are unequal. (Were I to phrase this by saying that they are different, I would offend fewer student sensibilities—but I should not be paying the students the tribute of frankness.)

We face a paradox. A certain amount of student criticism of the academic process is probably an indispensable corrective to its tendency to rigidity and involution. Free rein to student criticism, however, would end academic process—by eradicating real distinctions based on competence and experience. The solution proposed in the notion of "consent units" has a certain pragmatic efficacy, but it would in effect institutionalize at least two systems—one in which students would be the political equals of teachers and another in which the university

---

ture in Revolution by Holt, Rinehart and Winston, Inc., New York. For another view see Irving Howe's "Literary Criticism and the Literary Radical" (1971).

of 1963 would be perpetuated. It is absurd to suppose that these are our only alternatives. Can we not devise institutional means for student participation in the academic process which will not only recognize student rights but also call upon students to exercise responsibilities which they alone can meet? Something like student representation on certain academic bodies may be appropriate—representation in proportions which, instead of expressing simple and arithmetic notions of equality, would reflect both functional differences and their complementarity.

Knowledge is not wealth: it cannot be redistributed by decree or appropriated intact. (True socialism, incidentally, rests not on notions of confiscation, but on notions of participation and responsibility.) There are many points on which student and faculty interests may and do conflict, but the withholding of knowledge, is not one of them. The university's teaching mission and the student demand for participation in the governance of the university may be reconciled—by the gradual induction of students into academic responsibilities. These considerations have even more force when applied to graduate students or to students in the professional disciplines. They also touch upon questions of governance insofar as these relate to relationships between junior and senior faculty.

Into what academic responsibilities, precisely, may students be inducted—particularly when most of them are not to become academics? We may recall the familiar argument about a knowledge-based society. Students as citizens of that society, as future members of its work force, will be called upon to make general judgments on issues often complex and technically specialized. Are teachers, however, merely technical experts at the service of the academic polity? The analogy does not quite hold—unless we adopt the vulgarism of defining ourselves as "resource persons." The only justification for giving students a role in the determination of academic issues is that this will improve their education—by improving, as well, the quality of the teaching they receive. The kind of institutioanlized mechanism required, then, will be one which obliges faculty to take account of student opinion, while not subordinating faculty to that opinion. It will also provide a space for student experiment—and subject that experiment to rigorous academic criticism by the faculty. It is clear, I think, that this view of students in education rests on the notion that there are still objective structures of culture which it is the university's task to transmit. If there are not, everything else does come into flux.

Institutional Pronouncements

What of direct political pronouncements by the university? However the university is categorized, and however it is governed, it is difficult to imagine many occasions upon which it can speak corporately for a majority of its members—and be listened to. Insofar as a majority of the teachers, students, and administrators of a university have sharply defined convictions on public issues, there is no reason why they cannot have recourse to conventional political mechanisms for their expression. These would include the activities open to all citizens. The political activities of student bodies might well come under this rubric, with the qualification that the student body cannot commit the entire university to a political stand.

The argument is unsatisfactory. Suppose that there are matters at issue which bear directly on the teaching function of the university. It has been argued, and with no little justification, that the continuation of the war in Vietnam created national conditions under which that function was rendered impossible. Suppose, too, that in a society fragmented and equipped philosophically only with a (spurious) doctrine of pluralism, the university is the sole institution which can seek to articulate a higher public interest. Here, we would do well to distinguish between university and university community—but the supposition still merits reflection. Can the university as a whole speak in the name of—or, more precisely, for the sake of—that interest? Universities are not directly chartered by societies to represent their better or higher selves. Hegel once said that in accepting punishment, a judicially condemned person is in fact making obeisance to his higher self— embodied in, or represented by, the state. The reasoning will hardly satisfy many taxpayers when they confront official promulgations by universities of political opinions they do not like. My own view is that there are moments when universities may and can speak out on public issues, but that such moments are likely to be rare ones. The degree of unanimity within a university which would make such a pronouncement effective is not likely to be attained every other day. Moreover, if universities are to speak as corporate entities, they will have to undergo (in the United States at least) profound changes in governance.

The case of faculty pronouncement is a special one. Political stands taken by student bodies, in contradistinction to those taken by student groups, may not commit the university. The same is true of stands taken by the corporate faculty—but these declarations will appear to commit the university to a far greater degree than the utterance of student opinion. Here, again, I see no objection in principle to the faculty's taking a collective stand on certain issues—although the practical objection that faculty energies might better be spent on other matters, in the usual course of events, is a persuasive one. (I myself would rather persuade trade union leaders in Springfield than department chairmen in Amherst of the rightness of a given political position: the unionists are more influential.) There may well be moments when the corporate faculty of a university will wish to make political pronouncement. The principle of parsimony might well govern its use of this possibility—as well as what it says when it does use it.

The idea of a higher public interest, on which this section of the chapter rests, requires comment. At first glance, two criticisms of the notion that the university is peculiarly fitted to articulate it are in order. The first, which I have already mentioned, concerns those who would make the university a major agency in social change, if not revolution. Why suppose that rephrasing its political tasks in another rhetoric will, in the end, constitute less of a burden? The second criticism follows from the first: What about the press, the other makers and leaders of public opinion, and, above all, our politicians? Is not the articulation of the public interest their task? It certainly is, and there is nothing that can relieve them of responsibility for assuming it. Perhaps, however, the university can remind them of their responsibility—especially since a realistic view of the American political process does not show that inordinate interest attaches to the idea of a higher public interest. Political discussion, often enough, concerns competing and contending particular interests. The university's custody of the cultural tradition, its relative freedom from direct alignment with the major powers of society (in the best case), and its continuous examination of current doctrine and practice are all preconditions for its functioning as a special sort of interest group, a spiritual interest group. The university's pedagogic mission, then, does not concern only the young. It extends to the larger society. Especially in a society in which social and technological decisions frequently escape the control of an empirical or pragmatic politics, the university's reflective capacity is not simply a mode of abstract political thought. On special occasions, it can become the source of concrete political judgment. That, in turn, presupposes that the university takes seriously its public educative task.

Some Brief Conclusions

I have expended much space on the university and politics, but in the final analysis, the political implications of university activity are most important when they concern the processes of teaching and learning. Put another way, the politically most important element at a university is its teaching and learning. I have just referred to the distinction between the university and the university community. What is more important in the contemporary United States—the tortured discussions among faculty and students of the propriety of an institutional political role or the actual influence exerted, politically, by the university opinion?

As a larger fraction of the relevant age group enter higher education and as the composition of the labor force changes, the political significance of the university will increase. Already, important elements in the political elite, the professions, the media of communications, and corporate management are extremely responsive to university opinion. The struggle for control of the university is less an institutional one than an intellectual (or spiritual) one. In that struggle, it cannot be said that the party of dissent, of antagonism to the conventional values of a technobureaucratic civilization, has been defeated. Indeed, a technobureaucratic civilization may have to live with a profound inner contradiction. To reproduce itself, it requires knowledge. The conditions for the accumulation and transmission of knowledge, however, are precisely those which encourage criticism of its social organization: the development of university institutions and the culture these generate and then diffuse in the wider society. The Soviet Union has attempted to deal with the contradiction by limiting advanced education to rigorously specific sequences—only to have it explode at the very apex of its technobureaucratic system, among the pure scientists of the Academy of Sciences.

It will be seen that I give a large meaning, here, to the term *politics*. The university cannot promulgate new values for society, nor can it impose new institutions upon a political community unwilling to develop these. It can, however, raise society's consciousness of its own conflicts—and hold out to the political community alternative definitions of reality. But it can do so only at risk to itself—the risk of incurring the wrath of those whom it will offend by challenging (if only implicitly) their sloth, culpability, or greed. A university unable to make the challenge, however, is a university unworthy of its traditions.

Summary

The university's most important contribution to politics is an indirect one. The attitudes, capacities, knowledge, and sensibilities it transmits are increasingly important to a society dependent upon an educated labor force and upon applied knowledge as an indispensable element of administration and production. Yet the university is rent by a contradiction between its legacy and its present functions. We are witnesses of (and participants in) the demise of the liberal university. The liberal university addressed a public and transmitted a culture in which knowledge and a moral conception of its use were joined. The liberal university formed persons for autonomous performance in the society. The inexorable growth and differentiation of knowledge itself, the change from a market society to a bureaucratic one, has altered the university. It has become technocratic, producing knowledge for the use of specific social agencies. The technocratic university may be understood by what it lacks. It does not speak to an educated public, but its several components serve specific markets, groups, and clients. Most important, it has abandoned the notion that it is custodian of a coherent high culture. By *high culture,* I mean a system of sensibilities, values, knowledge, and techniques transmitted formally from generation to generation. High culture, if it is to be acquired or altered, requires self-conscious effort and reflection. Effort and, indeed, reflection are certainly not absent from the technocratic university. Its highly specialized activities, however, do not entail the cultivation of a general culture. The technocratic university imparts specialized knowledge, but has no specific conception of the place of knowledge in a larger context. The technocratic university, in other words, has activities but not purposes. There is, of course, a liberal remnant in the technocratic university. Unless and until the idea of the public educative role of the university can be given new historical context, the institution is likely to lack clarity as to its political and social functions.

Meanwhile, many of its activities are political in implication. The recent radical critique of the university's responsibility for the uses of the knowledge (and knowers) it produces. The radical proposal that the university ought to reverse its alliances and serve groups it previously neglected has interesting implications. It presupposes a university which is pluralistic because it offers its resources to every competing and conflicting segment of a torn society. There is, of course, no justification for the university's serving only certain agencies and publics, and not others. On the present assumptions of the technocratic university, a reversal of alliances (or, at least, a broadening of alliances) is a moral and a political necessity. However, there may be a different political function for the university, one connected not with the close relationship of scholarship to social interests but with a more autonomous role for thought. The university, in a fragmented and divided society, may be a repository of a higher and more general idea of the public interest.

Suppose, however, that the university's components and members do not agree on the definition, direction, and expression of the public interest? This chapter holds that occasional direct political pronouncements by the corporate university, the corporate faculty, or the corporate student body are legitimate. There are other and more effective ways, however, in which the university can serve the public interest. The university has a responsibility, as the repository of the intellectual resources used in the society's political life, to think in genuinely critical and pluralistic terms. Genuine intellectual pluralism in scholarship, teaching, and recruitment is an ideal not easy of attainment. Above all, the university will have to cultivate thought which transcends the present conventions and possibilities of society. These conventions are, often enough, built into the university's conceptions of academic propriety, into the canons of the several disciplines, into the assumptions of the social technology administered by the university. A pluralism consisting only of the conversion of the university into a cockpit for contending group interests would also, in the end, ignore the critical vocation of thought. The university's greatest service to society may at times consist in rendering none.

The university does engage in a range of activities which impinge directly upon society—above all, in the area of applied inquiry. Universities exercise formal control over the researches of their faculties. It may be useful, however, to experiment with forms of faculty control of research by bodies like faculty research councils. This would apply not only to faculty members' activities as private consultants or citizens (outside the university) but above all to university commitments to large-scale projects. Here the university's decision to proceed with a project does constitute a kind of endorsement. The recent discussion of university employment and investment policy entails similar considerations. It is reasonable that decisions in these areas should involve a wider segment of the university than previously.

We touch, finally, on the question of the internal democratization of the university. There is no mechanical correspondence between internal democratization and more effective service to American democracy. Some university hierarchies are quite legitimately based on profound distinctions of knowledge, experience, and competence. A university is not a microcosm of the larger polis. However, an increase in the transparency of decision making within the university and public promulgation of the explicit criteria for decisions may contribute to the university's educational effectiveness. The issue of democratization, however, is attached to the larger question of what interest the university serves. It will have to rethink its mission in cultural and pedagogic terms—and even then, it will be difficult enough to formulate a new set of principles which can lend dignity to its practice.

References

Adorno, T. W.: *Minima Moralia*, Suhrkamp Verlag, Frankfurt, 1951.

Allen, Jonathan (ed.): *March Fourth: Scientists, Students and Society*, The M.I.T. Press, Cambridge, Mass., 1970.

Alliot, Rector (ed.): *Cahiers des Universités françaises, Cahiers 1*, Armand Colin, Paris, 1971.

Altbach, Philip G., and Patti Peterson: "Beyond Berkeley: Historical Perspectives on Student Activism," in "Student Protest," *Annals of the American Academy of Political and Social Sciences*, Philadelphia, vol. 395, pp. 1–14, May 1971.

American Association of University Professors: *Policy Documents and Reports*, Washington, D.C., 1971.

"An die Macht," *Der Spiegel*, no. 49, pp. 81–82, Nov. 29, 1971.

Anrich, Ernst (ed.): *Die Idee der deutschen Universität: die Fünf Grundshriften aus der Zeit ihrer Neubegrundung durch klassichen Idealismus and romantischen Realismus*, Wissenschaftliche Buchgesellschaft, Darmstadt, 1964.

Aron, Raymond: *La Révolution introuvable*, Fayard, Paris, 1968.

Aron, Raymond: "De la Condition historique de la sociologie," *Informations sur les Sciences Sociales*, vol. 10, no. 1, February 1971.

Arrowsmith, William: "The Idea of a New University," *The Center Magazine*, vol. 3, no. 2, pp. 47–60, March–April 1970.

Bell, Daniel: "Quo Warranto," *The Public Interest*, no. 19, pp. 53–68, Spring 1970.

Bell, Daniel: "The Post-industrial Society: The Evolution of an Idea," *Survey*, no. 79, 1971*a*.

Bell, Daniel: "Religion in the Sixties," *Social Research*, vol. 38, no. 3, pp. 447–498, Autumn 1971*b*.

Ben-David, Joseph: *The Scientist's Role in Society*, Prentice-Hall, Inc., Englewood Cliffs, N.J., 1971.

Bettelheim, Bruno: "The Anatomy of Student Dissent," in Sidney Hook (ed.), *In Defense of Academic Freedom*, Pegasus, New York, 1971.

Birenbaum, William: *Overdrive: Power, Poverty and the University*, Delta Books, Dell Publishing Co., Inc., New York, 1969.

Birnbaum, Norman: "The Arbitrary Disciplines," *Change*, vol. 1, no. 4, pp. 10–20, July–August 1969*a*.

Birnbaum, Norman: *Crisis of Industrial Society*, Oxford University Press, New York, 1969*b*.

Birnbaum, Norman: "Reviews," *Change*, vol. 2, no. 2. pp. 48–55, March–April 1970*a*.

Birnbaum, Norman: "Reviews," *Change*, vol. 2, no. 4, pp. 60–67, July–August 1970*b*.

Birnbaum, Norman: "Reviews," *Change*, vol. 2, no. 5, pp. 69–74, September–October 1970*c*.

Birnbaum, Norman: "Reviews," *Change*, vol. 2, no. 6, pp. 72–80, November–December 1970*d*.

Birnbaum, Norman: "Reviews," *Change*, vol. 3, no. 4, pp. 68–71, Summer 1971*a*.

Birnbaum, Norman: *Toward a Critical Sociology*, Oxford University Press, New York, 1971*b*.

Birnbaum, Norman: "Up against the Wall in Bookcases," *The New York Times Book Review*, May 16, 1971*c*. pp. 48–50.

Birnbaum, Norman: "Marx in '71: The Heavenly City of the Twentieth Century Philosophers," *Worldview*. vol. 15, no. 1, pp. 15–20, January 1972.

Blau, Peter, and Otis Dudley Duncan: *The American Occupational Structure*, John Wiley & Sons, Inc., New York, 1967.

Bourdieu, Pierre, and Jean-Claude Passeron: *La Réproduction*, Éditions de Minuit, Paris, 1971.

Bourne, Randolph *War and the Intellectuals*. Harper & Row, Publishers, Incorporated, New York, 1964.

Bouwsma, William, J.: "Learning and the Problem of Undergraduate Education," in John Voss and Paul L. Ward (eds.), *Confrontation and Learned Societies,* New York University Press, New York, 1970.

Brustein, Robert: *Revolution as Theatre: Notes on the New Radical Style,* Liveright Publishing Corporation, New York, 1971.

Brzesinski, Zbigniew: *Between Two Ages,* The Viking Press, Inc., New York, 1970.

Carnegie Commission on Higher Education: *Dissent and Disruption: Proposals for Consideration by the Campus.* McGraw-Hill Book Company, New York, 1971.

Chenu, Pierre: *La Théologie au douzième siècle,* Vrin, Paris, 1957.

Chomsky, Noam: *American Power and the New Mandarins,* Pantheon Books, a division of Random House, Inc., New York, 1967.

Chomsky, Noam: *Problems of Freedom and Knowledge,* Pantheon Books, a division of Random House, Inc., New York, 1971.

Clark, Ronald William: *Einstein: The Life and Times,* The World Publishing Company, Cleveland, 1971.

Cockburn, Alexander, and Robin Blackburn (eds.): *Student Power,* Penguin Books, Inc., Baltimore, 1969.

Coser, Lewis: *Men of Ideas,* The Free Press, New York, 1965.

Crews, Frederick: "Offing Culture: Literary Study and the Movement," *Tri-Quarterly,* nos. 23, 24, Winter-Spring 1972; also in George Abbott White and Charles Newman (eds.), *Literature in Revolution,* Holt, Rinehart and Winston, New York, 1972, pp. 34–56.

Crisis at Columbia: Report of the Fact-finding Commission Appointed to Investigate the Disturbance at Columbia University in April and May 1968, Vintage Books, Random House, Inc., New York, 1968.

de Beauvoir, Simone: *Memoirs of a Dutiful Daughter,* Andre Deutsch, London, 1959.

de Beauvoir, Simone: *The Prime of Life,* The World Publishing Company, Cleveland, 1966.

Dewey, John: *Human Nature and Conduct,* Henry Holt and Company, Inc., New York, 1922.

Durkheim, Émile: *La Science sociale et l'action,* Presses Universitaires de France, Paris, 1970.

Eisermann, Gottfried: *Die Grundlagan des Historismus in der deutschen National-ökonomie,* Ferdinand Enke Verlag, Stuttgart, 1956.

Eulau, Heinz, and Harold Quinley: *State Officials and Higher Education,* a report prepared for the Carnegie Commission on Higher Education, McGraw-Hill Book Company, New York, 1970.

Faber, Sir Godfrey: *Jowett: A Portrait with Background,* Faber & Faber, Ltd., London, 1957.

Galbraith, John K.: *The New Industrial State,* Houghton Mifflin Company, Boston, 1967.

General Education in a Free Society, Harvard University Press, Cambridge, Mass., 1945.

Gerth, Hans, and C. Wright Mills (eds.): *From Max Weber: Essays in Sociology,* Oxford University Press, New York, 1946.

Gilbert, James B.: *Writers and Partisans: A History of Literary Radicalism in America,* John Wiley & Sons, Inc., New York, 1968.

Goodman, Paul: *The New Reformation: Notes of a Neolithic Conservative,* Random House, Inc., New York, 1970.

Gorz, André: "Detruire l'université," *Les Temps Modernes*, no. 285, April 1970.

Gorz, André: "Technique, techniciens et lutte des classes," *Les Temps Modernes*, no. 301–302, August–September 1971.

Habermas, Jürgen: "Die Scheinrevolution und ihre Kinder," in *Protest-bewegung und Hochschulreform*, Suhrkamp Verlag, Frankfurt, 1968.

Habermas, Jürgen: *Toward a Rational Society*, trans. by Jeremy Shapiro, Beacon Press, Boston, 1969.

Habermas, Jürgen: "Die deutschen Mandarine," in *Philosophische-politische Profile*, Suhrkamp Verlag, Frankfurt, 1971a.

Habermas, Jürgen: *Knowledge and Human Interests*, Beacon Press, Boston, 1971b.

Hennis, Wilhelm: "Freiheit und Verantwortung der Wissenschaft," in *Bund der Freiheit der Wissenschaft: Die Gründungskongress in Bad Godesberg am 18. November 1970*, Markus Verlag, Köln, 1970.

Himmelfarb, Gertrude: *Darwin and the Darwinian Revolution*, W. W. Norton & Company, Inc., New York, 1968.

Hofstadter, Richard: *The Age of Reform*, Alfred A. Knopf, Inc., New York, 1955.

Hofstadter, Richard, and Walter Metzger: *The Development of Academic Freedom in the United States*, Columbia University Press, New York, 1955.

Hofstadter, Richard, and Wilson Smith: *American Higher Education: A Documentary History*, The University of Chicago Press, Chicago, 1961, vol. 2.

Hook, Sidney: *Academic Freedom and Academic Anarchy*, Cowles Publishing, New York, 1970.

Horowitz, Irving Louis: *The Rise and Fall of Project Camelot*, The M.I.T. Press, Cambridge, Mass., 1967.

Howe, Irving (ed.): *Voices of Dissent*, Grove Press, Inc., New York, 1959.

Howe, Irving: "Literary Criticism and the Literary Radical," *The American Scholar*, no. 41, Winter 1971.

Hutchins, Robert: *The Higher Learning in America*, Yale University Press, New Haven, Conn., 1936.

Jones, Ernest: *The Life and Work of Sigmund Freud*, Basic Books, Inc., Publishers, New York, 1953–1957, vols. 1, 2.

Kadushin, Charles, et al.: "How and Where to Find the Intellectual Elite in the United States," *Public Opinion Quarterly*, vol. 34, no. 1, Spring 1971.

Kaysen, Carl: *The Higher Learning, the Universities, and the Public*, Princeton University Press, Princeton, N.J., 1970.

Keniston, Kenneth, and Michael Lerner: "The Unholy Alliance against the Campus," Carnegie Commission on Higher Education, Berkeley, Calif., 1971. Reprinted by permission of *The New York Times* Company.

Kerr, Clark: *The Uses of the University*, Harvard University Press, Cambridge, Mass., 1963.

Klawitter, Robert: *Degrading Education*, New University Conference, Chicago, 1969.

Kuhn, Helmut, et al: *Die deutsche Universität im Dritten Reich*, Piper, Munich, 1966.

Kuhn, Thomas: *The Structure of Scientific Revolutions*, 2d ed., The University of Chicago Press, Chicago, 1970.

Lasch, Christopher: *The New Radicalism in America*, Alfred A. Knopf, Inc., New York, 1965.

Lasch, Christopher: "Educational Structures and Cultural Fragmentation," in

John Voss and Paul L. Ward (eds.), *Confrontation and Learned Societies,* New York University Press, New York, 1970.

Lasch, Christopher, and Eugene Genovese: "The Education and the University We Need Now," *New York Review of Books,* pp. 21–27, Oct. 9, 1969.

Lefebvre, Henri: *Positions contre les technocrates,* Gonthier, Paris, 1967.

LeGoff, Jacques: *Les Intellectuels au moyen-âge,* Éditions du Seuil, Paris, 1957.

Leibfried, Stephan (ed.): *Wider die Untertanenfabrik,* Pahl-Rugenstein Verlag, Köln, 1967.

Lichtheim, George: *Europe and America,* Thames and Hudson, London, 1963.

Lilge, Frederic: *The Abuse of Learning,* The Macmillan Company, New York, 1948.

Lipset, S. M.: *Rebellion in the University,* Little, Brown and Company, Boston, 1972.

Lipset, S. M., and E. C. Ladd, Jr.: "College Generations—From the 1930's to the 1960's," *The Public Interest,* no. 25, pp. 99–113, Summer 1971a.

Lipset, S. M., and E. C. Ladd, Jr.: "The Divided Professoriat," *Change,* vol. 3, no. 3, pp. 54–60, May–June 1971b.

Lynd, Staughton: "Restructuring the University," New University Conference, Chicago, 1970.

Macciochi, M. A.: *Dopo la revoluzione culturale,* Feltrinelli, Milano, 1971.

McDermott, John: "The Laying on of Culture," *The Nation,* vol. 208, pp. 296–301, Mar. 10, 1969.

Maier, Hans, and Michael Zöller (eds.): *Die andere Bildungskatastrophe: Hochschulgestze statt Hochschulreform,* Markus Verlag, Köln, 1971.

Mankoff, Milton and Richard Flacks: "The Changing Social Base of the American Student Movement," in "Student Protest," *Annals of the American Academy of Political and Social Science,* Philadelphia, vol. 395, pp. 54–67, May 1971.

Mann, Golo: *Deutsche Geschichte des 19. und 20. Jahrhunderts.* S. Fischer Verlag, Frankfurt, 1958.

Mannheim, Karl: *Ideology and Utopia,* Harcourt, Brace & World, Inc., New York, 1952.

Marcuse, Herbert: "Charles Reich—A Negative View," *The New York Times,* p. 41, Nov. 6, 1970.

Marx, Leo: "Susan Sontag's 'New Left' Pastoral: Notes on Revolutionary Pastoralism in America," *Tri-Quarterly.* Nos. 23, 24, Winter–Spring 1972; also in George Abbott White and Charles Newman (eds.). *Literature in Revolution,* Holt, Rinehart and Winston, New York, pp. 552–575, 1972.

Mayhew, Lewis B., and Patrick J. Ford: *Changing the Curriculum,* Jossey-Bass, San Francisco, 1971.

Meiklejohn, Alexander: *The Liberal College,* Marshall Jones, Boston, 1920.

Meyerhoff, Barbara: "The Revolution as a Trip." in "Student Protest," *Annals of the American Academy of Political and Social Science,* Philadelphia, vol. 395, pp. 105–116, May 1971.

Michels, Robert: *La psicologia sociale della boheme e il proletariato intellectuale,* Academia di Scienze Morali e Politiche della Societa Reale, Naples, vol. 54, pp. 181–199, 1931.

Moynihan, Daniel Patrick: *Maximum Feasible Misunderstanding.* Basic Books, Inc., Publishers, New York, 1969.

Nagel, Julien (ed.): *Student Power*, Merlin Press, London, 1969.

"Neutrality or Partisanship: A Dilemma of Academic Institutions," Carnegie Foundation for the Advancement of Teaching, Bulletin 34, New York, 1971.

New University Conference: *The Radical Teacher*, Chicago, 1969a.

New University Conference: *The Student Rebellion*, Chicago, 1969b.

The New York Times, May 11, 1970, p. 15; July 9, 1970, p. 21; July 24, 1970, p. 1.

Nisbet, Robert: *The Degradation of the Academic Dogma*, Basic Books, Inc., Publishers, New York, 1971.

Ohmann, Richard: *Politics and Professional Organizations: A Radical View*, Modern Language Caucus of the New University Conference, Chicago, 1968.

Organization for Economic Cooperation and Development: *Reviews of National Science Policy: The United States*, OECD Publications, Paris, 1968.

Organization for Economic Cooperation and Development: *Science, croissance et société*, OECD Publications, Paris, 1971.

Orlans, Harold: "Social Science Research Policies in the United States," *Minerva*, vol. 9, no. 2, January 1971. (Reprinted as Brookings Institution Reprint no. 207, 1971).

Perkins, James: *The University In Transition*. Princeton University Press, Princeton, N.J., 1966.

Pliven, Frances, and Richard Cloward: *Regulating the Poor*, Pantheon Books, a division of Random House, Inc., New York, 1970.

Rauh, Morton A.: *The Trusteeship of Colleges and Universities*, McGraw-Hill Book Company, New York, 1969.

Regents of the University of Wisconsin: "Report of the Investigating Committee," papers of the board of regents of the University of Wisconsin, Sept. 18, 1894, in Richard Hofstadter and Wilson Smith, *American Higher Education: A Documentary History*, The University of Chicago Press, Chicago, 1961, vol. 2, p. 860.

"Report of the Committee on Academic Freedom and Tenure of the American Association of University Professors," 1915, in Richard Hofstadter and Wilson Smith, *American Higher Education: A Documentary History*, The University of Chicago Press, Chicago, 1961, vol. 2, pp. 860–878.

Report of the President's Commission on Campus Unrest, Washington, D.C., 1970.

Richter, Melvin: *The Politics of Conscience*, Harvard University Press, Cambridge, Mass., 1964.

Ringer, Fritz: *The Decline of the German Mandarins: The German Academic Community, 1890–1933*, Harvard University Press, Cambridge, Mass., 1969.

Rossanda, Rossana: *L'anno degli studenti*, Dedalo, Bari, 1968.

Roszak, Theodore (ed.): *The Dissenting Academy*, Pantheon Books, a division of Random House, Inc., New York, 1968.

Rudolph, Frederick: *The American College and University*, Alfred A. Knopf, Inc., New York, 1962.

Schelsky, Helmut: *Abschied von der Hochschulpolitik*, Bertlesmann Universitätsverlag, Gütersloh, 1969.

Scheuch, Erwin: *Die Wiedertäufer der Wohlstandsgesellschaft*. Markus Verlag, Köln, 1969.

Schnapp, Alain, and Pierre Vidal-Naquet: *Journal de la commune ètudiante*, Éditions du Seuil, Paris, 1969. (English translation, Beacon Press, Boston, 1971).

Schumpeter, Joseph A.: *History of Economic Analysis,* Oxford University Press, New York, 1954.

Schwiebert, Ernest: *Luther and His Times,* Concordia Publishing House, St. Louis, 1950.

Science for the People, Scientists and Engineers for Social and Political Action, Jamaica Plain, Mass., various issues, 1968–1972.

Selznick, Philip: *The T.V.A. and the Grass Roots: A Study in the Sociology of Formal Organization,* University of California Press, Berkeley, 1949.

Simon, John G., Charles W. Powers, and Jon P. Gunnemann: *The Ethical Investor: Universities and Corporate Responsibility,* Yale University Press, New Haven, Conn., 1972.

Sontheimer, Kurt: "Die reputierliche Mauschelei," *Die Zeit,* Dec. 17, 1971.

Spaeth, Joe L., and Andrew M. Greeley: *Recent Alumni and Higher Education: A Survey of College Graduates,* a report prepared for the Carnegie Commission on Higher Education, McGraw-Hill Book Company, New York, 1970.

Stammer, O. (ed.): *Max Weber und die Soziologie Heute,* Mohr (Siebeck), Tübingen, 1965.

Teodori, Massimo: *The New Left: An Anthology,* McGraw-Hill Book Company, New York, 1970.

Thibaudet, Albert: *La République des professeurs.* B. Grasset, Paris, 1927.

Touraine, Alain: *Post-industrial Society.* Random House, Inc., New York, 1971.

Trilling, Lionel: *The Liberal Imagination,* The Viking Press, Inc., New York, 1950.

Trilling, Lionel: *Beyond Culture,* The Viking Press, Inc., New York, 1968.

Trow, Martin: "Expansion and Transformation of Higher Education," paper presented to the American Sociological Association, Boston, September 1970. (Mimeographed.)

U.S. Office of Education: *Equality of Educational Opportunity,* Washington, D.C., 1966.

"The Universities," *The Public Interest,* no. 13, Fall 1968.

Venturi, Franco: *Roots of Revolution,* Alfred A. Knopf, Inc., New York, 1960.

Veysey, Laurence R.: *The Emergence of the American University,* The University of Chicago Press, Chicago, 1965.

Wallerstein, Immanuel, and Paul Starr (eds.): *The University Crisis Reader I, II,* Random House, Inc., New York, 1971.

Weber, Max: "Science as a Vocation," in H. H. Gerth and C. W. Mills (eds.), *From Max Weber: Essays in Sociology,* Oxford University Press, New York, 1946.

Weber, Max: *The Methodology of the Social Science,* trans. by Finch and Edward Shils, The Free Press, Glencoe, Ill., 1949.

White, Morton: *Social Thought in America,* The Viking Press, Inc., New York, 1949.

Whitman, Alden: "Middletown Revisited: Still in Transition," *The New York Times,* Dec. 3, 1970, p. 49.

Wicker, Tom: "America and Its Colleges: End of an Affair," *Change,* vol. 3, no. 5, pp. 22–25, September 1971.

Wilson, Woodrow: "Princeton in the Nation's Service." in Richard Hofstadter and Wilson Smith, *American Higher Education: A Documentary History*, The University of Chicago Press, Chicago, 1961, vol. 2.

Withey, Stephen B., et al.: *A Degree and What Else? Correlates and Consequences of a College Education*, a report prepared for the Carnegie Commission on Higher Education, McGraw-Hill Book Company, New York, 1971.

Wolff, Robert Paul: *The Ideal of the University*, Beacon Press, Boston, 1969.

Wolin, Sheldon S., and John H. Schaar: *The Berkeley Rebellion and Beyond: Essays on Politics and Education in the Technological Society*, New York Review of Books, Vintage Press, New York, 1970.

Acknowledgments: The research on which this chapter rests was in part supported by the U.S. Office of Education (OEG 1-9-0900640117) and the Division of Higher Education and Research of the Ford Foundation. I much appreciate the support of the Office of Education and the Ford Foundation.

I am much indebted to Messrs. James Ackerman, Carl Kaysen, David Riesman, Verne Stadtman, and Laurence Veysey for their critical comments.

9

What Really Happened at the Sorbonne

It is with some hesitation that I venture to write about the French government's cultural conference, which met at the old Sorbonne in February (1983). Unlike most of its most frenzied American detractors, I was actually there. Unlike them, too, I do not find that having to deal with ideas or persons French induces an immediate crisis of intellectual and personal identity. In Paris, I did not think of myself as a provincial who would use the cultural equivalent of the wrong fork, but as a visitor from one metropolis to another.

Our nations do have different views of the public role of culture. American Protestantism (and, not quite paradoxically, our religious pluralism) renders us uneasy at cultural intervention by the state. No doubt, the absence of a Department of Culture never deterred school boards, college presidents, and library committees from imposing their views of first and last things upon much of the nation. They did so, however, locally—and cultural creation proceeded elsewhere, if often unnoticed by a sizeable fragment of the nation. The National Endowments for the Arts and the Humanities are hardly surrogates for a European ministry of culture. The foundations are more plausible candidates for that designation. Even they are hybrids, half private, half public. American presidents, to be sure, have recently advanced into cultural combat. John Kennedy declared at Yale that there were no longer any political arguments in economics: only technical questions remained.

The late president can be forgiven; he must have been listening to his Harvard advisers. President Reagan has cultural notions which, if they embarrass and enrage at least half the nation, are strenuously argued. Our politics has not lacked ideas: Jefferson, Calhoun, the first Roosevelt, and Wilson were our compatriots. Skilled ideological topographers can discern occasional rises even in the present flatness of our political landscape. Still, the cultivation of the spirit is a matter many Americans find contentious and difficult enough without calling upon the state.

The French state, by contrast, has always been involved in culture. Perhaps this is a legacy of Catholicism. If so, the lay republic did not hesitate to assume it. Catholic and anticlerical, bohemian and bourgeois, liberal and Marxist, have battled for the national psyche for generations—in politics and out of it. Artists, writers, and thinkers are public figures. De Gaulle at the height of his power addressed Sartre as "Cher Maître." Nevertheless, intellectuals do not make French politics. The two recent republics have been dominated by technocrats—economists, engineers, lawyers. They embodied rationality without philosophy, technique without passion. The artists and intellectuals retreated to their publishing houses, studies, studios, and universities—which, indeed, most of them had never left. Their obsession with structuralism, with culture as a system of codes, with the unconscious as the site of language, betrays a hermetic resignation. The work of deconstruction fits nicely into this sequence—deconstruction doubts that there is a world at all. An earlier generation of radical intellectuals thought the point was to change the world. Their successors seek only to interpret it. At first sight, it is surprising that a Malraux presided, as De Gaulle's minister of culture, over the early stages of this dismal sequence. The ideas he brought to the regime, however, were ones he articulated a decade before it began—just as Gaullism is fundamentally the thought of a brilliant young officer between the wars.

Now the Socialists rule France, with some help from the dispirited remnant of the Communist Party and miscellaneous radicals and Gaullists. The technocrats remain sovereign. Mitterrand, a literary figure whose entire style bears the imprint of the Third Republic in which he grew up, seems uncomfortable about that. Many artists and filmmakers, intellectuals, and writers support the regime. Perhaps they anticipated reenacting the revolutionary drama of 1968, when the Latin Quarter seemed to be the capital of a new world. The slogan of that springtime, all power to the imagination, has become a distant memory. The winter of austerity has descended upon France. The surrealist dream of art becoming life is not prominently inscribed on the government's program. The social groups indispensable to the success of French socialism are discouraged, and a pervasive disappointment is evident. True, the cultural budget has been doubled, and so has the one for scientific research. It is vulgar, however, to suppose that any nation's intellectuals live for grants and jobs alone. (That may well be the case, let it be said, for those neoconservative intellectuals who advance the thesis to denigrate their adversaries.) They actually live for ideas, and in France as everywhere else, new ideas, new sensibilities, are hard to find.

The Paris conference was an effort to restore some of the regime's *élan*. Jack Lang, the imaginative minister of culture, had been the dean of a law faculty and a theatrical producer before taking office. At a UNESCO meeting in Mexico City in 1982, he had criticized the world-wide diffusion of commercial television products as a form of cultural imperialism—and had named "Dallas." He was promptly marked by our anxious philistines as anti-American. He had compared Melville unfavorably to Françoise Sagan, the noise could not have been greater. Lang was joined in planning the conference by Mitterrand's adviser, the gifted economist Jacques Attali. When the hosts assembled a list of American participants, they turned to their friends—those sympathetic to the regime. That made a certain amount of tumult in our country inevitable. Had the guest list resembled a list of authors from *Commentary*, Mitterrand would have earned almost as much praise for his cultural prescience as for his firm stand on the Germans' duty to take American missiles. In fact, he did our nation's cultural standing abroad a service by not inviting our intellectual vigilantes. The uninvited were also done a service: they are the sort of people made uneasy by unfamiliar surroundings. Lang and Mitterand were interested in the common problems we now face, not in the compulsive iteration of values already dubious in the nineteenth century. Their selectivity, however, was interpreted here as a form of intervention in our own cultural civil war.

In the end, 150 foreign guests and 300 French figures assembled at the Sorbonne. In a gesture to Leopold Senghor, former president of Senegal and once a teacher of French literature, the conference theme was given as "Creation and Development." The original title was to have been something like "Culture Confronts Crisis"—and that would have been more specific in its very vagueness. What (or whose) culture, and what crisis? These questions dominated the proceedings.

Artists, film directors, musicians, painters, writers in the group far outnumbered the economists, historians, philosophers, and scientists. Could the imagination find a way out of our society's economic immobility, its political stasis, its psychological inertia? The creators turned the conference's (well-laden) tables on our hosts. Ask not, they said, what culture can do for you: ask what you can do for culture. Perhaps the most striking element of the dialogue was the position taken by the participants in pinstripes: economists, bankers, and technocrats from French state industry. Persons who habitually count, they voiced a not-quite-ascetic readiness to change their ways. We needed, they said, new ideas of quality to replace the quantitative thought of our society. Wassily Leontiev declared that structural unemployment would grow as machines increasingly performed mental functions. We would need new conceptions of the division of labor, of work itself. The artists and writers, in effect, instructed the technocrats not to flee their responsibilities for the administration (or misadministration) of society to that last refuge of political scoundrels, spiritual values. The German director Voelker Schlondorff and the all-purpose Italian thinker Umberto Eco warned that culture brought not peace, but a sword. Culture's task was to make society unsure of itself, to provoke crises. Some of the other creators responded in a way reminiscent of the celebrated meeting between Sam Goldwyn and George Bernard Shaw. Asked about the encounter, Shaw declared that the misunderstanding had been complete. Goldwyn had wanted to talk only about art and he, Shaw, only about money.

Imagine, then, Francis Ford Coppola, Jacques Derrida, John Kenneth Galbraith, Jacques LeGoff, Norman Mailer, Gabriel Garcia Márquez, Alain Robbe-Grillet, Giorgio Strehler, Wole Soyinka, and Iannis Xenaxis in one room. Add a group of scientists and some of France's higher civil servants. The result did not resemble that Bosch painting of the Tower of Babel, but was more like one of his pictures of play. Some of the most interesting encounters of the conference occurred in the corridors, at the receptions. Most of the American reporters present (in contrast with their European colleagues) were made uneasy by these elements of chance and play. One great American cultural hero, apparently, lives: Babbitt. In his spirit, a few of his journalistic compatriots seemed to be obsessed by what the conference cost. The most plausible explanation is that they found intellectual argument itself difficult.

Argument there was: beneath the seeming disorder of a multiplicity of themes, uttered in a variety of tongues, some central ideas were entirely audible. The aesthetic, the transcendental dimensions of existence were threatened by humanity's struggle for sheer survival. Humanity had fashioned traditions to master that struggle. These, however, were also threatened: by the industrial fabrication of culture. When tradition lived, it could too easily ossify. The task of re-creating tradition at times was insurmountable. In depicting this situation, the artists, film directors, writers displayed more energy, maybe more naïveté, possibly more courage, than those from the more reflective disciplines. David Riesman once contrasted the exuberance of the French intellectuals, promulgating philosophies of despair with untrammeled delight, to the lugubrious earnestness of America's optimists. At the Sorbonne, the contrast was not between nations but between genres. Those of us who came from the social sciences were sicklied over with the pale cast of thought—or, at least, of our thoughts. The technocrats, by contrast, gave the impression of being free of doubts, but sure that the problems they evoked were real. Used to direct and linear statement, these worldly figures (most of them French) confirmed the worst intuitions of the rest of us. Argument could begin, after a surprising agreement on an initial diagnosis.

The conference was divided into three discussion groups. Given our numbers, six might have been better. I participated in one ("Creation and Social Change") presided over with authority and elegance by a medical scientist, the cancer specialist Leon Schwarzenberg. There were thirty or so statements, although the chairman and I later agreed that we had heard three and only three ideas. (We also agreed that this was an unusually high score.) The two other groups, to judge from *rapporteurs* and participants alike, dealt with the same problems, and in much the same way.

It was not surprising that a conference convened by a Socialist government discussed the democratization of culture. What was surprising was the (relative) absence of cant. The idea of progress was conspicuous by its absence. Cultural populism in its vulgar forms was almost equally invisible. Given our familiar anxieties about technocratic domination, it was interesting that the technocrats raised the problem of citizenship. If citizens are not to be at the mercy of experts, they must have the knowledge to argue with them. If our contemporaries are to overcome electronically induced mediocrity, they require access to the means of reflection. The old socialist theme of the appropriation of the means of production returned, in transmuted form. How can the means of cultural production be made available? For the moment, we know that very few Renault workers read Pascal, few IBM employees read Hawthorne. In these circumstances, visions of our nations as heirs to the ages are derisory. A realm of universal creativity seems an absurdly utopian dream.

These were some of the systematic discontents of the industrial societies. The very vocal spokesmen for the Third World in our midst had other complaints. The theme of the defense of distinctive cultures against homogenization was heard. Leopold Senghor, speaking half in African parables and half in citations from western classical and modern literature, figured as the conscience of the gathering. The difficulty was, that his view of a distinctive African cultural model (sometimes termed "Negritude," sometimes "the African way to socialism") owes at least as much to Rousseau as to African sources. A defense of the particular, then, can hardly substitute for a relentless search for a human essence.

That phrase sounds like something out of the past. The dramatists and, above all, film directors at the conference are, in one sense, traditionalists. They are the heirs of the tradition of social depiction, of historical discourse, of the early modern novel. (The novelists are, by and large, using other aesthetic means.) It was they who, at the conference, declared themselves to be advocates—defenders of a humanity threatened everywhere by famine, poverty, tyranny, and war. Even, or above all, their efforts to penetrate the surface of everyday existence in the prosperous and relatively stable societies had didactic intent. I report, of course, their own understanding of their work. At the conference, the participants from film resembled those from government in their plain speaking—and those from science in their passion.

The theme of cultural imperialism was invoked. Actually, there were only three references to "Dallas." One was from Amos Kenan, who complained that in Tel Aviv, where he lived, it was impossible to make peace, war, or love while "Dallas" was being shown. The Italian director Ettore Scuola complained that the children of Milan might or might not know something of the history of Lombardia: they knew "Dallas." I said that the problem was not "Dallas" but the industrial fabrication of culture. If "Dallas" had victims, the American public was certainly to be numbered among them. (I was also able to do a bit for our cultural relations in Central America. At one point, I found myself sitting next to the cultural minister of Nicaragua. Father Ernesto Cardenal. He was somewhat reserved at first, but when I told him that I had successfully sued the CIA for opening my correspondence, the atmosphere warmed appreciably.) In fact, most of the anti-imperialist rhetoric of the conference was directed against France—by an African historian and an Algerian film director.

No one at the conference, alas, was able to deal with a contradiction. The defenders of cultural pluralism inveighed against domination. The burden of the conference, however, was that nothing or no one exercised domination any longer. No one cultural model was canonical, and the very substance of culture was a matter increasingly obscure. Most of the programmatic statements at the meeting, like Senghor's, approached these matters diplomatically—that is, they ignored them. Mitterrand, to his credit, did better in a speech which closed the conference, but which should have opened it. He called for an extension of the idea of creativity to include the work of those managing our institutions and our technologies. No doubt, this was (on the eve of an election) a political opening to France's *cadres,* its managerial and technical elites. It was also an implicit renunciation of one conception of culture, confined to formal humanistic pursuits. Let us say that it was not a Compiègne Forest for humanism, but a program for a new Tennis Court Oath. There were other dimensions to the president's remarks, a not-quite-articulated idea of a new relationship between culture and routine. He also depicted a France which was ready to abandon its old claim to being the world's cultural capital in favor of a position as one pole of attraction in a multipolar world. There was, finally, little that was ethnocentric or provincial in the intellectual hospitality the visitors experienced.

On one point, those of us in the American universities can allow ourselves a rare moment of self-congratulation. The presence at the Sorbonne of artists and writers was somewhat unusual. Even after the recent sequence of reforms, the French universities generally adhere to rather traditional views of the disciplines proper to higher education. The creative arts are taught (and housed) elsewhere. Our own universities have become, for better or for worse, centers of cultural production. Moreover, even if much of what passes for interdisciplinary work is trivial or vacuous, in the best cases we are able to transcend rigidity. No doubt the moving spirit has been hard to sense in North America recently. When it descends, at least the vessels are ready. As for John Kenneth Galbraith's encounter with Sophia Loren at the conference, perhaps that shows how generously these days we need to draw the boundaries of higher education.

Most of the Americans present were confirmed in what we had never doubted. Our nation is a cultural superpower. Our art, film, literature, and music (even, occasionally, our social science) are known everywhere. They interest others because they express our conflicts and failures, as well as our triumphs. Susan Sontag, to be sure, warned the conference not to "overestimate" our culture. She complained of the lack of financing for her films. That is, no doubt, regrettable—but hardly irrefutable evidence for irreversible national cultural decline. Certainly, we should invest more in culture (and education). The lesson of the conference for us may lie elsewhere. Was it only twenty years ago that some ideological hit man or other scoffed at the artists and writers who had the impertinence to doubt the competence and good faith of the generals and technocrats directing the war in Vietnam? Perhaps we should reflect, anew, on the political value of the American imagination.

That possibility, it appears, disturbs the conference's American critics immensely. Among them, Raymond Sokolov of the *Wall Street Journal* is an exception: he was there, and actually knows French and French culture. He provoked a transatlantic tempest by declaring that contemporary French culture was null. He later explained to me that he did not mean to denigrate French history and social science, but that the arts and the novel were disappointing. What really irritated him, I gather, was what he took to be the supreme arrogance of the French: the very idea of the conference struck him as mistaken. Perhaps—but had he complained less and listened more, he might have disturbed his paper's readers by reporting that a good many serious thinkers suppose that our acquired notions of economy and work no longer correspond to reality.

The prize for systematic malice and obdurate philistinism, however, has to go to the *Washington Post*. The conference was covered by a promising younger journalist, Michael Dobbs. The difficulty is that Dobbs had just come to Paris, was just learning French, and managed to attend only the very end of the final session and a reception. Someone at the *Post* produced an editorial comment entitled "Shame of the Intellectuals," the burden of which was that it was unfair to criticize "Dallas" when one of the characters was seriously ill. Presumably, the *Post*'s editorialist decided that the issues raised at the meeting were beyond him (or her). Those at the conference who asserted that we lack any common discourse which is neither trivial nor vulgar, one gathers, have a point.

These, however, were relatively minor defects. Two of the *Post*'s columnists, George Will and Jonathan Yardley, took the conference as an excuse for convincing displays of chauvinism and *ressentiment*. Will quoted at length from works of Mailer and Sontag which he disliked. He accused the American participants of having "rented" themselves to a government of the left. Will is a frequent speaker at business associations: it is difficult to believe that he donates his services. His criticism of the rest of us must rest on one of the tenets of the age of Reagan. We actually went without fee: no more convincing evidence of the incapacity of some of our intellectuals can be found than in our want of healthy avarice. Will, at least, had the honesty to attack us on political grounds. Yardley, by contrast, is one of those critics who is unable to think in ideas of more than one syllable. Like Will, he knew as much about the conference as Dobbs told him—which is to say, nothing. Yardley proceeded to discover an eternal conflict between art and politics. The conflict, it has to be said, was tailored to the event. Many of his columns praise otherwise obscure writers for "patriotism" (not criticizing the Vietnam war). Others celebrate the virtues of ordinary persons—virtues which seemed exhausted in their accepting our class system by decently averting their eyes. Yardley's incoherence was so great that the key to his rage must be sought elsewhere. His column was printed, actually, next to a report on a reception given for the British royal family by the Annenbergs. The *Post* entitles the section in which it mixes the arts, culture, and the most trivial sort of gossip "Style." In this case, the only thing evident in the *Post* was its absence.

The French newspapers, on the other hand, dealt with the entire conference according to their political predilections. The pro-Socialist press was more or less positive, the press of the right more or less critical. Even the criticism, interestingly enough, was often muted: Mitterrand takes intellectuals seriously, and those who penned polemics against Lang (much disliked by some, occasionally for reasons which will not stand scrutiny) have guild interests to defend. *Liberation*, on the left, did deride the event as a "cultural high mass," but *Le Monde* was respectful, calling it the first meeting of "the international of the imagination." Most of the press responded irritably to American criticism, and especially to Sokolov, who soared to a brief notoriety which could not have been greater had he suggested burning the Bibliothèque Nationale. The French correspondents in America were insightful enough to report that American criticism was conditioned by our own cultural politics. Meanwhile, the visible fusion of culture and politics in attitudes to the event on both sides of the Atlantic confirms its initiators' intuitions. The two are inextricably connected.

Index